D1564172

HARD GRAFT IN HONG KONG
SCANDAL, CORRUPTION AND THE ICAC

H. J. Lethbridge

Hard Graft in Hong Kong

Scandal·Corruption·the ICAC

HONG KONG
OXFORD UNIVERSITY PRESS
OXFORD NEW YORK MELBOURNE
1985

Oxford University Press

Oxford London New York Toronto
Kuala Lumpur Singapore Hong Kong Tokyo
Delhi Bombay Calcutta Madras Karachi
Nairobi Dar es Salaam Cape Town
Melbourne Auckland

and associated companies in
Beirut Berlin Ibadan Mexico City Nicosia

© Oxford University Press 1985
First published 1985

ISBN 0 19 583896 3

OXFORD is a trade mark of Oxford University Press

Printed in Hong Kong by Ko's Arts Printing Co.
Published by Oxford University Press, Warwick House, Hong Kong

PREFACE

THE Independent Commission Against Corruption (usually referred to by its initials as the ICAC) was set up in February 1974. It has been in existence, then, for over a decade. From time to time the Commission has been subject to severe criticism; but over the years the population has come to accept the organization as a necessary part of the administration of government and as a mostly uncontroversial and permanent feature of Hong Kong life.

The Commission has introduced an element of equity, sorely lacking before, into the economy and the society, a society stratified by very marked differences in wealth and status; for the Commission's agents strike at people in both high and low places and the Commissioner does not discriminate between persons belonging to the local or expatriate communities, the Chinese and non-Chinese. The ICAC has thus helped, unwittingly, in reducing the opprobrium attached to the term 'colony', a rather sinister designation these days.

In 1974, I was one of the Colony's many residents who greeted the Commission's birth with acclamation and enthusiasm. My enthusiasm and interest in its fortunes have not flagged. In 1973 the Governor, Sir Murray MacLehose, declared in the Legislative Council Chamber that the problem of corruption could only be mitigated by the creation of a special body to deal with the corrupt. I believed he was right when he spoke those words; and I still believe in his assessment of the situation in Hong Kong. This book, then, is the product of a decade of interest in the ICAC's work, history, and its fortunes. It does not, however, make any attempt at prediction. It is too soon to speculate about how the Chinese Communists will treat the ICAC in 1997, when they will play a major role in Hong Kong's future. Nevertheless, I doubt whether they will then wish to disband the organization, established by a colonial administration. For China itself now suffers from much corruption in its public life and has taken violent steps to eliminate corrupt officials and party members, and has reported that it has done so.

I did not contact the ICAC until I was working on my final chapter; then I got in touch with the Commissioner, Mr Peter Williams, and asked him if he would read my manuscript. He did so, and made very helpful suggestions, mostly of a factual nature. I also wish to thank Mr Gerald Harknett, Director of Operations, and his deputy, Mr Norman Whiteley, for reading portions of the text and also pointing out some errors. No one in the Commission attempted to influence my assessments of the facts. In every way, the Commission's staff were most helpful, quick to respond to my letters.

Thanks also go to Professor Mary Turnbull, Dr Norman Miners, and Dr Ian Scott, each of whom drew my attention to certain documents or books that I found useful. The first draft of *Hard Graft in Hong Kong* was typed by Mrs Hilda Chan, the Department of Sociology's secretary, who produced a very pleasing typescript. Finally, I wish to thank Professor Murray Groves, a friend and colleague, for supporting my endeavours.

HENRY LETHBRIDGE
Department of Sociology
The University of Hong Kong
May 1984

CONTENTS

Preface   *v*
Acknowledgements   *viii*

1. The Nature and Forms of Corruption   1
2. Scandal and Corruption, 1842–1941   24
3. The Star Ferry Riots and the Issue of
        Corruption   54
4. The Origins of the ICAC: The Control of
        Corruption   82
5. The Independent Commission Against
        Corruption   104
6. The Partial Amnesty   126
7. The ICAC Extends its Scope   159
8. Conclusion   194

Appendices   222
Bibliography   232
Index   244

ACKNOWLEDGEMENTS

THE author and publisher wish to make grateful acknowledgement to the following for permission to reproduce photographs: Associated Press; Government Information Services; the Public Records Office of Hong Kong; *South China Morning Post*; and George Webber.

I

THE NATURE AND FORMS OF CORRUPTION

'I can resist everything except temptation'.

Oscar Wilde, *Lady Windermere's Fan*

THE study of corruption has engrossed political scientists, sociologists, and historians for many years; but the popularity of the subject increased significantly in the 1960s, if one takes as an index the annual volume of books and articles published on the topic. Yet, since the 1960s, the decade of protest, the subject has lost a little of its savour, possibly because so many other important issues have since emerged to capture the interest of scholars and the public. At the same time, the British, stereotypical imperialists, who once (in cliché) owned an empire on which the sun never set, have since 1945 gradually freed themselves from their colonial incubus, so that today Hong Kong remains an anomaly, a relic of a largely defunct and widely condemned system.

America, on the other hand, in response to the Cold War and its own spectacular obsession with Communist infiltration of the Third World, has demonstrated a growing involvement in the underdeveloped and developing nations. It has taken over (if we politely ignore the Russians) Britain's role, not in the older sense of actual possession of foreign territory but as an interventionist in the politics and economies of the newly independent states. Americans are now arraigned, in Marxist jargon, as neo-imperialists; they are engaged, radical critics assert, in controlling weaker countries through the medium of economic power, or military might.

The British at first were sanguine about the destinies of

their former colonies. They pursued a policy, although often under intense nationalist pressure, of granting independence to territories that strongly desired it. The British believed that the new states, influenced by the implantation of English institutions, especially legal institutions, would be able to go it alone, would mature into sensible nation-states, in structure not unlike Great Britain—democratic and meritocratic, obedient to the rule of law and stabilized by the benefits of constitutional government. Not surprisingly, in retrospect at least, the new African states, for example, dismissed their former mentors and went their own way. They severed the colonial umbilical cord. Their leaders imprisoned political opponents (so had the British), improvised one-party systems, and veered sharply away (with some important exceptions) from the British model. '*Enrichissez-vous!*' appeared to be the dismal slogan of the new ruling élites. More importantly, for purists and moralists, corruption effloresced. (There was the celebrated case of a West African minister's wife who imported a gold bed. Where had the money come from?)

One influential post-war study—*Corruption in Developing Countries* by Ronald Wraith and Edgar Simpkins, published in 1963—took as its major theme the renaissance of corruption, especially the political variety, in West Africa, where 'dash' (tips, bribes, emollient gifts) was a traditional custom. The authors wished to discover what had gone wrong. Why had standards fallen so swiftly after independence? They concluded, among other matters, that the cure for African corruption was:

The evolution of a public opinion, which must follow the spread of education, which rejects corruption because it is morally wrong or because it is scientifically inefficient, or both ... The further growth of the professional class, and its resolve to raise its ethical standards by increasing association.

Wraith and Simpkins viewed corruption as primarily a moral problem, akin to taking or trafficking in drugs, being a practising homosexual, a thief, or a prostitute; activities that

2

one should not indulge in because they are intrinsically wrong ('sinful' in older diction). If corrupt behaviour could be reduced, for example, by moral education, social conditioning, or by inculcating professional standards and codes, then it follows the problem would largely fade away. That is no doubt immaculately true. If people were more honest—to choose a banal example—there would be less crime. But no one knows how to produce 'better' citizens. Even the Soviet government has not been able, since 1917, to replicate many copies of its model 'socialist man' (a superior species of humanity, it asserts, since he is motivated by altruism, 'capitalist man' by egoism).

Wraith and Simpkins concluded that corruption has a common cause—greed. 'The wrong that is done', they averred, 'is done in the full knowledge that it is wrong, for the concept of theft does not vary as between Christian and Muslim, African and European, or primitive man and Minister of the Crown'. As Colin Leys drily comments, 'Emotionally and intellectually, this seems to be in a direct line of descent from the viewpoint of those missionaries who were dedicated to the supression of native dancing. The subject seems to deserve a more systematic and open-minded approach'.

The moralistic approach, as typified in their study, should not be dismissed summarily. For it is indeed an essential ingredient of the work of the Community Relations Department of the Independent Commission Against Corruption (ICAC), whose task is both educational and propagandistic. As its director writes: 'It [the Department] has the responsibility of enhancing the public awareness of the evils of corruption and harnessing community support for the Commission's effort'. So long as the limitations of the moralistic approach, or perspective, as an explanatory theory are understood, there is no reason to criticize the ICAC's attempt to promote better standards of public and private behaviour and to encourage greater interest in the problem. Le Play, the nineteenth-century French social theorist, explains: 'Every new generation is just an invasion of young barbarians that must be educated and trained. Whenever such training is by any chance neglected, decadence becomes imminent'.

American political scientists reject Wraith and Simpkins' narrow focus, for corruption is part of America's history; Americans have become habituated to its presence. Boss Tweed (1823–78), whose aldermanic associates were known as 'The Forty Thieves', is a figure of American folklore. The presidency of Andrew Johnson, 1865–9, was notorious for its many corruption scandals; that of Warren Harding, 1920–3, led to a number of investigations and prosecutions associated with the Teapot Dome scandal, the secret leasing by the Secretary of the Interior, Albert Fall, of naval oil reserve lands to private companies, from which deal Fall benefited to the tune of US$300,000. The private life of President Harding, who died suddenly and mysteriously in San Francisco, became public soon after his demise, when it became known that his administration was riddled with corruption, peculation, and nepotism, and that he kept a mistress, Nan Britton, whose embraces, she claimed, he once enjoyed in a coat-closet in the White House executive office. In the 1920s, Chicago was largely controlled by Al Capone; and Cicero, a suburb, by the mayor he had installed. While serving his novitiate, and on reconnaissance in Chicago's suburbs, the future great gangster informed his boss, Johnny Torrio, 'This is virgin territory for whorehouses'. And so it was. If theft is to fraud as prose is to poetry, then so is British compared to American corruption. This possibly explains why American political scientists and sociologists have developed a more realistic approach to the problem than others.

American political scientists see corruption as a process of informal influence, as part of the *informal* political system; and graft and the spoils system (the supplanting of civil servants on a change in government—to the victor belong the spoils) as an integrating force cutting across the many divisions in society—racial, religious, social, and economic—and as a means of rewarding underdogs (by, for example, placing them on a city's payroll). Many Americans perceive corruption as an unavoidable, though unattractive, feature of what they term the 'democratic process'. If this is so, then political corruption may serve important social functions, functions which a purely moralistic approach to the problem would tend to conceal. A 'functionalist' (sociological) or 'realistic' perspective on corruption, and its various forms, has thus developed in recent years and has been utilized to explain not only the role of graft in American politics but also corrupt phenomena in Africa, Asia, South and Central America, indeed anywhere. Key, in a 1936 study of the techniques of political graft in America, puts this neatly: 'Much of what we consider as corruption is simply the "uninstitutionalized" influence of wealth in a political system'. The investigation of rule-breaking may thus throw much light on the suppressed under-life and deviations of a society, which a study of legal norms or formal political systems can never do. To understand health, we need the concept of disease, of pathology. The two exist in tandem.

It should be added, in parenthesis, that although Hong Kong has politics, in the sense of interest groups and cliques, and 'politicians' (people's tribunes, many self-selected and self-elected), it does not experience much political corruption in the sense given to that notion by scholars; this is because the Colony lacks contesting political parties seeking votes, lacks universal suffrage, and a government chosen by the people. Hong Kong is a species of administrative state, governed by a corps of civil servants headed by a British-appointed governor. The evolution of District Boards (local government bodies) may well lead to greater political corruption as candidates jostle for the spoils of office and delude voters into supporting them; but, at present, the problem of political corruption is not acute, although a few purported cases have been investigated by the ICAC.

Wraith and Simpkins, as we have seen, were preoccupied with patterns of development in the new states, particularly in Africa, which had lost their 'seagreen Incorruptible', the British administrator. But Americans also, in the 1950s and 1960s, began to worry about the emerging pathologies of the new states, especially in Asia—South Vietnam, South Korea, the Philippines, Indonesia, and Thailand (a traditional society under modernization). Corruption was rife in all these countries, without exception, as well as in India with its mixed economy, part socialist and planned, part capitalist and unplanned. American advisors of all types reported an extraordinary prevalence of corrupt practices; the corruption and dishonesty of ruling élites; the exploitation of the masses, mostly peasantry; and the deflection of foreign aid, supplies, stores, and equipment into an ever-expanding black market or into the hands of government officials. American concern was neither disinterested nor missionary: it was utilitarian and self-centred. America wanted to protect these states from Communist subversion, made easier by governments which had lost their legitimacy through allowing corruption to infect every level of society. It was urged that the establishment of relatively incorrupt administration would win over the people to 'democracy' (Western style).

These events sparked off a debate in academic and government circles. Was corruption really so detrimental, so deleterious? Or did it sometimes have beneficial rather than baneful effects? Roughly speaking, this was an argument between moralists and functionalists, between absolutists and relativists. The controversy was foggy. There was no clear winner, probably because the embattled academics and men of affairs asked different questions; or, ironically, asked the same questions but expected different answers. An idea which is not clearly expressed can never be proved clearly wrong.

Some realists found what they were looking for in India, a highly bureaucratized society, with civil servants dominating the economy, not only the large public sector with its many state enterprises but also the private sector, where a system of licensing economic activity made the work of a businessman difficult or hazardous. In order to obtain an import or export permit, or the foreign currency for such a transaction, money had to change hands between entrepreneur and bureaucrat. A bribe in this case may be regarded as 'speed money'. Since

6

time is money in business, any measure that expedites the granting of a valuable possession—a document—will benefit the recipient of the licence. Again, as Tilman argues, the supply of valuable concessions controlled by a bureaucracy is far exceeded by demand from private citizens; this discrepancy between supply and demand inflates 'price', so that a corrupt 'black market' is likely to develop, and usually does. Corruption, in these circumstances, is regarded by realists as a lubricant maintaining the machinery of economic enterprise. From this perspective, it is beneficial, tonic not toxic. Unfortunately, this neat functionalists' apologia can be countered by suggesting that a bureaucrat is likely to delay issuing a perfectly legal licence because he knows an impatient businessman will bribe him to expedite matters. What are the costs, what are the benefits of this social practice? The answer is not as clear-cut as realists assume.

In 1964, a Harvard academic, Nathaniel Leff, published an article with the title (daunting to moralists) 'Economic development through bureaucratic corruption'. 'The question for us to decide', he declared, 'is whether the net effects caused by such payments and policy redirection are likely to favour or hinder economic development'. There is no need to reproduce all his arguments—some are contained in the previous paragraph—but one is ingeniously provocative. Corruption, his thesis runs, also performs the valuable function of a 'hedge' against the full losses of bad economic policy.

Even when the government of an underdeveloped country is proceeding actively and intelligently to promote growth, there is no assurance that its policies are well-conceived to attain its goals. In effect, it may be taking a vigorous step in the wrong direction. Corruption can reduce the losses from such mistakes, for while the government is implementing one policy, the entrepreneurs, with their sabotage, are implementing another. Like all insurance, this involves a cost—if the government's policy is correct. On the other hand, like all insurance, it is sometimes very welcome.

In this example, corruption is, on occasions, a *deus ex machina* which providentially saves a government from its folly or muddleheadedness. Even an incorrupt administration, a regime of saints, may unwittingly dissipate resources or hinder modernization, as the Chinese Communists did during the years of the Cultural Revolution. Goodness and godliness, estimable qualities in themselves, must be linked, according to this thesis, with appropriate technological solutions, if a society is to progress.

Finally, one last example of the approach variously labelled realistic, functionalist or sociological will be given. José Abueva, a Filipino, has examined the contribution of, in his words, 'nepotism, spoils and graft to political development'. He claims that all these corrupt practices may 'speed up political unification and stability, popular participation in public affairs, the development of a viable party system, higher levels of political and administrative achievement of maintenance of development goals, and bureaucratic responsibility'. In his concluding paragraph, he states that he does not 'intend this little essay to be a brief for nepotism, spoils, and graft ... I only wish to stress the neglected functional features in respect to some primary and urgent goals of democratic, and political development in many a developing nation'.

The three articles quoted from, by Tilman, Leff and Abueva respectively, are products of the 1960s when corruption became a key topic in governmental and academic discourse.

It would be interesting to know how these authors now view their theses and conclusions. Do they look back in some anger at their former naïvety? Or do they remain satisfied with their hard-headed analysis of the problem? For much has changed since the 1960s, including the perception of Janus-faced corruption. Those who wrote on the subject worked from certain premises, usually implicit rather than explicit; thus the political and ideological commitment of the inquirer should not be bracketed off, as it were, from his published findings. Nearly all American academics who examined the developmental problems of the new states, or those undergoing modernization, were funded by government agencies, by private foundations and conservative organizations, often covertly by the CIA. The countries in which they worked were allies of America, or territories which America wished to influence; their governments were committed, at least in theory, to the principles of private enterprise and the Free World. These sponsored researchers were inclined to look on the bright side and be persuaded that corruption was not so great an evil as purists, moralists, radicals, and Communists affirmed. Inevitably, they wore cultural blinkers. If America could contain a great deal of corruption and yet flourish, then why should this not be true of India, South Vietnam or South Korea? (For they were writing in a period of economic expansion, of boom and innovation.)

There were of course American Jeremiahs (similar in attitude to Wraith and Simpkins) and many cynical observers of the foreign scene, such as journalists, but they were not much listened to by policy-makers. Rather it was the rationalizing apologists of corruption who largely held the stage at that time; those who were apt to view corruption as a partial solution to, rather than a problem of, economic dilemmas facing developing nations, or as insoluble.

If, for the moment, we return to Hong Kong, it is plausible to suggest that any commissioner of the ICAC would not be swayed by functionalist arguments, however intellectually exciting these are. He would not be inclined, one surmises, to minute the Governor that the ICAC should be wound up and its staff deployed to investigate tax evasion, a problem as acute in Hong Kong as corrupt practices. The situation is similar to that of the professional thief who took an Open University course in sociology; on release he continued thieving, but now knew *why* he did so. An improvement in understanding— indubitably—but, for the community, he still remains a social nuisance.

The idea of corruption is conditioned by time and place; history and culture determine its perception. The term 'proto-corruption' has been coined to denote practices that today are labelled corrupt, yet in the past were not deemed to be so. It is important to stress that people have always distinguished

between 'normal' corruption ('honest graft' in American parlance) and 'pathological' corruption (an evaluation that re-
minds one of that between gourmet and gourmand). Extrava-
gant behaviour far beyond the norm has always been subject
to censure from moralists and moralizers, just as a medieval
schoolman or casuist distinguished canonically between a fair
and an extortionate price. Sir Robert Naunton remarked, in
his *Fragmenta Regalia*, that the Elizabethan Lord Richard
Sackville should more appropriately be called 'Sack-full'
rather than 'Sack-ville' because of his rapacious talent for en-
riching himself and his family. On the other hand, Pepys, the
celebrated diarist and Secretary of the Admiralty, was regarded by his contemporaries as an honest servant of the
Crown because his acquisitiveness was not outrageous but
moderate, by the standards of his time. Forms of proto-
corruption have been transmogrified by the flow of history
into criminal offences in most countries, for ethical standards
change as society itself evolves.

Examples of proto-corruption may be detected in all ancient
civilizations and pre-modern states (but to a lesser degree
in nineteenth-century Europe once rational bureaucracies,
with professional codes, were instituted). Proto-corruption
flourished in Stuart and Hanoverian England; and it existed
on an even more extensive scale in France under the *ancien
régime*, because of the size of the bureaucracy, its larger
population, and the greater wealth of the country. In England, under the Stuarts, the sale of office to the highest bidder
was a common device used to raise revenue (an office was
regarded as a commodity that could be traded by auction).
Other examples of proto-corruption were sinecures, which
gave the recipient an assured income, but no duties; tax farm-
ing, which meant the renting out of administrative functions
to private citizens; and the sale of titles, such as peerages, to
those who sought to validate their newly acquired wealth by a
prestigious title. (Surprisingly, the trade in titles was revived
by J. Maundy Gregory during Lloyd George's last years as
Prime Minister, a period of political jobbery and corruption

when £10,000 was a starting price for a knighthood. Gregory acted as an 'honours broker' until his prosecution in 1933 under the 1925 Honours (Protection of Abuses) Act. He, of course, was not acting as an agent for the monarch but, he claimed, for political parties.)

Proto-corruption flourished in myriad forms in traditional China, where it was largely unavoidable because of that country's system of administration. It continued to flourish after the 1911 Revolution, in the Republican, War-lord, and Nationalist periods, until the establishment of the People's Republic in 1949; after that date, the re-making of Chinese society affected its incidence, its scale and its volume. However, since the eclipse of the Gang of Four and the introduction of more liberal policies, it appears to have revived, especially in Guangdong, Hong Kong's neighbouring province. Its re-emergence on a grand scale was symbolized by the public execution in January 1983 of Wang Zhong, Secretary of the Heifeng county Communist Party Committee, on charges of corruption and embezzlement.

Proto-corruption in China was an institutionalized practice. But it should be noted that, as in England, exorbitance was deplored by Confucian moralists and condemned by censors (members of the Board of Censors, an internal control organ, whose official duty was, in Fairbank's words, 'the ferreting out of cases of treason, misgovernment, or maladministration and [the] reporting [of] them directly to the emperor'). Examples of blatant malpractice and flagrant corruption in the civil service could not be ignored by the censor, especially if they were likely to arouse the ire of the populace and lead to disturbances. The censor acted, to a certain degree, like a latter-day Ombudsman ('grievance man'), an independent official appointed to investigate complaints against administrators, someone who mediates between citizens and the government.

The salaries of Chinese officials were notoriously small; the district magistrate's particularly so. Yet, although ranking low in the hierarchy of officials, it was he who played the key role in administration. As Ch'ü notes: 'It is no exaggeration to say that the local administration was in the hands of magistrates. Without them it would have been at a standstill'. The magistrate was the official closest to the people and the person whom anyone with a grievance or case was likely to approach for rectification or arbitration (though it is true to say that Chinese were always reluctant to have dealings with officialdom, a disturbingly shadowy and problematic world for the average man). Much corruption centred on the magistrate's *yamen* and on his underlings—the clerks, gate porters, and runners—who were all local men, unlike the magistrate.

Dynasty after dynasty, emperors and their senior officials were made aware of the perversions that appeared routinely in the workaday world of the bureaucracy, of its members' lapses and descent into corruption, into exaction and dishonesty. The Board of Censors monitored grave infractions of the penal code or examples of serious deviant behaviour among the educated élite, and passed the information upward. The Chinese had a vast span of time—more than thirteen hundred years— in which to appreciate the misdeeds of officials, for the examination system, the cornerstone of the Chinese state apparatus, was introduced as early as the Sui dynasty (589–698) and was finally abolished only in 1906 (the last examinations were held in May 1904). The old scholar-officials were then put out to grass; they were the living dead, superseded by administrators who looked more to European or Japanese models of the civil service than to the traditional system, now swept aside by the tide of reform.

To check nepotism and venality, the state had insisted that no magistrate could serve in his natal province or take up appointment in one where his wife was born. The magistrate came as a stranger to, and normally spoke a different dialect from, the population he was sent to govern. He was thus, in theory, unencumbered by swarms of relatives or networks of clansmen. But the pressure to become corrupt arose more from the paucity of his official emoluments, a problem which the state attempted to solve by providing additions to his nominal salary. As Chang Chung-li writes:

It was supplemented by an extra allowance called *yang-lian*, meaning to 'nourish incorruption'. This allowance, which was many times the amount of the regular salary, was given in recognition of the fact that the regular salary was too low for positions with so much responsibility and so much opportunity for financial gain. In some positions a small extra allowance was given for administrative expenses, the so-called *gong-fei*.

The examination system imposed an enormous psychological strain on a candidate. In order to succeed, he had to devote himself fanatically to his literary education, to memorize a total of 431,286 characters in order to master the classics; and had to discipline himself severely from about the age of eight, through pubescence and early manhood, always watched over by an anxious and admonishing family. By the time he became a *jin-shi* ('presented scholar', the highest degree in the examination system) he was likely to feel his country owed him more than a living; or, in a more extreme case, that the world should be his oyster (after all, in Freudian terms, he had experienced much instinctual renunciation). Moreover, a candidate who finally achieved his ambition and was appointed to the civil service had now to maintain his dignity and live in an appropriate style, consonant with his station: he must protect his 'face'. It is not surprising, surely, that many were forced into proto-corrupt practices or even into obviously illegal activities. The civil servant's official role presented him with an implacable dilemma: a conflict between the demands of Confucian morality, the ideal of rectitude, and, on the other hand, the monstrous claims of real life. This is not to say that there were no correct, incorrupt, rigidly moral officials: there always were. The mandarinate, like any large body of men, contained the full range of human types, from the good to the bad, from the strong to the weak. The majority ritualistically conformed, but even this allowed much proto-corruption, acceptable to the authorities, who knew that ideal and reality are never likely to coincide.

A *yamen* contained not only the magistrate's official residence but was also the abode of his private secretaries and of numerous clerks, runners, and messengers, as well as personal servants and attendants. Subordinate staff indulged habitually in much petty corruption, almost a customary practice, known to all. Before a supplicant or a person with a grievance could obtain access to a magistrate, whose chambers were located at the rear of the *yamen*, and kowtow before him, he must pass through a screen of minor officials. The latter were in a strategic position to 'squeeze' all those who entered requesting an audience. The very architecture of the building, with underlings occupying the outer courtyard (where the main gate was, protected by a 'spirit wall'), helped to promote bribery, chicanery and exaction. The spirit wall, erected outside the main gate, was designed to keep out evil influences; it did not protect the public, however, for it was guarded by rapacious door-keepers, ever on the look-out for perks. The magistrate could not oversee everything that went on at street-level where the great public and subordinate staff confronted each other. Chinese thus became accustomed to the need for providing gifts or bribes before any action was taken (as in Hong Kong's hospitals, where once it was customary to tip an amah; if not, no bedpan would appear).

Chinese who came to Hong Kong after 1842 as transients, temporary sojourners, or permanent residents could not leave behind them, as so much discarded lumber, their cultural experiences; they carried these, as if shackled to a ball and chain, into their new world. They arrived with cultural expectations about how officials were likely to act, and react; they had their own folklore of officialdom. To a large degree, their expectations were confirmed in encounters with the European inspectorate, with the petty officials on whom senior administrators had to rely, since the former (who were subordinate staff) were too often revealed in Chinese eyes as even more greedy, crooked, and devious than their simulacrums in China. However, 'there is no settling the precedency', as Dr Johnson affirmed, 'between a louse and a flea'.

The pervasion of corruption in Hong Kong after 1842 cannot be blamed entirely on migrants or increasing Chinese settlement; nor on the folklore that *all* civil servants, especially junior officials, were always open, potentially, to business, if the price was right, the bribe big enough. There is no simple cause and effect explanation. What can be deduced is that Chinese perceptions and attitudes must be taken into account, as an important factor, in any attempt to understand the prevalence of corruption among *both* locals and foreigners, for members of each community did, at times, collude and break the law. There was extortion, with an exploiter and a victim, but there was also much consensual graft. Clearly, many arguments may be marshalled to account for the phenomenon: the enormous gulf between the Chinese majority and Western minority; the wide gap in understanding, the mutual misunderstandings; as well as the difficulties that arose from the imposition of an alien legal system with its mystifying conceptions, a system which had evolved in a vastly different social context. Again, attention should be focused on the values of the colonials, on how they reacted to their isolation on the shores of China, cut off from the conventional social controls that operated in their homeland. Resident in Hong Kong they could live more dangerously, though covertly; they had less to fear from the law than if they had remained in their own countries. They experienced what André Gide has termed *dépaysement*, a moral disorientation, a condition induced by an unfamiliar environment, like a roistering soldier in an occupied town. We should not exaggerate for pre-war Hong Kong was extremely conventional and middle-class; but, nevertheless, Europeans were freer in Hong Kong and less likely to be paralysed by the threat of criminal proceedings. All these conditions made corruption a little easier to indulge in. Hence, infractions were more likely to occur. Social controls were weaker; enforcement less stringent; dereliction commoner.

The term 'corruption' has been used extensively in this chapter; the text should suggest that what is labelled 'corrupt' is a creation of social perception, of social judgment and evaluation. Certain types of behaviour—actions and transactions—are stigmatized by the word. This is a consequence of the evolution of norms and legal rules, of moral codes and values. Broadly speaking, the concept implies moral deterioration, in the biblical sense, a fall, a declension from some higher, finer standard. The word has its special resonance; it is an emotive concept. In a narrower sense, it denotes what the law depones are criminal offences, as in the Prevention of Bribery Ordinance of 1971, and its various amendments, the instrument by which many corrupt officials and members of the public have been caught. Standards, need one say, change over time; proto-corruption becomes stark corruption, a criminal offence. Much of what we regard nowadays as venal has developed, it follows, from shifting perceptions of the role of public servants. It is necessary, then, to digress a little and comment upon standards of conduct in public life and on the emergence of bureaucracy and the rise of professional civil services.

Until the 1850s, in Britain, recruitment into government service was a matter of departmental patronage, jobbery, and nepotism. One of the reforms to which Bentham and the Utilitarians attached great importance was the replacement of the traditional system of patronage and nomination by one of selection by competitive examination, carried out by an impartial body, free (at least in theory) from all political influence. A Civil Service Commission was, therefore, established in 1855; by 1870, the principle of recruitment by competition had been accepted by Parliament and had taken root, largely as a result of the endeavours of Sir Stafford Northcote and Sir Charles Trevelyan. Those who wished to become administrators, to enter the administrative grade, had to proceed along this charted route. In fact, this apparently novel method of selection had been introduced to India as early as 1854, when Macaulay succeeded in making entry into the Indian Civil Service (the famed ICS) dependent upon passing a number of set papers—the best got in. Macaulay's innovation was an adumbration of the future meritocratic state, a reward for diligence and intelligence.

Although Carlyle in 1850 called bureaucracy 'the continental nuisance ... I see no risk or possibility in England', his foresight was at fault. Bureaucracy (government by central administration; the Continental practice) has constantly increased, so that the public sector is now the largest employer of labour in Britain. The historian Ramsay Muir defined bureaucracy as 'the exercise of power by professional administrators' (an apt summary of conditions in Hong Kong, where civil servants appear to be accountable only to God). Concomitant with reforms in the civil service, extending from 1855 to 1875, a professional code of ethics evolved. This may be best described as a distinction drawn between a civil servant's public office and his private affairs; he should not use his office in a private capacity to enhance his income, as in Stuart England. The new type of official, recruited by competitive examination, was well paid, a member of a hierarchical service, with an elaborate division of grades and functions. He was expected to live within his income, to live in a seemly mode. He was, as an administrative officer, a member of an élite group (ironically the public's 'most obedient servant', a view not always shared by aggrieved consumers of the services he provided). In principle, he was expected to be totally incorrupt; to uphold high standards of conduct in public life. The same code applied to the various colonial services and, more relevant to us, to Eastern cadets, to Hong Kong cadets, introduced into the Colony in 1861, at first ostensibly to provide competent interpretation. Compared with their Chinese counterparts, British officials were not underpaid; their conditions did not compel them to become venal. They were members of a modern rational civil service. They were also more closely supervised since Britain was geographically small, united by a railway system, and administration was centralized in London. Chinese officials, on the other hand, were thinly scattered over a vast territory, in a country with poor communications and an enormous population. Foreigners have often visualized

China as extraordinarily homogeneous and monolithic, inhabited by 'look-alike' and 'think-alike' people, conformists to a man. This was never so. In reality, China was marvellously diverse; it contained many divisions and distinctions: various languages (dialects), many ethnic groups (the Manchus had a culture of their own), geographical and climatic extremes, as well as important contrasts between northerners and southerners. Administration was simpler in tiny, compact Britain; and administrators there were easier to supervise and control.

The opening of the British civil service to the clever was almost completed by Gladstone's action on 31 May 1870 to recruit officials by competitive examination, with the exception of the foreign and education departments. This development profoundly changed the nature of corruption in England and greatly extended its ambit, for the innovation implied, and indeed necessitated, the raising of standards of conduct in government and in public life generally, in sum, the 'moralization' of administration. It transformed proto-corrupt practices, inherited from the past, from the pre-modern period, into corruption amenable to the criminal law. By 1875, the entire public service was included within the examination system, so that every post was competed for. The sale of office, recruitment by nomination, jobbery, and nepotism, all had been largely extinguished. This important change was complemented later by legislation—the Public Bodies Corrupt Practices Act of 1889, and the Prevention of Corruption Acts of 1906 and 1916. The British now expected civil servants, as well as those who served in local government and on various public bodies, to exhibit much higher standards than in the wicked past, when the few monopolized power and administration, and democracy was limited.

Any attempt to raise standards will increase the number of deviants in society, for more persons will be put outside its moral boundaries, now re-drawn. Rigid enforcement of the law will also help to amplify the total of known deviants, just as changed standards of child care have revealed a new problem, that of battered babies and of cruelty to children. The changes outlined in the preceding paragraphs did not eliminate corruption in Great Britain; this cannot be done simply by administrative fiat or legislation. What is forbidden may still flourish, perhaps even more abundantly, as society and the economy evolve. The reforming Liberal ministries of Campbell-Bannerman and Asquith (1905–15) displayed, for example, much financial corruption and great scandals, such as the Marconi case of 1912, which implicated the Attorney-General, Rufus Isaacs (later Lord Reading). The problem is always exacerbated by economic growth and the creation of wealth (for concomitantly the dividends from corruption tend to enlarge). This also holds for a rapid expansion in the public sector, an increase in the number of public servants, not all of whom will abide by the civil service ethic of incorrupt administration. It is widely accepted that corruption, like crime in general, or prostitution in particular, cannot be eliminated. Most people, therefore, are reasonably happy with stabilized conditions, with no marked or visible change in the scale and volume of corrupt practices. But this is a situation difficult to obtain, even when an ICAC or similar control body has been set up to correct the problem. Rule-breakers have a nasty way of accommodating themselves to innovation and challenge, and of outflanking the defences set up against them.

That corruption on a large scale existed in modern Britain was made plain in the 1974 Redcliffe-Maud Report on local government rules of conduct (Cmnd. 5636) and the 1976 Salmon Report on standards of conduct in public life (Cmnd. 6524). The latter dealt with the so-called 'Poulson affair'. John Poulson had set himself up as an architect in 1932. By the late 1960s he owned and controlled a firm which reputedly had the largest architectural practice in Europe, employing a staff of around 750. Poulson worked mostly for the public sector, putting up homes, hospitals, and other types of public buildings. The enterprise was in fact world-wide in scope and operated wherever there was a demand for its services.

The Salmon Report states: 'We do not know exactly when Mr Poulson first resorted to corrupt methods in order to obtain work, but we have reason to believe that it was as early as 1949/50'. One of Poulson's main aides and fellow conspirators was T. Dan Smith, then leader of the majority Labour group and chairman of the planning and building committees of the Newcastle-upon-Tyne City Council. Later, he became chairman of the Northern Economic Planning Council, and of other public bodies. He was a man with much patronage to offer. What Smith did for Poulson—they worked hand in glove—was to appoint councillors of various local authorities as paid 'consultants' to one or other of the fourteen public relations companies he controlled. The 'councillor-consultants' were expected to use their influence to see that Poulson's company got the contracts it wanted. Poulson, Smith, and the various local councillors benefited from this comfortable arrangement, and the great architectural firm from a steady flow of work. For various reasons, Poulson went bankrupt in 1972. This meant that the Official Receiver now had access to his books and papers. Cross-examined during his public examination in bankruptcy, Poulson allowed a number of facts to emerge which suggested he had been engaged with others in corrupt practices. In June 1973 he was proceeded against under the Prevention of Corruption Acts and was convicted in February 1974. A large number of senior public servants were also prosecuted as a result of wide-ranging investigations by the police.

As the Salmon Report states:

The information ... shows that over the years Mr Poulson had succeeded in corruptly penetrating high levels of the civil service, the National Health Service, two nationalised industries and a number of local authorities, involving in one case the chairman of a police authority ... We doubt whether Mr Poulson would ever have been prosecuted but for his bankruptcy and his habit of meticulously preserving copies of everything he wrote or was written to him—however incriminating these pieces of paper might be.

The Report contains the statement: 'We do not believe that the growth of the public sector necessarily creates greater risks of corruption'. The use of the word 'necessarily' might suggest that the commissioners could not make up their minds about the matter or that they were split into two groups, that some probably believed it did make a contribution to corruption, as argued above. The Report continues:

Nevertheless, the fortunes of companies and individual citizens have undoubtedly been increasingly influenced by the decisions of central government and other public institutions. Any situation in which public authorities exercise controls or have business to offer is potentially vulnerable to corruption ... A significant minority does not measure up to acceptable standards.

It is interesting to note that the Royal Commission on Standards of Conduct in Public Life was set up in the same year as was Hong Kong's ICAC, 1974, although of course there is no direct connection between the two events; on the other hand, the 1970s was a period when many corruption scandals surfaced, some with international ramifications (such as the Lockheed imbroglio). The 1970s came at the end of a period of growth in many domestic economies and in world trade, before the price of oil shot up. The point needs no underlining: economic growth, an expansion in trade, a buoyant market, these provide more opportunities for the corrupt, the dishonest, and the greedy.

So far no definition of corruption has been attempted, and that has been deliberate. It is better to do so after circling the problem and providing a few examples of its nature and types. A definition adopted by some political scientists and sociologists is that by Nye. He writes (in a style that gives social science a bad name among the literate) that corruption may be defined as:

Behaviour which deviates from the formal duties of a public role (elective or appointive) because of private-regarding (personal, close family, private clique) wealth or status gains: or violates rules against the exercise of private-regarding influence.

His definition is at least comprehensive, if glutinous. McMullan, on the other hand, presents a more commonsensical and readable interpretation:

a public official is corrupt if he accepts money or money's worth for doing something that he is under a duty to do anyway, that he is under a duty not to do, or to exercise a legitimate discretion for improper purposes. Institutions have official aims, the human beings that work them have personal aims. The ideal relation between the individual and the institution is that the individual should be able to satisfy his personal aims in harmony with, and while forwarding, the official aims of the institution.

This is a helpful way of looking at the problem. Although McMullan is concerned with the public rather than the private sector, the last part of his statement would apply to individuals working for any business enterprise.

One can of course avoid definitional problems and say, *tout court*, that corruption is what the law states it to be, and none other. Even if we agree that this is so, the problem of interpreting the law has to be faced. There are three main ingredients in the legal offence: first, it has to be shown by the prosecution that a gift or consideration was given or offered by one party to another (this is objective and a matter of evidence); second, that the gift or consideration was given, or received, as an inducement or reward for services to be rendered or already rendered in relation to official duties (this is subjective, broadly speaking, for it involves a mental element or *mens rea*, that is, a guilty mind); and third, that the transaction took place corruptly (here again, the problem of *mens rea* intrudes). The law itself provokes exegesis and interpretation, disputes about meaning.

The man in the street knows, too well, when he is being 'squeezed'; he is not stuporous, flat on his back, when involved in graft or extortion as practitioner or victim. All those, in Hong Kong, engaged in business, commerce, or industry know full well that commissions are illegal unless the receiver has his employer's consent. It is said that no good deed goes unpunished, so the civil servant who does a service for a friend, and infringes the law, is likely to be called on to do so again; but he need *not* comply. Corruption is a rational act, associated with benefit. It is not a sleepwalker's occupation, not a mysterious happening; people do not drift into it unwittingly, like a child into a wild wood full of dangerous creatures. Those who are corrupt or allow themselves to be corrupted always take pains to erase their tracks; they wish to remain invisible, ghosts in the economic machine. A person does not need to read the Theft Ordinance to find out he has picked a pocket or mugged an old lady. The definition of corruption, whether legal or sociological, is certainly of importance to lawyers and scholars; but the man in the street has a good enough working knowledge of social behaviour to know what corruption is.

Technical problems face all legal draftsmen. The 1971 Prevention of Bribery Ordinance has been amended several times in order to close loopholes in the law and to make it a more efficient instrument for catching the corrupt. The process is unending, for the venal element in the population—law breakers—is often as sharp and wary as law-makers, often more so. Cases that come to court, some celebrated, some routine and hardly noticed, reveal only the tip of the iceberg: the 'dark figure' (unreported or undetected events) is difficult to determine. This is because, firstly, much corruption is consensual and those parties involved in the transaction obtain satisfaction from the, almost contractual, arrangements. Even in obvious cases, not all victims will report the facts, for various reasons, to the police or the ICAC; the possibility of invoking reprisals from strong-arm men being only one of a number of motives for not doing so. This problem—the enigma of the dark figure—is important because any upward trend in reporting the offence does not necessarily imply an increase in scale and volume, although it might mean that.

2
SCANDAL AND CORRUPTION,
1842–1941

'The heart is deceitful above
all things, and desperately wicked.
Who can know it?'

Jeremiah 17:9

No attempt will be made in this chapter to provide a chrono-
logical history of Hong Kong corruption; only a few cases,
exemplar, will be discussed. That corruption always flourished
in Hong Kong is indisputable; that its forms have not markedly
changed can be demonstrated. The real problem is to determine how far the practice infected the higher levels of government, and that is not easy. At lower levels it was rampant and
institutionalized, a customary habit known to all. Every government attempt to enforce its prohibitory and regulatory
laws normally created fresh opportunities for the corrupt.
Thus, in the 1890s, legislation designed to force all house-
holders to whitewash their homes regularly (a precautionary
measure to control endemic plague in Taipingshan) directly
encouraged corruption; it did so by providing an opportunity
for sanitary inspectors to report the whitewashing as having
been done when clearly it had not. No one checked their reports. And if someone had, no doubt he too might have been
susceptible to bribery.

The early history of Hong Kong may be likened to that of
an American frontier town or the pioneering days of the Aus-
tralian colonies. The new settlement attracted growing numbers of speculators, adventurers, shady lawyers and shysters,
men on the make (and take), as well as Chinese crooks,

Triads, brothel-keepers, legions of whores, and opium-den proprietors. The merchant class of both races was prepared to cut corners, to sail close to the law—for who wanted to settle in this insignificant spot when he could do better at home? Who envisioned a life sentence in Hong Kong, then notorious for its high mortality rate?

The new colony was a law-breaking one; and the law could only be enforced spasmodically and erratically; it impinged mostly on the labouring classes. The denizens of Hong Kong did not carry six-shooters on their hips; for European Hong Kong was a distorting mirror of mid-Victorian England— outwardly respectable, conservative, conformist, snobbish, and Sabbatarian. Men dressed for dinner. Women wore gloves, richer ladies the latest Paris fashions. But beneath the lacquer was a frantic scramble for wealth, with the intruding reminder that life was short on the China coast. Nigel Cameron has called Hong Kong a 'cultured pearl'. But from another perspective it was 'uncultured', uncultivated, proudly mediocre and philistine, a society in which money spoke, as it does today, with a deafening voice. It lacked both an English aristocracy and a Chinese mandarin class. Given these attributes, one should not expect its new citizens to have been models of civil comportment, paragons of virtue, Bayards of business. Social and economic conditions at that time created and encouraged corruption. Hong Kong was a classic example of Pareto's élite of *speculators* (foxes), by which this Italian sociologist meant manipulative entrepreneurs, the crafty, cunning masters of money, in contrast to *rentiers* (lions), men of breeding and feudal instincts.

An important change came about in 1861 with the introduction by Sir Hercules Robinson, the Governor, of 'Hongkong Cadetships', the recruitment into the civil service by competitive examination of educated young men from the British Isles to act as interpreters, for whom there was then a great need. There was, however, a still greater need for trained administrators and these the cadets quickly became. They began to take over key appointments so that by the end of the century most heads of department were cadet officers (administrative officers, as we now call them). A cadet expected to rise, grade by grade, to the top, to become a departmental chief, the gifted or fortunate to achieve a colonial secretaryship or governorship, if not in Hong Kong then in some other colonial possession.

Before 1861, officials had been recruited from all sorts and conditions of mankind, many being former naval or military officers. Sir Hercules' scheme introduced 'public administration' into Hong Kong and a career in the Hong Kong civil service became sought after by many a public schoolboy who lacked parental means or by those who failed entrance into the prestigious Indian Civil Service.

The cadets were all of British stock (the first Chinese, Paul Tsui, was appointed in 1948). They came from conventional middle- or upper-middle-class families, and were largely educated at English public schools and at Oxbridge. But there was always a large component of Scots and Irish, in the main from the same social stratum (the professional classes), though some Scots had humbler origins. Cadets formed a small élite within the civil service, sharing the same background, education, aspirations, and values. They were paid, by Victorian standards, good salaries, enjoyed high social status, and could look forward to a more than adequate pension. They were an élite, but also a caste, separated from the executive grade by education, social background, income and position. They were also distinct from the taipan class—'The aristocracy of the Moneybag', to use Carlyle's phrase—by superior education and a disdain for trade and commerce. And in Hong Kong, unlike Shanghai, the official took precedence. As a group, cadets were not inclined to accept bribes. Moreover, they did not marry into the Chinese, Eurasian or Asiatic communities, for a mixed marriage would have affected their career. This was not entirely a matter of racial prejudice but rather a device to prevent cadets from collecting large numbers of Chinese or non-European relatives, with the possibility that a cadet would be exploited by his relatives or encouraged

CHAPTER TWO

to indulge in nepotism. The cadet was thus not only separated
from various segments of the European community but also
from the non-European community. Hong Kong, as it
were, was divided into 'officers and gentlemen' and 'other
ranks'.

The assertion that cadets were not inclined to accept bribes
is not really controversial, although it is conjectural. In the
period 1861–1941 no senior official was dismissed for corruption (the cases of Mitchell-Innes, Forrest, and Steele-Perkins
will be mentioned later). Those few who either resigned or
were dismissed were not charged with a criminal offence but
with incompetence; some who resigned did so in order to take
up a more lucrative post, such as R.D. Starkey who left government service in 1866 to join the North China Insurance
Company, in Shanghai. Cadets and other senior officials were,
to repeat, well-paid and enjoyed many privileges, including
paid leave and housing. The temptation to accept bribes cannot have been great, unlike the underpaid Imperial Chinese
magistrate who was forced into acceptance so as to maintain a
seemly way of life. Nor were officials allowed to engage in private business, as some had done in the early days of the Colony, when there had been much involvement in land and
property speculation. Again, later in the century nearly all
senior officials lived in the European-reserved Peak District
and had few contacts with the local population except on cere-
monial occasions. They were not permitted to marry into the
non-European community but were tightly enclosed in their
own. In brief, they were presented with few opportunities for
becoming corrupt and experienced little temptation to do
so. More importantly, the volume of economic activity was
small compared with today: Hong Kong was then mainly
an entrepôt.

The occupational and social separation of cadets and senior
officials from *pong-paân* (European supervisors, overseers, inspectors, low-level management staff) and from the Chinese
community, especially the coolie class, labourers, artisans,
and shopkeepers, did, however, provide opportunities for

27

much small-scale corruption and extortion, as it still does to-day. The attempt to regulate the Chinese population was in the hands, necessarily, of the police and numerous inspectors of one type or another, most of whom were European. The latter mixed with Chinese not only occupationally but often socially or sexually, as they lived in quarters of the town inhabited also by non-Europeans (Wan Chai, for example). The inspectorate was a focus for corruption; the standards of its members were lower because their economic position was precarious; they could not afford to be too high-minded; and, in any case, they had not been trained in the principles of *noblesse oblige* or strongly influenced by the standards of the emergent Victorian middle and professional classes.

Leo Goodstadt has referred in the *Far Eastern Economic Review* to a former governor (nicknamed 'Cumshaw') 'allegedly so corrupt that he needed an entire ship's hold to carry away his loot on retirement'. The acceptance of gifts by government servants, although subject to regulations, was not uncommon before 1941. Even the incorruptible Sir James Stewart Lockhart (1858–1937), Colonial Secretary of Hong Kong, 1892–1902, received and officially accepted presents from Chinese community leaders and Chinese dignitaries in Hong Kong and, as Commissioner, in Weihaiwei. After retirement, a number were proudly displayed in his Kensington flat. He could not, at times, refuse a gift without causing the donor to lose face, or breach the rules of Chinese etiquette, equivalent to not returning a polite bow in public from a leading citizen. Non-acceptance, in certain situations, would have been interpreted as a snub, as a politically maladroit action.

Gift-giving was a traditional Chinese custom and Hong Kong and Weihaiwei, British-administered territories, were overwhelmingly populated by Chinese. A gift, together with its acceptance or reciprocity, may symbolize any number of conditions or relationships; for example, gratitude, love, deference, superiority or inferiority, and patron-client status; or, on the other hand, contempt, 'one-upmanship' (as Stephen Potter insidiously insists, 'If you're not one up you're one down').

The value of a gift in itself may provide social information about the donor and/or recipient.

It is not always easy to avoid making crass retrospective judgments nor to avoid applying the standards of the present to the past. Even the currency of words, and standards, has changed in a comparatively brief period: thus the Victorian cad has become today's *homme moyen sensuel.* The sinister purport of the gift was not so obvious to the nineteenth-century intelligence, for today we have been educated into an understanding of the sociology of corruption, become more aware, sentinel. But there is little hard evidence to suggest that gifts seriously corrupted the majority of pre-war senior civil servants, in that they declined to do what they should have done or did what was clearly criminal or illegal. As the poet T.W.H. Crosland said, untruthfully alas, of himself: '... there are many things he might have sold and did not sell'. Before 1941, officials were expected to seek advice on whether to accept gifts (and probably most complied if the value of the gift was significant). The point made here is that at the upper levels of government gifts were received routinely, as tributes to office, but few pay-offs in cash were ever proffered or accepted. This is surmise, of course; but the standard of living generally maintained by retired senior civil servants would seem to confirm that this was true; so, too, does a scrutiny of a selection of wills deposited at Somerset House. There is no reason piously to conclude that all were angels, only that few were fallen ones.

There is a difficult thesis to confront, that the nullity of cases meant that the law was not enforced, that detection was acutely difficult (for corruption rarely leaves a spoor), or that no one in high office bothered much about the matter. The rather cynical counter-argument is that before the war the amount of money invested in corrupt practices must have been at an extraordinarily low level compared with the present because Hong Kong's GNP was minimal—and the businessman, entrepreneur, crook, or speculator did not have large sums to dangle enticingly before the eyes of wavering civil servants. A man may have his price, but if the price is not right he is likely not to be moved, and will remain secure in his probity. In stark terms, opportunities for corruption were then scanter and the sums of money involved smaller. However, the finances of a governor are not usually scrutinized, monitored, or investigated, so perhaps Leo Goodstadt's story is not all legend, for no one is claiming that there was *no* graft before 1941, an absurd proposition as we shall see.

In June 1897, John Joseph Francis, a leading public figure and Hong Kong's most eminent QC, sent a brief missive to the Captain Superintendent of Police informing him that illegal gambling houses were operating in the Western District of the town. It seems plausible to argue that Francis' note was intended to discomfit the Captain Superintendent, F.H. May, a cadet officer. Two years before, Francis had returned to the Governor a silver inkstand presented to him in recognition of services rendered in the 1894 epidemic of bubonic plague. He had been 'miffed' that May, a colleague on the Permanent Committee of the Sanitary Board, of which Francis was chairman, had been *more* honoured than he. As he expatiated in a long letter to the Governor: 'The gift of a silver inkstand from the Governor of Hong Kong is, Your Excellency will pardon the expression, so ludicrously inadequate to the services rendered'. May had been honoured with a CMG: did Francis expect a KCMG? The knowledge that illegal gambling was flourishing, as Francis intimated, under the noses of the men he commanded, must have perturbed May, for he had often been assured by detectives that the evil had been suppressed.

On 21 June 1897 May personally led a raid on one of the houses, which turned out to be the headquarters of a large gambling enterprise. The premises were sedulously searched and a number of compromising and incriminating records seized. It soon became clear that a high percentage of the police force had been paid regularly—bribed—so that gambling houses would remain inviolate. May had thus, thanks to Francis, stumbled upon the existence of a gross case of 'syndicated corruption' (as the ICAC now designates this particular abuse of public office), the presence of a large-scale protection racket, which involved both Chinese and European officers, of junior and senior rank. May was not an inexperienced Captain Superintendent—his appointment dated from 1893—and it must have irritated him to know that Francis had better 'inside' knowledge of the 'bad hats' of Hong Kong than had he.

May, a hard-working and efficient official, acted swiftly, with the full support of the government, backed by the Colonial Office. He set about decimating his force, especially the detective branch, by dismissals. The final tally, as given in the *Hong Kong Government Gazette* for 12 March 1898, was: one European inspector convicted of receiving bribes and sentenced to six months' imprisonment with hard labour; three inspectors and one sergeant dismissed; two inspectors and two sergeants forced to resign; and two sergeants and one acting sergeant not re-engaged. Another sergeant resigned voluntarily. Nineteen Indian police were also dismissed; forty-four Chinese police either resigned or were dismissed. May added, sombrely, that there were '49 Asiatic Policemen still serving whose names were on the list'. Altogether, the police lost about half their establishment.

May's ruthless culling eliminated nearly the entire detective branch, the body of professional 'thief-takers'. One casualty was Chief Detective Inspector William Stanton, born in Liskeard, Cornwall, who had joined the force in 1873 as acting sergeant. He was the local expert on Chinese secret societies, the author of 'The Triad Society or Heaven and Earth Association', first published in *Thё China Review*, but later issued, in 1900, in book form. Another was the celebrated Inspector Quincey, distinguished because he had been General Gordon's protégé. When Gordon took the city of Quin-san in 1863, he enlisted 2,000 defeated Taiping rebels in the 'Ever Victorious Army' (the Imperialist force Gordon commanded). One prisoner taken was young Quincey, whose English cognomen was adapted from the place where he was found. Gordon, who had a penchant for waifs and strays, sent Quincey to be educated in England at a regimental school. In 1870 he was brought back to Hong Kong and enlisted in the police. He now spoke very good English; his deportment was that of an Englishman; and he wore Western dress. His rise was steady: he was the first Chinese to be promoted to the inspectorate. And his fall was spectacular. It reinforced the European stereotype that *all* Chinese police were venal, and that Quincey was no exception. Localization in the police suffered a setback from which it took decades to recover.

The only European convicted and imprisoned was Inspector Job Witchell. Witchell, a Gloucestershire man, transferred from the Bristol Constabulary to the Hong Kong police in 1880. Like Stanton and Quincey, he was an experienced officer, a great loss to the force. He was convicted of receiving bribes and sentenced to six months' imprisonment with hard labour. Witchell was unfortunate because in his case, unlike the others, May had found the intermediaries through whose hands the money had been passed to Witchell, and they had turned Queen's evidence. At his trial Witchell expostulated: 'I have a family of five children and a European wife, my Lord, solely dependent on me. My sole estate in Hong Kong ... $1,198 for ten years'. His only consolation: he was taken to Victoria Gaol in a sedan chair.

A *Hongkong Telegraph* editorialist animadverted:

The chair coolies, the coal lumpers, the 'water rats' and the native and domestic servants gloried in the fact that an Inspector of Police had at last been found out in the gravest and most revolting dereliction of duty that it is conceivable an officer in his position could be guilty of.

Strong words; but not all level-headed persons agreed with them. It is illuminating to read Dr (later Sir) James Cantlie's comments on the gambling scandal. He wrote (in 1898):

At the present moment there is considerable scandal in connection with the acceptance of bribes by European police, and men of great local experience are being got rid of because they took 'tips'; surely a well-understood purloin of the police in all countries ... The Chinese members, if not quite reliable as regards their moral tone as police, are invaluable aids in the detection of crime. A leading member of the detectives is Inspector Quincey, 'Chinese' Gordon's old 'boy'. Unfortunately he has also fallen under the ban of the purists, and he has been dismissed the force. Surely his connection with his great master, and the dangers and perils he endured in his behalf [sic], might have saved him from this indignity. One can only be thankful that Gordon did not live to see this further 'neglect' heaped upon those he already endured at the hands of his 'grateful' country.

Cantlie was a distinguished surgeon, an authority on tropical medicine, and, until 1896, Dean of the College of Medicine for Chinese, the Hong Kong medical school where Sun Yat-sen studied. His views are interesting because they mirror the mixed feelings with which some Victorians viewed corruption, as venial rather than venal at the lower levels of society, where wages and salaries were low. A certain amount of 'squeeze', Cantlie implied, was simply a perk attached to the policeman's occupation.

What the general public then thought of the police is perhaps revealed in the *China Mail* of 4 August 1897. The editor wrote:

We are convinced the Police Force has never been free from corruption. Gambling-houses, brothels, pawnshops, are the mainstays of the blackmailer: and perhaps the millennium of honesty and cleanliness will never blossom into full flame, because it is the nature of the Chinaman to pay hush-money.

Ironically, low-level corruption had been amplified by government action, by the puritanical attempt to turn Hong Kong into a moral society, by legislation. *Hoi polloi*, on the other hand, were enthusiastic about gambling (as were Europeans who congregated at the Happy Valley racecourse); they did not regard indulgence as a serious vice; and, in a territory where men greatly outnumbered women, especially *good* women, most males found brothels to be not only places of pleasurable recreation but also a biological necessity. Missionary mortifications were not for the average man. And because this was so, the police were always able to supplement their meagre salaries with squeeze.

Hong Kong—it is an obvious point—was not unique in harbouring corrupt policemen. In 1877 the famed London Metropolitan Police, the prototype of many professional forces (with the marked exception of the French), experienced a similar scandal, after which a large part of its detective force was imprisoned, dismissed, or resigned. Those involved were senior, and hence experienced, detective officers. This scandal is usually referred to as the 'Turf Frauds' or the 'de Goncourt Case' and is the subject of a study by George Dilnot, *The Trial of the Detectives* (1928).

It originated in a series of frauds perpetrated by Harry Benson, an extremely intelligent, well-educated young man, a confidence trickster and swindler of genius, who had opened a number of 'bogus' betting establishments. His downfall came about when he attempted to entice the rich Comtesse de Goncourt, who lived in France, into investing £30,000 (she had already parted with £10,000) in his betting schemes. Her alarmed French lawyer, once he knew of Benson's solicitations and appreciated the Comtesse's credulity, informed Scotland Yard. For several years Benson had been defrauding a gullible public of large sums of money with the connivance of detectives at the Yard. He and his confederates had not been apprehended because they were always given advance warning of attempts to track them down. By various inducements, and by subsequent blackmail, Benson had involved many detectives in his deceptions. They did not seriously investigate his dubious and movable enterprises. The trial of the detectives on a charge of conspiracy to obstruct justice (a common law offence) started on 24 October 1877. It was, up to that date, the longest trial in the history of the Old Bailey.

In this instance, the participating detectives had been corrupted by an exceedingly sharp and manipulative young man. As for the Hong Kong scandal of 1897, it is now impossible to determine how or when the syndicated corruption arose. But the lesson to be drawn from both cases is clear: corruption is a latent occupational disease for all law enforcers, if only because they maintain a symbiotic relationship with the

34

CHAPTER TWO

underworld; they participate in, to a lesser or greater degree, a criminal subculture, they frequent the same milieux. And police informers, who play a key role in all detective work, are also members of the criminal fraternity or live on its fringes. This is not a black-and-white world, of good and bad, but a grey *terrain vague*, where hunter and hunted may come to share the same ambiguous values and grow estranged from the conventional world.

On the other hand, with each career step forward a policeman tends to separate himself from the dingy workaday world of the detective or the man on the beat. Inevitably, with elevation, he tends to become more of a 'desk wallah', walled in by paper, minuting files that circulate unceasingly at higher levels. The man at the top is thus often remarkably ignorant, as was May, of the world as it is at street level. He becomes an administrator, a bureaucrat preoccupied with the minutiae of organization. This dilemma remains. Possibly it can never be solved satisfactorily.

Other public servants, not only police, were found to have been suborned during the period, such as Sanitary Inspector Thomas Hore. He was charged with receiving bribes from gambling-house keepers. These were not passed on directly but to his Portuguese mistress. In the course of his official inspections, Hore had noted with interest that some premises he visited had gambling paraphernalia on display. He profited from the knowledge and was paid to keep silent. It should be emphasized that in the 1880s the government could not be too particular in the recruitment of those who filled the lower grades: they could only choose from a small number of Europeans resident in Hong Kong. These were mostly a rum lot: beachcombers, discharged seamen or soldiers, drunkards, debtors, the flotsam and jetsam of the British Empire. The Cantonese referred to the European inspectorate as *pong-paân* (help-manage) as contrasted with *taai-paân* (bosses) and distinguished between them: the first could be got at, the second less so.

Hore, for example, had been Chief Usher to the Shanghai

Supreme Court but had been sentenced in 1888 to five years' penal servitude for criminal assault. He served his sentence in Hong Kong's Victoria Gaol and on release was taken on as an inspector in the Sanitary Department. He was a man with a criminal record, a boozer and womanizer; but he was British and the inspectorate was mainly staffed by Europeans, some Eurasians and Portuguese. The privilege was not normally granted to Chinese. It is, needless to say, not surprising that corruption flourished in the lower reaches of government.

That corruption extended far beyond the domain of the police was made clear by the lengthy report of the Commission of Inquiry into the Public Works Department (PWD), published in 1902 as a sessional paper. It was revealed, once again, that corrupt practices flourished blatantly at the lower levels of the PWD where *pong-paân* and Chinese met face to face. The Director of Public Works, William Chatham, admitted to the Commissioners that he could not exercise proper supervision and gave as his reason that 'there is such an immense amount of office work at present that it is impossible to find time and go round and look after the staff and inspect works'.

The inspection of works was carried out, therefore, by executive engineers (those with trade qualifications rather than university degrees, unlike cadet officers), many of whom were suspected of conniving at botched work after receiving *douceurs* from local contractors, a 'satisfied customer' species of corruption. This did not necessarily mean the payment of cash but conciliatory presents of value at Christmas or Chinese New Year, or at any other time. European overseers and Chinese foremen were also alleged to be particularly prone to accepting bribes, as one would suppose. Chatham was asked specifically whether he thought 'overseers are bribed to allow the use of improper materials or an insufficiency of materials, such as lime or cement'. He did not give a straight reply to that question. He was offended by the questioner's insinuation. But he did admit that European overseers generally were not made of the 'right stuff'.

CHAPTER TWO

In his speech on the 1898 financial estimates, the Governor, Sir William Robinson, opined:

I must refer with great regret to the grave irregularities which have recently been shown to exist in the Police Force and in other departments of the Government Service amongst the subordinate officers ... I fear there can be no doubt that these irregularities have been in existence for many years.

The government's alarm was expressed in a new ordinance, the Misdemeanours Punishment Ordinance, which became law on 23 February 1898. The new legislation was enacted, as the Attorney-General informed the Legislative Council, 'for the more effectual punishment of bribery and certain other misdemeanours'. He declared: 'In Hong Kong no power of inflicting hard labour on offenders convicted of accepting or offering bribes exists, and this state of affairs should not be allowed to continue'. In effect, the maximum punishment for the offence was now set at two years' imprisonment with or without hard labour or a fine not exceeding $500, or both. The Ordinance thus provided for more severe punishment—the imposition of hard labour (a penal distinction which has now vanished: today imprisonment is not differentiated into categories). The 1898 Ordinance became the basis for all the legislation that followed dealing with bribery and corruption.

The introduction of a more severe penalty is a standard official response to a crime that has shaken the public's confidence in law and order or to one that has been given great publicity in the press. An increase in penalty should be seen as an expressive act, the reflection of a current mood. But enactment is never enough; enforcement is necessary. The 1898 Ordinance did not create any special body, within or without the police, to investigate allegations of bribery and corruption. The problem was left, as before, in the hands of the police. Corruption among 'subordinate officers' (the group especially referred to by Sir William Robinson) continued. The gambling scandal had simply erupted, caused great perturbation, and subsided. A scapegoat, Witchell, had been humbled in a public trial, and many others dismissed or forced to resign. There was no follow-up. The government, in 1898, thought the matter had been largely dealt with, the bad apples removed and replaced by better. The social reasons that gave rise to corruption were not seriously examined, for that would have necessitated a critique of the fabric of government and society in Hong Kong.

In 1941 two great scandals disturbed Hong Kong, and especially the British community, and reinforced doubts as to the integrity of its civil service. Each gave rise to allegations of widespread corruption. The first resulted from the setting up on 18 November 1940 of a new Immigration Department, an outcome of the Immigration Control Ordinance of that same year. R.A.D. Forrest, a veteran cadet officer with over twenty years of experience in government service, was appointed its first head. Before that date, problems arising from uncontrolled immigration and emigration had been handled principally by the police or the Secretariat for Chinese Affairs. The need for a special department had been created by the massive influx of refugees, panicked into flight from South China by the Japanese invasion of, and military operations in, Guangdong Province in 1938. Over half a million Chinese fled to Hong Kong between 1938 and 1940. This very rapid expansion in the size of the Hong Kong Chinese population created difficulties for the government and strained its resources and capacity to govern efficiently.

The newly established Immigration Department was necessarily a makeshift affair. Staff were recruited hurriedly without much vetting. Many had no previous experience of government service; some were simply opportunists; a few, the innately corrupt, must have scented opportunities for squeeze or peculation. Eight European and seventeen Chinese Assistant Immigration Officers were quickly recruited. The former were a mixed lot and included a Frenchman, a White Russian, and a Hungarian. Only one was already working in the civil service when appointed to his new post. The Hungarian, for example, set up a studio in his office for quick passport photo-

graphs and signed 'official' cheques without the countersigna-
ture of his superior. The rush to obtain certificates of residence
led to chaos since most Chinese feared, wrongly in fact, that
without a chit from the Immigration Department they would
be deported back to China, into the hands of the beastly and
ferocious Japanese. By its very nature, the new Immigration
Department created conditions for chicanery and corrupt
practices, 'paying for convenience' as we now say. Rumours
swiftly spread about malpractices, malversation, and administrative inefficiency. On 28 February 1941 the Governor, Sir
Geoffrey Northcote, appointed a Commission of Inquiry
under the chairmanship of Sir Athol MacGregor, the Chief
Justice. In mid-June their report was issued. It was a scathing
document. It bluntly stated that Forrest was an irresponsible
incompetent, unfit to run a government department. He was
allowed to 'resign' and left the Colony for England. In retrospect, he was a very lucky fellow. Sir Athol MacGregor, who
had excoriated Forrest in his report, continued to live on the
Peak and was resident there when the Japanese overran Hong
Kong. He ended up in Stanley Internment Camp and expired
in October 1945, his death hastened by malnutrition and
other ills occasioned by his Japanese captors. Forrest, on the
other hand, outlived the war and ended up as a lecturer in the
School of Oriental and African Studies at the University of
London.

   Forrest was only the second cadet to have been sacked since
the cadet scheme was introduced in 1861 by the Governor, Sir
Hercules Robinson. The first had been N.G. Mitchell-Innes,
blamed in 1893 by the Secretary of State, the Marquis of
Ripon, for allowing defalcations to occur in the Hong Kong
Treasury, of which he—Mitchell-Innes—was the appointed
custodian. (This delinquent cadet also survived the grave crisis in his affairs. Later he became deputy governor of a gaol in
the north of England and as an inspector in the English Prison
Commission retired on pension in 1919.) Both Mitchell-Innes
and Forrest, be it noted, were held *accountable* for the respective
misdeeds of their subordinates. Since 1945, as we shall see, the

principle of accountability has not been applied so stringently as before the war to remove or weed out the incompetent or corrupt from the public service. Only one senior cadet has been forced to resign since the end of the war, because, so it is alleged, the Governor disapproved of his social life. A great deal of lateral shuffling of posts has occurred, a device commonly used to shift an official from one job to another, where it is hoped he will be less of a danger to the public he purportedly serves.

Forrest, need it be said, was not himself corrupt and was probably as efficient, or innocuous, as most of his cadet colleagues. But he had been placed in a most difficult position: to create a new department from scratch, and in a great hurry. He could only recruit staff from a depleted pool of Europeans resident in Hong Kong in November 1940 and from Chinese about whom little was known. At heart, he was a scholar, an excellent linguist who wrote, as Sir Victor Purcell comments, 'a notable book on the Chinese language'. Appointed to the Hong Kong civil service in 1919, aged 26, he soon mastered the routines of administration, not too difficult a task in those less trying inter-war years. He was, as it were, a victim of the Colonial Office dogma of the 'omnicompetent generalist': the belief that a trained administrator should be able to switch, like a professional dancer, from position to position, from tempo to tempo. Today, although this notion has not evaporated, the need for experts and specialists in government is more widely appreciated.

The immigration imbroglio, with its intimations or undertones of corruption, was almost totally eclipsed by the great air-raid precautions (ARP) scandal later in the same year, 1941. The background to this event may be given briefly. The Spanish Civil War had demonstrated the vulnerability of civilian populations to bombing from aircraft. The need to protect, in particular, those who lived in cities or worked in factories, shipyards and docks, was quickly recognized. Even before Britain declared war on Germany in September 1939, air-raid precautions schemes had been devised; and in 1938 the colonies were instructed to institute plans similar to those in Britain. As early as 1938, a sum of $50,000 was included in the Hong Kong financial estimates. The amount voted by the Legislative Council for air-raid precautions increased markedly from year to year, so that by 1 October 1941 total expenditure had reached over $8 million, a very large sum in those pre-inflationary years.

Wing Commander A.H.S. Steele-Perkins, accompanied by his wife, arrived in Hong Kong by ship on 16 March 1938 to take up his duties as Hong Kong's first Air Raid Precautions Officer (later upgraded to Director of ARP). Born in 1887, he had joined the Royal Navy as a midshipman in 1905. During the First World War he served in the Royal Naval Air Service, transferred to the Royal Air Force in 1918, then back to the Fleet Air Arm in 1928. He was a man of wide and varied experience—an expert—when he reached Hong Kong, having also served on the Committee of Imperial Defence in the early 1930s, followed by five years in the Home Office, advising on air defence. For as early as 1935, the Home Office had started to prepare schemes on paper; and, under the energetic leadership of Sir John Anderson, began in 1938 to implement them in Britain. A good organizer, energetic and sanguine, with all the gusto and bounce of the old-style naval officer, Steele-Perkins took his job most seriously, lecturing to somewhat languid colonial audiences on the need to prepare Hong Kong for future air attacks, a realistic notion in 1938 since the Japanese had reached the border of the New Territories and, at times, had trespassed into British territory.

ARP costs were limited, in 1938 and 1939, mainly to the payment of personal emoluments, the supply of badges and other equipment, official publications, and fees for lecturers. Then, in November 1940, the Legislative Council passed a supplementary vote of $1 million for underground shelters, in the form of tunnels excavated from Hong Kong's hillsides. The 1941 Budget provided a further sum of $4 million. The lack of air-raid shelters for the mass of the population had been strongly criticized in 1939 by the Chinese Unofficial members of the Legislative Council; and reports of the awful effects of bombing in Europe had, of course, been registered by the Hong Kong Defence Committee, composed of unnamed members of the armed services and government departments. Both sets of facts, and others, had powerfully concentrated the government's mind on the problem of air defence. The go-ahead was thus given in late 1940 to tunnel the granite hills. This was not a task the government itself could easily under-take; an understaffed PWD was not able to cope with this grand project. The actual tunnelling and construction work was therefore contracted out to Marsman Hong Kong China Limited, a company based in the Philippines (then under American governance) and controlled by Jan Marsman, a Dutchman with American nationality. A new government de-partment, the ARP Department, had already been created in 1939, with Steele-Perkins as Director, so that now the Wing Commander was a key participant in a great engineering proj-ect to shelter a large part of the urban population, on both sides of the harbour. Steele-Perkins was no sluggard; he joyfully took over supervision; but his enthusiasm outran his vigilance.

There is a parallel here with the exposure of the immigra-tion scandal earlier in the year, as rumours started to filter back to senior government officials about irregularities in the administration, supervision, and financing of the work carried out by the ARP Department. It should be stressed that in 1941 the European, largely British, community was small and tight-knit. Those who mattered nearly all belonged to the Hong Kong Club or met at the Hong Kong Hotel (known as 'The Grips') in Pedder Street. Gossip could hardly be con-tained, as tongues wagged over drink after drink and suave discretion disappeared. Gossip is a social lubricant, a way to make friends and influence people. It was, however, the Hong-kong and Shanghai Banking Corporation which officially sounded the alarm. This great institution, the linchpin of Hong Kong, had potent influence; its magisterial voice was always listened to by those in authority.

CHAPTER TWO

The precipitating factor was the blacking out of the Bank's headquarters at 1 Queen's Road, Central. For this task the Bank had been allotted $500 by an ARP official but had accomplished it for only $87. The disparity was so great that an alarmed banker reported the facts to a senior government official. On 8 April 1941 a Commission of Inquiry was instituted under the chairmanship of the Puisne Judge, P.E.F. Cressall, a newcomer to Hong Kong: the other Commissioners were L.C.F. Bellamy, General Manager of Hong Kong Tramways; S.H. Ross, an accountant; and, as secretary, a cadet officer, K.M.A. Barnett. (Oddly, the last three were all Freemasons. Masonry is, arguably, itself a social 'conspiracy': and scholars have stressed similarities between it and Chinese secret societies.) The Commission's terms of reference were, among other matters:

To inquire into and report upon (1) matters disclosed at a recent departmental investigation into charges against a Government officer (since dismissed) concerning the payment of a cheque for $500 for work done for the Government of this Colony and coming under the supervision of the architectural branch of the Air Raid Precautions Department, and (2) the practice and presentation of contractors' accounts for such work and of their certification by Government officers, and (3) in particular, as to whether gifts in cash have been received by any Government officer from contractors engaged in constructional work supervised by the architectural branch of the Air Raid Precautions Department ...

The Commission sat from 14 August to 7 November 1941. Although the public hearings were reported at inordinate length in the newspapers, no document on the inquiry was ever published or made public, for the Japanese invasion of 8 December 1941 supervened. Cressall, now a captive of the Japanese, took a draft into Stanley Internment Camp with him as part of his sparse impedimenta.

The press, however, day after day did unfold a startling tale of how the ARP Department conducted itself and of government ineptitude. W.F. Carman, the American manager of Marsman's operations in Hong Kong, blandly informed the

43

Commissioners that the government reimbursed his company for the cost of all stores or equipment bought, plus ten per cent commission or profit. In other words, the government had been charged ten per cent on its own property. This meant that the higher the costs of the construction work the greater the profit for Marsman Hong Kong China Limited. There was no need for economy: ten per cent was the ineluctable profit on all work. Yet more extraordinary was the discovery of the number of firms involved and paid off. Bogus cartage or transport companies had been rapidly formed. These then passed on the work to smaller companies; the latter in turn subcontracted the work to smaller units; wives and relatives, without any experience in the field, then entered the commerce. The original bogus firm or firms simply pocketed the forthcoming ten per cent. There had been no proper supervision by the ARP and Public Works Departments; no monitoring of work; little supervision or financial control.

Captain C.C.A. Hobbs, a former Royal Engineer, at that time chief architect to the ARP Department, and on secondment from the PWD, was called to give evidence. He did not appear, and was found to have shot himself. An executive engineer in the PWD, in charge of the construction of ARP tunnels, attempted to commit suicide (it must be presumed), for he was admitted to hospital suffering from self-induced acute poisoning. He had already been charged with having accepted $2,000 from one of the contractors, but had been released. But the centre-piece of the inquiry, at least in the eyes of the public, was the Wing Commander himself, A.H.S. Steele-Perkins, whose private life suddenly became very public. His relationship with a Miss Mimi Lau, a secretary, was relentlessly probed by the Commissioners. Miss Lau (Lau Kum-ding) informed them that she was the divorced wife of General Fan Tak-sen and that she had come to Hong Kong in 1937. She had worked for several news agencies but was now employed as a secretary by the Chiap Hua Manufactory Company. It emerged that her duties were not onerous, as she spent only an hour or so in her office on working days. She had met Steele-

Perkins when he first arrived in the Colony but a deep friendship had only developed in early 1941. She had visited him at his Peak residence and, since her flat was only a few yards from ARP headquarters in Morrison Hill Road, Happy Valley, waved daily to him from her window.

Miss Lau's visits to the Peak caused eyebrows to rise; but the explanation was simple. In July 1940, most British women had been evacuated, Mrs Steele-Perkins to Australia. There was thus an acute shortage of women within the European community, but many desirable Chinese, Eurasian or Portuguese women on its social margins. The British matriarchs, the memsahibs of Hong Kong, the guardians of Peak values and decorum, had largely vanished by 1941, had departed to such places as Australia, Singapore or India. It was at this sexually exiguous time for the British male that Miss Lau renewed her acquaintance with the Wing Commander and visited him, always chaperoned she said, at his residence, 292, The Peak, or dined with him in company down-town. But what the Commissioners really wished to elicit was whether Miss Lau acted as a go-between for the Chiap Hua Manufactory Company. Was she a vamp, manipulated by shrewd Chinese businessmen to seduce a lonely man from his public duty? (If all this sounds stagey or melodramatic—fustian—to a modern reader, he should be reminded of the terrific impact, between the wars, of the trial of Lieutenant Norman Baillie-Stewart of the Seaforth Highlanders—'The prisoner in the Tower'—who was sentenced to five years' penal servitude in 1932 for communicating military secrets to Germany. His downfall had been occasioned by infatuation with a blonde German maiden. The reality of the *femme fatale* theme was accepted by most clubmen in the 1930s.)

Chiap Hua certainly had benefited from rumours of impending war. It was given a contract by the ARP Department to supply concrete blocks (breeze blocks) for the tunnel shelters. A tender for their delivery at 38 cents each had been rejected in favour of one at 49.25 cents from Chiap Hua, a company that as yet had had no experience in making such articles. These Chiap Hua blocks (facetiously referred to by the public as 'Mimi Lau blocks') were later checked by the Professor of Civil Engineering at the University of Hong Kong, who testified that only 46 out of 100 examined withstood the specified pressure of 1,500 lbs. Chiap Hua, an officially approved company, employed Miss Lau at a salary of $200 a month. Surprisingly, she deposited $5,000 in her bank account within a period of six months. It is now not possible to penetrate all the mysteries unveiled by the inquiry. The Commissioners were foxed by the evaporation of so many documents and accounts, the disappearance of witnesses, the perjury or forgetfulness of others. And no report of the findings was ever published. The draft copy that Cressall took into Stanley vanished after his death on 8 April 1943. Cynics have suggested that this was destroyed by a PWD official named in the document. It is, however, more likely that the abandoned bundle of typescript was utilized either as lavatory or writing paper, for both were in very short supply in Stanley in 1943, as Jean Gittins' detailed account of life there confirms.

The facts disclosed at the public hearing and given great publicity by the press caused, one imagines, anguish in government circles, for this was the second great scandal within the year. While the Commission was still sitting, the new Governor, Sir Mark Young, announced on 31 October 1941 that he had appointed Sir Athol MacGregor, the Chief Justice, as a special commissioner:

To inquire into and report ... on all such matters as may be brought to his attention affecting the existence of corruption in the public service of this Colony; to consider whether improvement can be effected in the arrangements in force in individual departments of Government for detecting and checking corrupt practices; and to advise generally on the manner in which effect may best be given to the desire of Government and of the community as a whole to stamp out corruption in the public service ...

Sir Athol was left little time in which to get to grips with the problem of corruption within the colonial government for, as noted, the Japanese invaded on 8 December and Sir Athol, together with the British community, was interned throughout the war. (The Japanese, one should add, did not succeed in eradicating corruption; new forms appeared as they imposed their own administration and rules on the occupied territory.) Sir Athol had no time in which to prepare a report. It is not known whether he presided over many closed sessions in his chambers, examining witnesses. He was, after all, a very busy man, with numerous public or official duties to perform.

Sir Geoffrey Northcote left Hong Kong on 8 September 1941. The Puisne Judge, P.E.F. Cressall, came on board ship to say farewell and in private conversation informed him of many incriminating matters that had come to the knowledge of the Commissioners. Sir Geoffrey at once wrote to the Colonial Office declaring:

Several Government officers are under the gravest suspicion of having taken bribes or presents ... I feel sure that in Downing Street you will agree that these stables should be swept as clean as possible ... I fear that the other disturbing outcome from the anti-graft Commission report is going to be the revelation of serious laxity in the control of Government expenditure, at any rate on defence works ... All this leaves me with a nasty taste in my mouth on my departure hence, and I feel somewhat culpable myself.

In early November, Sir Mark Young, the new Governor, informed Whitehall that he had set up another commission (Sir Athol MacGregor's). However, he was more optimistic than Sir Geoffrey and affirmed: 'The number of black sheep is greatly exaggerated in the public mind'. Sir Mark Young was new to Hong Kong and probably lacked knowledge of its secret history, the subterranean ramifications of corrupt practices. He had not been long in the Colony when he evinced such complacent views, unlike some clubmen and old China hands, cynical observers of the colonial scene, who believed that most things were up for sale in Hong Kong.

Robert S. Ward, the American author of a study of Japanese occupation techniques, calls Steele-Perkins 'an able

and energetic Englishman' and avers: 'Assured that, no matter how much his rashness might be deplored, his integrity
was absolutely unquestioned, the Englishman went off to India'. He left, in fact, in early November, at the expiry of his
contract, to take up a similar post there. No evidence directly
linked Steele-Perkins with corruption. He was, one concludes,
an innocent abroad, gulled by Chinese entrepreneurs and dishonest PWD engineers and inspectors, all British. There was
nothing special about his friendship with Miss Lau. She was a
lively, lissom, fun-loving young woman; he was middle-aged
and alone. The rest was chemistry. The Chiap Hua management knew of Miss Lau's friendship with the ARP Director
and doubtless hoped to profit from it; that was why they engaged her as secretary and gave her no work to do. Her role,
as we would say today, was public relations. G.B. Endacott
soberly concludes:

It is clear that since the [ARP] work had to be pressed on with
quickly, normal government safeguards were by-passed and that not
enough trained supervisory staff were available. Still what appeared
to be dishonest collusion between Government officers and contractors to divert money into their own pockets through bogus companies cannot be completely excused on these grounds.

The danger that arose from the traditional Chinese subcon-
tracting system was commented upon in H.R. Butters' 1939
Report on labour and labour conditions in Hong Kong. He
complained that the system was particularly vicious in building construction 'where it is not a question of splitting a contract among several sub-contractors but of subletting a whole
contract through several intermediaries who all take their
profit until the actual contractor who does the work may receive so little that he scamps his work or goes bankrupt and is
unable to pay his labourers'. In the case of the ARP tunnels,
the contractors not only scamped their work but were richly
paid for so doing, as Endacott implied.

Shanghai, which had a British population of over 5,500 in
1915 (9,000 in 1936) could be compared experimentally with
Hong Kong, to determine whether the same social and eco-

nomic forces were at work in each territory to promote corrupt practices. But the task is extremely difficult, for no specialized study has appeared as yet on Shanghai corruption and sources and records are scant or inaccessible; only indirect evidence or hearsay is available. What one can safely assert is that, generally speaking, corruption flourished in Shanghai on a far grander scale if only because the extent of economic enterprise was much larger in Shanghai, a city strategically located on the Chang Jiang (Yangtze), the largest Chinese river and one of the longest in the world. Moreover, between the wars the pace of industrialization was swifter in Shanghai than in Hong Kong. The Shanghai International Settlement, which dated from 1854, was administered by a 'Taipan oligarchy' (to use Hawks Pott's nice term). It was governed by an elected Municipal Council, chosen from a select list of ratepayers, all of whose members were usually businessmen (the first Chinese was admitted, under pressure, in 1928). Corruption in Shanghai's heyday was an established way of life, penetrating every segment of society. As Noel Barber relates:

If a European financed the construction of a tenement block for the poor, more often than not the Chinese builder would water down the cement, the salaried Chinese landlord would demand a kickback from prospective tenants, and the Chinese policeman would demand a fee for 'protection'. The European never got to the bottom of it.

But Shanghailanders, as they liked to call themselves, did not regard corruption as in any way a major social problem (nor curiously did missionaries who were more upset by sins of the flesh, and by idolatry and apostasy). They regarded it as a social nuisance to which they must accommodate themselves, as they had with Eastern squalor, epidemic disease, beggars, guilds of thieves and burglars, secret societies—all immemorial and persistent attributes, at that time, of urban life in China. As an international city, a foreign enclave—a truly open city—the Municipal Council could not control the quality of its population nor reject the swarms of Chinese from all classes who periodically poured into its environs and demesne when conditions worsened in China. It became, especially between the wars, a haven for refugees and the dispossessed and a Mecca for criminals from all countries, for no passport was needed for entry. Émile Buisson, born 1902, guillotined 1956, one of France's most notorious post-war public enemies, served part of his apprenticeship in crime in Shanghai, trafficking in arms, drugs and women. As he reminisced of pre-war Shanghai: 'Un type qu'avait un peu de culot faisait fortune' ('Any bloke with a bit of cheek would make his fortune'). It was a home for the *déclassé*, the *déraciné*, for international crooks and confidence tricksters. The notorious Trebitsch-Lincoln (1879–1943), former British Liberal MP, convicted German spy, and international swindler, made Shanghai his base in the 1920s and died there, a Buddhist convert. In sum, Shanghai was no rose-garden; it was a jungle where all stalked the same prey—money.

Conditions were different in Hong Kong, for its colonial administrators were made constantly aware of the 'tut-tutting' of Whitehall officials. As a group, the civil servants of Hong Kong were accountable finally to London, not to ratepayers. The moral and social standards of the British homeland had to be adhered to, at least in public or in theory; and these standards were typically enshrined in Hong Kong legislation, as with Ordinance No. 3 of 1901 (an ordinance to amend the criminal law as regards certain indecent outrages and assaults) which was copied from the English 1885 Criminal Law Amendment Act (the law which snared Oscar Wilde in 1895). Paradoxically, Shanghai flourished despite its inherent, inexpugnable corruption; and Hong Kong survived in the inter-war period and was no obvious victim of its subterranean ramifying system of corruption. Corruption had, perhaps, accelerated the pace of development in that it helped cut through red tape and baffling officialdom.

This might suggest that corruption is a *moral* rather than social or economic problem, one created mostly by insistence on creating or maintaining certain standards of private and public behaviour. It seems likely that Shanghai's ruling élite,

its Taipan oligarchy, saw corruption as a problem largely insoluble, one which unwisely investigated might give rise to
grave public scandal and produce few useful returns. Shanghai, after all, was controlled by a small number of proverbially
hard-faced businessmen, those who wished to make the world
safe for private enterprise. Hong Kong, to reiterate, could not
afford to be as liberal or antinomian: each political system had
different emphases. As Sydney Smith said of two housewives
screaming insults at each other from upper stories of a narrow
Edinburgh street: 'These two women will never agree: they
are arguing from different premises'.

One should not, of course, exaggerate the lawlessness of
Shanghai. Attempts were made periodically to suppress its
burgeoning vice. Brothels staffed by American women were
closed in 1906; Chinese brothels in 1920. But the trade continued, sometimes camouflaged, often openly. A Chinese
madame, whose establishment was nicknamed the 'Vice-
Consulate' for the services it provided to the community, was
not put out of business until the Communists arrived. Shanghai only indulged at times in a certain amount of window-
dressing, when missionaries made a fuss. The problem of vice
was largely insoluble because the Municipal Council's supervisory staff and inspectorate were prepared to protect illegal
establishments, at a price.

Even this brief and episodic survey of pre-war corruption
should reveal that the forms of corruption have not markedly
changed, only the dimensions of the problem. Syndicated corruption, the satisfied customer variant, paying for convenience, protection rackets, extortion, squeeze, kickbacks, and
commissions, all then existed in a primal state. Corruption
infected not only the police, a classic source, but *all* government departments that provided any opportunity for its
occurrence. The main victims, as always, were the masses
who lived in tenement blocks, low rental areas, or in the rural,
tradition-bound New Territories. Corruption was an unofficial tax levied on all those who laboured or who lived ex-
iguously on the fringes of private enterprise—factory workers,

artisans, craftsmen, shop assistants and small shopkeepers, clerks and others. The rich, on the other hand, used the bribe commonly as a species of speed money to hurry things up, such as a permit, licence, official document, contract; or to get what they wanted but could not expeditiously or legally obtain.

The majority of Europeans were not subject to this unofficial system of taxation—they were outside the net—but many were prepared to accept dubious kickbacks and commissions in the course of their daily work (income tax, it should be noted, was first introduced in Hong Kong in the 1947 Budget). Taipans, the cream of the business world, depended on compradors to do their dirty work. Compradors, often referred to as the 'Chinese manager' or 'Chinese business-manager' of a European-owned firm, were either Chinese or Eurasian for they needed, as middlemen or go-betweens, to speak Cantonese and be conversant with the themes of Chinese society. Taipans normally turned a blind eye to the comprador's activities, so long as profits were guaranteed. Many Shanghai compradors were originally Cantonese, from Hong Kong, who had transferred from one port to the other, for a degree of bilingualism was an essential attribute of their profession. Like wild geese, they, together with numerous Shanghai entrepreneurs, flew back to their natal home when the Communists took over Shanghai in 1948–9. Acclimatized to corruption, compradors, and Shanghai businessmen and industrialists, brought back to Hong Kong more sophisticated techniques of corruption. They did not flinch from using their acquired knowledge to sponsor new business enterprises in a fresh environment, colonial Hong Kong.

It has also been argued in this chapter that senior civil servants were, in the main, incorrupt; that their background, training, situation, and conditions acted as prophylactics against becoming corrupt. Directors of the PWD, who often worked their way up from the ranks, might be suspect, but in all honesty we do not know whether this was really ever justified; though we can assert that lesser lights in the PWD were sometimes not averse to inflating their salaries with pay-offs from contractors and others. The real problem lay with gifts. What effect did a gift—not cash—have upon decisions taken by senior civil servants? Again, we simply do not know the answer. All we can say, priggishly, is that the gifts should not have been received, but once received should have been returned. And returned many of them were.

3

THE STAR FERRY RIOTS AND THE ISSUE OF CORRUPTION

'"It's always best on these occasions
to do what the mob do."
"But suppose there are two mobs?" suggested Mr Snodgrass.
"Shout with the largest," replied Mr Pickwick.'

Charles Dickens, *Pickwick Papers*

AT nine in the morning on 4 April 1966, a young Chinese arrived at the Star Ferry concourse, Hong Kong side, and took up a position between the subway and the turnstiles. He wore a black jacket with white inscriptions painted on it. They read: 'Hail Elsie! Join hunger strike to block fare increase', 'Democratic' and, in Chinese characters, 'Oppose gambling'. The young man, a mysterious portent and an extraordinary figure in undemonstrative Hong Kong, remained all day at his post like a sentinel and left only when the ferries stopped running at night. The next day, 5 April, he returned to his vigil at eleven in the morning, a magnet for youth. The press and the radio soon referred to the solitary demonstrator as 'The Hunger Striker' and revealed that he was one So Sau-chung, a translator who lived with his family in Happy Valley. Later in the day, at about four in the afternoon, he was arrested for obstruction and passed, as it were, into history, for he played no part in the rioting that ensued on that and the following nights.

So's idiosyncratic public protest—there had been nothing like it in Hong Kong's history—was the initial event in a chain that culminated in the so-called Star Ferry riots, three nights of violence, looting and arson. These disturbances convulsed the community, agitated the police and alarmed the government. They were a turning-point in post-war Hong Kong and marked the beginning of the end (though not the total extinction as yet) of attitudes and policies inherited from pre-war days. The riots demonstrated that Hong Kong had a 'problem of youth' and that the balance of social forces had shifted significantly since 1945. The six-month period of confrontation with Maoist elements in the following year, 1967, tended to mask the importance of the Star Ferry riots but it is possible to show, by historical and sociological analysis, that 1966 is a crucial date in the modernization of Hong Kong, that afterwards the Colony was never quite the same.

The rioting in Kowloon on the nights of 5–8 April 1966, although provoked by the Hunger Striker's arrest, was really inspired by earlier events, by the Star Ferry Company's application on 1 October 1965 for an increase in fares on the grounds that operating costs had risen yet the general fare structure had remained unaltered since 1946. The company wanted first-class fares to go up from 20 to 30 cents and second-class fares from 10 to 20 cents. The government approved a compromise five cents' increase for the former with no increase in the latter. Opposition to the proposed change soon flared up. One of the most active campaigners against the increase was an Urban Councillor, Mrs Elsie Elliott. She launched a signature-collecting campaign and, on 23 November, presented a petition to Government House with a total of 23,000 names appended and announced that a further 100,000 had been promised. The Reform Club, of which Mrs Elliott was a leading light, did much to educate Chinese opinion about the issue. Mr Brook Bernacchi, Barrister-at-law, Chairman of the Reform Club and, like Mrs Elliott, an elected member of the Urban Council (a rare breed in those days), also spoke out against the proposal and organized opposition to its implementation. This popular campaign, led by 'populist' leaders, appealed not only to the notion of self-interest—the fear that the cost of living would rise—but touched also on larger social and moral issues. Should the government, for example, allow a public utility company to exploit the population when it was purportedly making a healthy profit? Should the voice of the people be hearkened to? Or should the government listen only to the sonorous tones of the prominent?

It seems, at first sight, extraordinary that the travelling public should have become so dismayed by the prospect of a five cents' increase in first-class travel between Kowloon and Hong Kong Island, for second-class passengers faced no additional levy and most workers journeyed the cheapest way. What the public feared, one concludes, was a general rise in the cost of living after a period of steady economic growth since the Korean War. In January 1965 the Canton Trust Bank, a small Hong Kong Chinese undertaking, had failed and its 114,000 depositors were paid only 25 per cent of their deposits. Many lost, at least temporarily, the bulk of their savings. In February the much larger Hang Seng Bank also found itself in difficulties, when a run by clamoring creditors started. Backed by the government, the Hongkong and Shanghai Banking Corporation, Hong Kong's mightiest financial institution, then stepped in and took over the failed bank. The crisis now ended, and confidence was restored. The run on a number of indigenous banks stopped, with the collapse of two and the taking over of a third. But the sight of long queues of anxious depositors, serpentining around buildings in the central business district, was disturbing to those Chinese with memories of inflation and bankruptcy in Nationalist China and the final collapse of its worthless currency. Other economic indications, such as the decline of the real estate market, together with a number of related critical economic trends, could also be adduced to explain the anxiety and nervousness that then infected local people. There is, however, no point in indulging in any detailed economic analysis to demonstrate authoritatively that in early 1966 the economy was either sound or unsound. It is clear that many people had begun to worry about their future livelihood; there was an almost neurotic belief that things were getting worse. As the Report of the Commission of Inquiry nicely and wisely states: '... it is sometimes not the facts which count so much as what people think to be the facts and, as we have seen, there are a number of people in Hong Kong particularly sensitive to any suggestion of general price inflation'. In brief, in early 1966 there were obvious tensions within the community, a flock of irrational beliefs, generated by fear and uncertainty about the future of the economy.

On the night of 5 April 1966, a demonstration march was arranged by So's young supporters, but So himself did not participate. It started soon after 9 p.m. from the Star Ferry Kowloon concourse, went up Salisbury Road, and turned into Nathan Road, the great Kowloon thoroughfare. About four hundred, mostly youths, took part in the boisterous, slogan-shouting protest march. A few demonstrators were arrested that night but little damage was done to property. The next night events were more violent. Once again a procession moved up Nathan Road, attracting growing support as the marchers, twisting and turning like lion dancers, progressed up and down the thoroughfare. The column of demonstrators was reminiscent of a children's crusade for its body was steadily infiltrated by boys, laughing and grimacing and showing off. This was the first night of sustained rioting with the police being stoned, or bombarded with flowerpots and other debris flung down from the roof-tops of high-rise buildings, such as the Chungking Mansion in lower Nathan Road. Further rioting took place on the nights of the 7th and 8th, but in diminuendo, for by the 8th the police were fully in control, and the riots were finally snuffed out that night. Over 1,400 persons were arrested during these disturbances, the great majority of whom were boys and young men. Only one rioter, an adult, was killed by gunfire, but destruction of property was widespread. One casualty was the Shui Hing Company, whose premises in Nathan Road were set ablaze. Many other buildings suffered from looting and vandalism.

The Hong Kong government had had little difficulty in explaining the 1956 riots, a faction fight between supporters of Mao and Chiang Kai-shek. The 1966 riots, on the other hand, were enigmatic in that no obvious political issues appeared to have been involved and no ideological element could be discerned. Moreover, the rioters were mostly untutored, uneducated young people and, in the main, politically illiterate or unmotivated. To find out what caused the riots, for the government and the public were vastly perplexed by the matter, a Commission of Inquiry was appointed on 3 May with the Chief Justice, Sir Michael Hogan, a veteran colonial civil servant, as chairman. The first public session began on 11 May; the last took place on 2 September.

The opening sessions were held, surprisingly, in the City Hall concert theatre. The audience lolling in the rows of tiered seats thus looked down on the large, brightly illuminated stage at which sat, like members of a court martial, the four unsmiling Commissioners. The setting was theatrical, the sessions a spectacle, with witnesses ushered in or out from the wings and the spectators cheering heroic figures like So Sau-chung or the intrepid and cheeky Lo Kei, a star turn and one of the original protestors. The terms of reference given the Commission were to inquire into and report on the Kowloon disturbances, the events leading up to them, and the 'causes thereof'.

As the inquiry progressed, there was a remarkable shift in focus, as though the scenario had been rewritten or the director sacked and replaced, so that spectators were soon led to believe that Mrs Elliott was the key figure in a *cause célèbre* concerning the police. Sir Michael and his three fuglemen thus drifted, unconsciously perhaps, into very murky waters. This came about largely through the questions raised by counsel for the police, presumably under instruction from his clients. These in turn led to counter-claims about police corruption.

The police had been faced with the same difficult problem put to the Commissioners by the government—what (or rather who) caused the riots? Policemen typically solve crimes by discovering a perpetrator; they are not trained to investigate the psychological or social background to crime; such issues have little relevance when they prosecute a case in court. What matters is hard evidence, fixing a crime to a person or persons (or, with corrupt policemen, fixing a person to a crime). Thus when the Commissioner of Police, Mr Henry Heath, and his senior officers pondered over the problem they were irresistibly driven into looking for individuals— 'personalities' in police jargon—who had instigated or master-minded the riots. They looked for agents. At first, they concentrated on Mr Brook Bernacchi who had had some very brief contacts with a few of So's original supporters. Then their sights became fixed on Mrs Elliott, a notorious public figure in police eyes. What the police hoped to develop through their counsel was a conspiracy theory, that the riots had been touched off by the activities of prominent members of the Reform Club, at that date the most radical association (that is, mildly critical of government policies) in Hong Kong. It was imputed that Bernacchi and Elliott were morally responsible for the destruction of public and private property in that they had encouraged young activists to break the law by organizing an illegal assembly (the protest march up Nathan Road on 6 May) or, at least, that they had not tried hard enough to dissuade them from taking action.

Mr Henry Heath, the Commissioner of Police, was a straightforward colonial policeman of the old school who had first come to Hong Kong in March 1935. He was representative of that generation of young Englishmen, in the 1920s and 1930s, who sought fame and glory, or security and a respectable job, in one or other of the many paramilitary police forces of the old British Empire, such as the Palestine Police. (Edgar Wallace's saga of 'Sanders of the River' supplied popular and potent reading for adolescents in the inter-war period and encouraged some, one imagines, to leave the homeland for a life of official adventure in Africa or Asia.) Heath was not a complicated man in any obvious way. He was certainly no intellectual; nor was he university-trained, but he had been a language student for two years in Guangzhou. It is necessary to make these points because certain moral issues surfaced during his lengthy cross-examination by Mrs Elliott's counsel and solicitor. When it came to questions about police corruption, it was clear that Heath was out of his depth discussing the problem and baffled by the turn his cross-examination took. That he was extraordinarily loyal to the force he commanded was patent. He could see no evil, at least little real evil, in his fellow policemen. The conspiracy theories, designed to explain the causes of the riots, did not emanate from him, one infers, but from lower down the police hierarchy, among a number of grossly corrupt police officers, whose careers would later be investigated by the ICAC. It is possible that Heath believed in some elements of the conspiracy theories because he regarded Mrs Elliott as a great public nuisance, a busybody who 'blitzed' the police with shoals of complaining letters. He informed the Commissioners that Mrs Elliott's correspondence—over 120 letters—had been brought together into a single file, which was kept at police headquarters for speedy reference. It is more likely, though, that Heath was sceptical, since the so-called evidence that buttressed the conspiracy theories was too fantastic, the lucubrations, as it were, of a very poor contriver of mystery stories.

Anyone who reads through the Commission of Inquiry's transcript, some 2,400 pages long, will be struck (certainly at p. 532) by an odd fact: apparently some police officers had been investigating the sexual habits of the arrested demonstrators, especially those who had visited the offices of the Reform Club or had spoken to, or had had previous contacts with, its officials. A study of the statements taken by Inspector Hurst from, for example, one Lee Tak-yee, will confirm that this was so. It is as though while inquiring into the Brixton riots, Lord Scarman had spent time collecting material on the sexual preferences of the black rioters and of those—white socialists, liberals, race relations experts, social scientists— who sympathized with or backed them. What had sex, an observer might well ask, to do with riots and rioting since the latter, surely, have social rather than individual causes, and the explanation of any collective phenomenon is likely to be more convincingly provided by sociological rather than bio-psychological factors? Does any historian believe that Napoleon's haemorrhoids, or the reputed troubles with his bowels, really explain why he lost at Waterloo?

It was Superintendent Ernest Hunt ('Taffy' Hunt to his familiars) who embarked on this line of inquiry in 1966. It is not certain whether this was an independent investigation, Hunt's very own, or whether he was directed to conduct it by more senior officers in the CID. He was then based at Colony Headquarters on the Island and was in charge of the Police Triad Society Bureau, a posting which put him in close touch not only with many types of villain but more particularly with Triads, the purveyors, protectors and controllers of so much lucrative vice in Hong Kong (gambling, prostitution, pornography, and narcotics). For a very corrupt policeman, it was a most marvellous placement, a plum job. Like a questing spider, he watched over a vast web, an elaborate nexus of criminal activities, and benefited, as we know, from his symbiotic relationship with the underworld, like lion and jackal so to say.

As Chief Inspector Michael Quinn affirmed before the Commission of Inquiry into Inspector MacLennan's case, in 1966 Hunt busied himself with collecting evidence about homosexuals. Together with a number of subordinate officers, Hunt hauled in a large number of suspected homosexuals and vigorously interrogated them. Some were held for over twenty-four hours without a charge being preferred: the purpose was information-gathering, not prosecution. Quinn, Hunt's subordinate, started to compile at this time his celebrated 'Black Book', a compendium of information about the 'gay fraternity' (to use his term). No one in authority has explained as yet why there was this particular flurry of police concern. No scabrous sexual scandal had surfaced since 1945, only routine cases of those caught *in flagrante*, so why this sudden focusing on a not very important criminal area?

At this point, one must of necessity indulge in some surmise and speculation and simply allow the reader to assess the sometimes tenuous evidence. The argument put forward here is that Hunt, like many a corrupt officer at this time, was being made uneasy by allegations of police corruption constantly iterated by Mrs Elliott and other reformers: what would happen if the government started to take these claims too seriously? Since 1945, the corrupt had not been seriously incommoded in their acquisition of illegal wealth. Many senior policemen had taken early retirement, in their forties or fifties, to spend their autumn years in sunny climes. Spain was a favoured haven, a 'Sybarita' where expatriates foregathered at cafés to drink their Sangria and chit-chat among themselves.

Hunt's investigations into the sexually deviant found no place in the Commission's Report published in February 1967. He had endeavoured to establish a link between some members of the Reform Club and a few young rioters—*amours singulières, amitiés particulières*— but was not able to substantiate his suspicions. The calumnies were simply not believed, and could not be developed in any useful way by police counsel. They were, in any case, irrelevant. Hunt has since spoken to the press on several occasions and his remarks (translated into Chinese as 'Hunt's Confessions') give some idea of his intentions in 1966–7. Briefly, he rationalized that while most policemen were on the take, certain detractors of the force were also repeatedly breaking the criminal law by indulging in homosexual practices. They were as morally flawed as those they condemned. There was a double standard, Hunt averred. These comments do not, however, exhaust the content of Hunt's mind in 1966, one imagines.

It is not implausible to suggest, then, that Hunt was mainly concerned to protect himself against future prosecution: for the good, good days would not necessarily last for ever. The dossiers he and his special team compiled in 1966–7 (and which have since mysteriously vanished) could be utilized to block trial and stigmatization; or at least might be helpful if and when it came to plea bargaining, something solid to put in the balance, to make the government's flesh creep. For political reasons, such sensitive information about homosexual civil servants and other prominent members of the community could not be disregarded. In 1975, when Hunt returned to given evidence at Godber's trial, he declared to local journalists that he was preparing his autobiography, a book which would 'blow the lid off Hong Kong', with its revelations of moral turpitude among the élite. As yet, this exposé has not appeared. It may well be that Hunt has found it difficult to switch, as it were, from baton to pen: the travail of composition is, after all, not likely to appeal to any playboy policeman, to a 'middle-aged juvenile', as Mr Justice Yang called him. But the tenor of his mind in 1966 is made clearer in his 'Confessions'. Hunt, a master of craft, at that date had his thoughts set on the future, fixed at a point when he might be unmasked.

Hunt's clandestine activities led nowhere in the context of the riots. His conspiracy theory, with its ripe insinuations, lacked conviction. It is time now to examine another, one which bedevilled the Commission, overshadowed its deliberations and caused Mrs Elliott to undergo a week's severe cross-examination by police counsel. It is given much prominence in the Report and is also described in *Crusade for Justice*, Mrs Elliott's autobiography. She claims that on the evening of 6 April 1966, a message was delivered to her home warning that a plot had been hatched in Mong Kok Police Station to discredit her status as a public figure. Her informant, she averred, was a Mong Kok policeman's relative. She would not give their names, and never did, in case they were victimized. The plot centred on the allegation that she had promised sums of money to those who would riot. The story appeared to derive from conflicting statements made by the incarcerated Lo Kei, who later asserted he had been repeatedly beaten to make him confess that Mrs Elliott had led him astray; but police officials admitted before the Commission that they did not believe in the 'Mong Kok Plot' allegation, and that is probably true. It was too absurd a confection for even them to accept.

Mrs Elliott has always claimed that the plot was organized

by Hunt and some corrupt Chinese police officers stationed in
Mong Kok, a district well supplied with brothels, massage
parlours, dance halls, opium divans, gambling stalls, and
other illegal enterprises. Over the years, Mrs Elliott had complained repeatedly of Triad activities and police corruption in
the Mong Kok division. Some of her letters were read out at
the Commission of Inquiry and her allegations rebutted by
Henry Heath, who asserted that little evidence had been
found to back up her stories. But the volume of Mrs Elliott's
complaints, her constant references to corruption, must have
made some guilty officers extremely uneasy. She was a woman
who knew too much. In time, she might be listened to more
sympathetically by those in authority. There might be a clean-
up campaign, as in an American city when reformers take
control. In 1966, the full extent of police syndicate corruption
was not generally known, although the poorer Chinese, members of the artisanate, proletariat, and lumpenproletariat,
were well aware of what was going on. They were simply not
listened to. The Secretary for Chinese Affairs only sampled the
opinions of respected Chinese community leaders, of those not
usually inclined to rock the boat or to be too radical or critical
in their views.

The end of the story is quickly told. Mrs Elliott was accused
of contempt by the Commissioners since she adamantly refused to reveal the name of her informant. She was neither
imprisoned nor fined but was sent 'to the bar of public opinion
where she must meet the censure and repudiation of all those
right-minded people who believe in the freedom of the innocent from the taint of unwarranted suspicion and in the principles of frankness and fair dealing in the affairs of men'. This
rather 'Buzfuzian' judgment did Mrs Elliott little hurt; on the
contrary, it consolidated her position among the poor and
needy. Her intransigence strengthened her hold over such persons, and others, and her circle of informants expanded, for
she could be trusted not to give them away.

The Report attempted to explain why the riots occurred
and why the overwhelming majority of the participants were

boys or young men, not adults as in 1956. It concluded, among other matters, that Hong Kong now had a problem of youth, following the pattern which had emerged in most post-war industrial societies ('Teddy boys', 'mods' and 'rockers' in Britain; *'blousons-noirs'* in France; *'Halbstarken'* in Germany). Hong Kong had given birth to its own *ah fei* and *laant-tsai*—drifters, delinquents, rebels (with or without a cause), a generation of alienated youth in sociological jargon. But there was scant mention of corruption as a possible social irritant; no highlighting of the fact that those who lived in the warrens of the poor, in tenement buildings, public housing estates, and squatter camps, had little confidence in the integrity of the average constable or detective. Throughout the 167-page Report the police were largely congratulated on their work in riot control and suppression. The Report examined the background to the riots, the various social conditions which might have precipitated the events, but neglected to show that the police force was part of that background.

On the other hand, daily accounts of the proceedings, which were given headlines and much space in the press, had evidently awakened the public to the fact that corruption was blatant and flagrant. Inadvertently, the Commission had opened Pandora's Box; unwittingly, it had publicized the problem of corruption, a problem which now emerged from the shadows. The Commissioner of Police's testimony had given little comfort. Asked whether there was more corruption in the police than other departments, he responded:

This is a rather difficult question. I would say that there is corruption in the police force, but that there is corruption in other government departments and ... indeed in commercial life and, in fact, pretty well every walk of life here in Hong Kong ... I would say this: that in terms of money the police force is probably not the worst, in spite of the fact that it is the biggest section of government.

He also provided an ingenious defence for police corruption by arguing that detectives needed bribes in order to pay their informers.

The Report concluded: 'We do not believe that political, economic and social frustration were the direct causes of the 1966 riots'. One must add that these factors are *never* direct causes but, as Neil Smelser's theory of collective behaviour postulates, may be one of the determinants of riots (conditions of the social structure that are permissive of riots). A more appropriate conclusion would have been Auden's lines: 'The situation of our time / Surrounds us like a baffling crime', for the Commissioners remained as befogged as the public about why the riots happened when they did.

The Report, nevertheless, had an impact on the government, especially on departments in close contact with the public. The police, one knows, pondered over its content and its implications and were concerned above all with the matter of public relations and the alleged communication gap between government and people. Edward Tyrer, Heath's successor, in his 1966–7 survey of police affairs, noted:

During the year the question of police / public relations has continued to occupy my attention. An informal committee including representatives of the public and the Director of Information Services sat with me to discuss ways of improving public relations. Amongst other measures referred to in the body of the report a programme of 'open days' was instituted whereby Divisional Police Stations were opened to the public who attended in crowds numbering thousands. They watched dog demonstrations, listened to the band and were shown around the station where exhibitions of police work were displayed. On less formal occasions parties of school children were invited to visit police stations in Kowloon and importance is attached to measures to increase such contact between the police and young people.

Mild reforms, unspectacular reactions—but a start. This was soon followed, in 1967, by the establishment of a post for a full-time police press officer, an important event historically for Hong Kong. From this innovation has grown the Police Public Relations Branch, an organization now commanded by a chief superintendent, with a strength (in 1984) of seventy-five police and information officers, and civilian staff.

The torpid and tradition-bound Secretariat for Chinese Affairs (SCA), in derivation a relic of the colonial nineteenth century, was also jolted by the riots and the controversies which surrounded those events. For many years, the main function of the SCA had been to provide a link between the government or administration and the Chinese population. One of its major tasks, supposedly, was to find out what Chinese felt about certain issues and to relay such information back to the Colonial Secretary and heads of department. It did not go about this task in any scientific manner—it employed no trained social surveyors or pollsters—but relied on the opinions of a picked body of respected and highly respectable Chinese community leaders. The SCA, in 1966, had become frozen in time, backward-looking, out of touch with developments within Hong Kong's highly urbanized population. Mr Ronald Holmes, the Secretary, admitted this in 1969. In discussing the importance of such associations as the Tung Wah Hospital Group, the Po Leung Kuk, the Lok Shin Tong (a benevolent association), *kaifong* and clansmen associations, and other bodies, he commented: 'We have however been very conscious that these traditional contacts do not for the most part necessarily reach the poorer people or those well-to-do people who are not interested in public activities or public life'. The SCA now wanted to establish links with the latter, with new social groupings, with 'mass society', as sociologists would say. (In 1969, the SCA became transformed into the Secretariat for Home Affairs, a more appropriate title in modern conditions, and less divisive.)

The SCA did not find it easy to change its role at first. Historically, it had been the guardian and protector of the traditional sector of Hong Kong; but the Colony was changing at a very rapid pace in the early 1960s. By attempting to preserve older social and political forms, which was part of its historical mission, to 'give face' to traditionalism, the SCA was in fact hindering the necessary process of modernization, an implacable constituent of industrialization. Hong Kong had developed by the mid-1960s into an industrial colony, a unique social or political form. It could no longer be governed as it had been in the 1930s, nor could moribund social institutions be preserved in perpetuity. During the industrial revolution, for example, no British government could have retained cottage industry, a dying economic entity, doomed as Marx and Engels demonstrated in theory. It took the SCA a little time to evolve something new. In 1968, Ronald (later Sir Ronald) Holmes, Secretary for Chinese Affairs, produced a blueprint for a City District Officer Scheme, an amalgam of the old and the new, a pseudo-novelty, a judicious compromise. It was an anthropological curiosity in an urban setting, an extension of the familiar role of the district officer, an incarnation which would have been recognized by students of the Empire, by former colonial administrators, and of course by those who lived in the New Territories, an area always administratively separate from the Island and Kowloon. This attempt to bring the SCA (now renamed) into the contemporary world derived from the Star Ferry riots, from the shock waves given off by an explosion of youthful discontent and, as we shall see, by the further impact of the 1967 'disturbances', as they were euphemistically labelled by government publicists. Both sets of events prodded, impelled the government to introduce reforms, to look more critically at its bureaucratic structures and policies. Modern Hong Kong was gestated in 1966 and 1967.

The Star Ferry riots were over. In February 1967, a verdict had been handed down, a judgment given. Corrupt policemen, one imagines, breathed a sigh of relief at total exculpation. Some notorious police villains, and their partners in crime, remained *in situ*, apparently untarnished by the many revelations of dubious conduct uncovered by the Commission of Inquiry; but some of these activities had been registered by Mr Charles Sutcliffe, who became the Commissioner of Police in 1969. Corrupt policemen were buoyed up by guilt, as Wilde would say, at having discomfited Mrs Elliott. But a clairvoyant, peering into his crystal ball, surely would have warned them that their lives would take a turn for the worse.

On 6 May 1967 a dispute between workers and management flared up at the Hong Kong Artificial Flower Works at San Po Kong. The Chinese 'Cultural Revolution' had come to the Colony, like an outbreak of rabies, and this was to be a more startling, and far longer, event than even the Star Ferry riots. The confrontation with Maoists lasted for six months but sporadic incidents continued well into 1968. The turning point came on 22 May when the police attacked a large mob outside the Hilton Hotel. The police had thrown a cordon across Garden Road to prevent dissidents from marching along the highway to demonstrate outside Government House. Provoked by a truculent mob, hysterically chanting the 'Thoughts of Chairman Mao', the police charged, batoning many, and arresting all those they could lay their hands on. The battered remnant was hauled off to the cells in police vans. Until that point, the police had played mainly a passive role, one of wait-and-see. Now they began to seize the initiative and applied increasing pressure on their opponents. By mid-July they were carrying out attacks on Communist premises and were arresting organizers and sympathizers. There is no need to catalogue these many episodes. John Cooper's *Colony in Conflict* (1970) provides all the relevant facts.

The 1967 disturbances had many consequences but only a few will be examined as germane to the theme of corruption. Overnight the police became heroes. They *were* heroes. They came into their own as a security force, as a paramilitary organization trained for combat. The public reacted with enthusiasm and gratitude, as the besieged do when they glimpse the pennons of their liberators. In these circumstances who could continue to make derisive remarks about 'bent' policemen? Thus criticism was, for the time being, muted and the problems thrown up by the previous year's riots discreetly forgotten. The great question was: Would Hong Kong survive?

Senior Superintendent Peter Godber, in 1973 Hong Kong's most notorious citizen, distinguished himself greatly at this time. He commanded a raid on the Spinning, Weaving and Dyeing Workers' Union in Tsuen Wan on the night of 28 July.

It was a difficult and dangerous but successful operation and resulted in thirty-three arrests and the seizure of useful documents. Godber was in the thick of the fight in those six tense months. Martin Woolacott of *The Guardian* interviewed Charles Sutcliffe, the Commissioner of Police, in October 1973, and reported the following conversation:

Godber is a man who was a very good officer and was a hero in 1967 ... this is where it was all a bit hard to take. He and I stood together in the riots and fought the bloody crowds together ... he was the very first man to take action against the communists in 1967. I issued the order and he carried it out.

Sutcliffe's lament came from the heart. He was upset by an expatriate's betrayal of trust. But Chinese policemen in 1967 also did not break ranks. Lampooned as 'running dogs' in the Communist press, they persisted in protecting the community and for once were genuinely popular. It was their finest hour.

As a result of the confrontation with Maoists—a playing out of themes originating in China—fifty-one people died, fifteen in bomb explosions, including several Chinese children. Ten police officers were killed and 212 wounded, some severely. Sympathy for the embattled police was widespread and steadily grew after 6 May. Thus a group of local businessmen set up a fund to further the education of police children. In a fortnight, donations reached $3 million. At the end of the year a grand total of $3.7 million had been subscribed to the Police Education Fund. The police—honoured by the Queen, in 1968, as the Royal Hong Kong Police Force—had preserved the status quo; there had been no humiliation of the colonial government as in Macau, where the Portuguese authorities were forced abjectly to confess their errors. Hong Kong neither bent nor broke before the storm. The Governor, Sir David Trench, continued, with aplomb, to play golf at Fanling, and cricketers continued with their ritual in Central as demonstrators raged around the Hilton Hotel and the lower reaches of Garden Road.

The disturbances had, in particular, one marked and important effect. During this period the police were fully engaged in riot control, in crowd management, in protecting public buildings, and in organizing raids on left-wing premises. They were also heavily committed to seeing that traffic flowed, that public transport operated, and that communications were kept open. After 6 May, they had therefore a multitude of tasks to attend to. The control of vice now had, of necessity, a very low priority. Much crime flourished, as though the force had folded its tents and melted away: but a lot went unreported. In 1919, a Liverpool police strike had led to the looting of many shops by opportunists; in Montreal, in 1969, when the police withdrew their labour, the same effects were observed. Occupied Denmark provides a classic example: in 1944, when the Germans removed all Danish police from their posts, robberies increased tenfold. In ordinary times, a police presence acts as a deterrent. Although it can never deter every potential law-breaker, it does exercise a powerful influence over human frailty. Inevitably, since the police were otherwise engaged, vice in Hong Kong started to mushroom. There was suddenly an efflorescence of 'dance halls', shadowy establishments in which no one tangoed but where the customer, amidst the heavy breathing, sat with a hostess in a cubicle or stall.

Traditionally, Hong Kong's extensive and persistent vice had always been controlled largely by Triads, or rather by the fragmented and competing groups of this once unitary political conspiracy to restore the Ming (Chinese) dynasty and oust the Qing (the Manchus). In law, Triad organizations are defined as 'Societies which use Triad ritual, or ritual commonly used by Triads, or closely resembling such ritual and including any part of such ritual, or who use Triad titles or Triad nomenclature' (Cap. 151). They are not defined in terms of their ideology or beliefs, because these have become attenuated over time and have lost clarity and shape. Police publications on secret societies (at least two have been published) have routinely contained a degree of illusion or make-believe. This is, perhaps, understandable, for Triads also act as police informers and benefit from that role. Thus some professional or full-time criminals have been allowed to continue with their life of crime with police connivance. And sometimes the pair—police and Triads—have colluded, to their mutual advantage, in exploiting the public.

Since the 1920s, Triads have usually leaned more to the Right than the Left, a collaboration cemented in February 1927 when the criminal underworld of Shanghai, controlled by secret societies, helped Chiang Kai-shek to put down the Communist-inspired insurrection in that city. When the Nationalists fled from China, between 1947 and 1949, many Triads emigrated to Hong Kong, including Lieutenant-General Kot Siu-wong, a Nationalist Triad official of long standing, who reorganized the secret societies, including the new immigrant members, into a pro-Nationalist support and intelligence group in Hong Kong. The Green and Red Bands (Ch'ing Pang and Hung Pang) from Shanghai are also credited with introducing heroin into Hong Kong after 1949. The 1956 riots, largely taken over and exploited by Nationalist elements and Triads, were a defeat for both. Between 1956 and 1960 over 10,000 Triad officers and members were arrested and charged, and over 600 were recommended for deportation. The survivors largely relinquished their political role and concentrated on the criminal exploitation of the community. At that time, crime was more acceptable than politics, paradoxically.

In 1967, the vast majority of active Triads collaborated with the police. As criminal entrepreneurs, they had no wish to see the austere, puritanical, kill-joy Maoists in control of lucrative Hong Kong, their golden goose. The hard-pressed police, as stated above, had little time to devote to them. The Police Triad Society Bureau, Taffy Hùnt's domain, was temporarily directed to other tasks: it became the Bomb Investigation Unit.

Ironically, then, the Triads played some part in maintaining the status quo, in preserving the fabric of colonialistic Hong Kong. In 1967 they were the unofficial and unacknowledged allies, a curious avatar, of the forces of law and order. Triad members supplied information about left-wing organizers, sympathizers and activists, and intelligence about the haunts and lairs of Maoists and dissidents. They doubled as police spies. Needless to say, in any great crisis one is likely to come across some strange bedfellows. After 1967 the crime rate rose markedly, not surprisingly, and criminal enterprise accelerated. So too, did corruption, police corruption in particular. The police, one surmises, rationalized that they had saved the Colony and, like any body of mercenaries, expected to be richly rewarded by a complaisant community.

So far this chapter has starred principally the police. This is intentional and not discriminatory. It was the specific problem of police corruption, highlighted in the 1966 Commission of Inquiry, that first attracted public attention and which, when Godber flitted from Hong Kong in 1973, led ultimately to the creation of the ICAC. Of course, as Henry Heath deponed, corruption was rife in Hong Kong, as prevalent as the common cold. From time to time particular scandals had aroused the community, but there had been no sustained campaign to educate the public about its scope and scale, to mobilize the population to combat it. The press only referred intermittently to bribery and corruption. It was Leo Goodstadt's article 'The Fixers', published in the *Far Eastern Economic Review* in 1970, with the words 'Squeeze is a way of life in Hong Kong' blazoned above it, which did much to educate at least the English-speaking public about the issue. This exposé advertised the presence of a major social problem and depicted its grim contours. In the 1960s, the community passively accepted a great deal of low-level, routine corruption as a necessary fact of life, like water shortages. It was generally assumed among Chinese that all government departments were corrupt to a greater or lesser degree, but markedly greater in the Police, Immigration, Transport, Housing, Resettlement, Public Works, and Education Departments. Why, then, did the government allow this situation to continue for so long? Why did governor after governor do so little? And why were so many citizens not prepared to speak out publicly about the problem?

The first two questions suggest obvious hypotheses: (1) the government was unaware of the problem; (2) it knew, but underestimated its extent; or (3) it recognized that corruption was rampant but refused to act energetically. The first may be dismissed as implausible. Senior officials are usually highly educated, a few have scholarly interests. They would have discovered from standard works on Hong Kong—those of E.J. Eitel (1895), J.W. Norton-Kyshe (1898), G.R. Sayer (1937), and G.B. Endacott (1958)—that the Colony had always been plagued by corruption, that at times departments had been honeycombed, heavily so at lower levels. Various government publications, such as the 1902 Report on the Public Works Department, shelved in the Colonial Secretariat Library, would have confirmed that this was so. Is it sensible to suggest, then, that the entire corps of administrators was permanently 'at prayer', out of touch with the vulgar flow of life outside office doors? Or that all had been suffering, as Nye Bevan accused Sir Walter Citrine, from a 'bad case of files', so distracted by bureaucratic 'gamesmanship' that they did not realize what was going on?

The second hypothesis seems, at first sight, more sensible. Since 1948, when the Prevention of Corruption Ordinance (Cap. 215) was introduced, or certainly after 1952 when the Police Anti-Corruption Bureau was set up as a separate, specialized unit within the CID, it is clear that the civil service had been alerted to the problem. But not to the degree that Singapore had been in the early 1950s when it established a Corrupt Practices Investigation Bureau, an independent body, and one of the models for the future ICAC. It is not easy either to confirm or reject the third hypothesis since it depends on subjective factors and interpretation, on the states of mind of those employed in Hong Kong in the 1960s. It is now difficult to ascertain what these were; and retrospective statements from those involved in policy decisions are today liable to rationalization and self-justification, a common response

74

among individuals who feel they are being judged, or have been remiss. Sir David Trench (Governor of Hong Kong, 1964–71), when asked on British television about corruption during his administration, sat before the cameras as rigid as a totem-pole, brusque and non-committal.

In October 1973, Sir Murray MacLehose, Trench's successor, admitted in his annual review of the Colony that 'the suspicion of corruption on a more extensive scale was better grounded that I had personally realized'. Sir Murray's illumination was inspired by Godber's flight from Hong Kong to the United Kingdom on 8 June and by all the publicity that emanated from the startling news. Even young Chinese students publicly demanded that the delinquent policeman should be brought back to face trial. Godber at that time was the highest-ranking official to have been accused of corruption since the end of the Japanese Occupation in 1945 (although from time to time some smaller fry had been imprisoned or dismissed from public service). These dramatic events, related in part in Sir Alastair Blair-Kerr's first and second reports, powerfully concentrated Sir Murray's mind on the problem of large-scale corruption. They had the same sharp impact on other members of the community. Sir Murray's comment, cited above, suggests that the government was aware that corruption existed but had no idea it was so far-reaching and occurred at such high levels. The true facts were simply not available at that time, early 1973; only rumour, gossip, and surmise could be tapped. One reason for this situation, the lack of hard data, is that the government had not, as yet, *isolated* corruption as a major social problem, one that needed to be attacked on all fronts; there had been no mobilization of the community to combat the evil. The third hypothesis, it follows, is not really tenable, not in the stark form in which it has been worded.

In the early 1960s, Mrs Elliott's complaints about corruption had irritated senior officials; most believed her claims were wild and not backed up by credible evidence. In a speech in the Urban Council on 1 February 1966, she made a number of allegations against police officers. The Colonial Secretary, Mr Michael Gass, was so enraged by her animadversions that he not only sent Mrs Elliott a letter disputing her facts but also sent a copy to the press. He asseverated, 'Such conduct on your part can only result in a loss of confidence by the public in the police force with a resulting reduction in the effectiveness of the efforts by that body to maintain law and order'. Ironically, Mrs Elliott's charges were often replied to by officers who were themselves corrupt, such as some in the Traffic Branch (a most lucrative source for corrupt money), but this Gass obviously did not suspect, for the information he utilized to rebut Mrs Elliott's allegations itself came from police sources.

Michael Gass (Sir Michael Gass in 1969) had moved in 1965 from the Western Pacific High Commission (Sir Arthur Grimble's *Pattern of Islands*) to become Colonial Secretary in Hong Kong. When the British Empire shrank, piece by piece, like Balzac's *peau de chagrin*, the prospects of advancement for colonial officials diminished correspondingly. Some transferred to Hong Kong; Michael Gass (and Sir Hugh Norman-Walker later) was among them. Born in 1918, he had spent most of his service on the Gold Coast and in the Western Pacific. Hence, he had acquired most of his colonial experience in underdeveloped territories, in Africa and the Pacific. It is not likely that he enjoyed the hurly-burly of politics in Hong Kong, a far more sophisticated society than any in which he had served, a society which contained not only cynical and educated Chinese but also a large European community not easily cowed by officialdom. He was certainly outraged—his letter makes this clear—by Mrs Elliott's repeated criticisms, especially in the Urban Council, of government servants, 'relying', as he put it, 'on the shield of privilege available to Urban Councillors'. He was particularly upset by her frequent attacks on the police. In 1966, the force was a paramilitary body and its main task was security. It was a formation trained to deal with riot, insurrection, and dissidence, like the Ulster Constabulary, and to protect the border and the outlying islands (in this work it was also supported by the Army). Its other duties—keeping the peace and enforcing the law, traditional police functions—were naturally important, but were not seen as so critical as maintaining the political stability of the Colony, on which commerce and industry necessarily depended. Mrs Elliott was therefore excoriated by highly conservative officials for 'selling the pass', for bringing the administration into disrepute, for making Hong Kong a more difficult place to govern. All cogent criticism was, at that time, regarded as political, as potentially subversive. In 1961, Kenneth Bidmead, Acting Commissioner of Police, declared in a radio talk: 'When I say that the Police Force is essential for the peace and internal security of the Colony I do not mean it is all-important, but rather that its very existence enables the daily life of the Colony to continue unhampered'. He roundly asserted: 'The public is apt to think that corruption is widespread in the Force. This is definitely not so'. Mr Bidmead's comments, one suspects, would have been applauded by all civil servants as excellent public relations, as the honest truth, more or less.

The last question posed—why members of the public rarely spoke out about corruption—has been partly answered, but needs further elaboration. The Chinese man in the street submitted to the practice as a fact of life; all those who operated without an official licence, like many hawkers and all *pak pai* drivers, or who were involved in any illegal enterprise or occupation, simply accepted bribery and extortion as an additional tax or cost, a small levy or fee which allowed them to stay in business. Rich Chinese, the élite of the businessmen, industrialists, and financiers, generally accepted the utility of corruption as a means of speeding things up within a sluggish bureaucracy (time is money, as the adage goes) or which allowed them to cut corners and enhance profits. If the price was right, they were always prepared to pay for convenience. 'Kickbacks' and commissions, on the other hand, were as traditional in Hong Kong as a 'Christmas box' to any British coalman, milkman, or postman.

European views were mixed, ambivalent. In the main, the British did not approve of corruption for they had been educated for well over a century to despise and condemn the habit. No one really disputed that it was wrong in principle. But in Hong Kong, where Chinese predominated and Westerners were greatly in the minority, all criticism could be interpreted as undermining the legitimacy of the colonial government (as Gass surely implied in his letter). Scandal was not good for the morale of the population; the unmasking of senior officials or prominent citizens would not promote the well-being of the community. There is, it should be stressed, no *moral* argument that favours colonialism as a social or political form: at least, no reputable political scientist or social philosopher has provided a convincing defence (and the same is true of the institution of slavery). The one *limited* justification for imposing alien rule over indigenous peoples has always been the notion of 'good government', the establishment of an efficient and incorrupt administration. This was (and is) the claim made by defenders of the British-controlled Indian Civil Service (ICS), a boast still accepted by some Indian scholars. To insist loudly in public that the Hong Kong civil service was ripely corrupt had, therefore, dangerous implications: it was *lèse-majesté*. Westerners—the British—were thus faced with a dilemma; they hovered between contrasting sentiments. Most compromised by not pushing the matter too far except in discreet private conversation. They adopted, *faute de mieux*, a double standard: condemnation of corruption in the home country, a degree of toleration within Hong Kong. Chinese intellectuals, whether of a Nationalist or Communist persuasion, had an escape hatch from this dilemma: they were able to argue that corruption was an inescapable consequence of colonialism; or exploiting another theme, that capitalism encouraged egoism, socialism altruism.

The estimated population of Hong Kong in 1967 was around 3.9 million, of whom 98 per cent were classified as Chinese on the basis of language or place of origin. The 1966 By-census did not give a figure for the size of the resident

European population; the report only declared that about
31,000 people, excluding transients, originated from Commonwealth countries and that most of these lived in urban
areas. Europeans thus formed a very small proportion of the
population; most were employed in government service, in
business or the professions, including teaching. They were all
beneficiaries of the juridical status quo, an historical fact
which sustained their livelihood and protected their position
as a privileged group within a large native population.
Sociologically, they would be ranked as 'middle-class' in
terms of income, style of life, interests and sentiments. This
minority, it follows, was not likely to throw up many radicals
or dissidents, critics or detractors of the colonial regime. To
attack the government too pungently was simply 'bad form',
'letting the side down'. In any case, civil servants were prohibited by colonial regulations from speaking out against, or
writing about, the way the administration conducted itself. If
the position had been different, if Europeans had been more
outspoken about what really went on in Hong Kong, the government might well have paid more attention to the twin
problems of bribery and corruption.

The only individuals who attacked government institutions
and policies with some persistence were members of the Reform Club and the Hong Kong Branch of the United Nations
Association, a few academics and a number of cranks, perfer-
vid letter-writers to the press. The legal profession, on the
whole, was mute on such issues; but lawyers form an important élite group in Hong Kong and are close to the Establishment. In this transitional period (the 1960s), Hong Kong suffered not only from Betjemanesque ghastly good taste but also
from the terror that someone would rock the boat and disturb
the comfortable equilibrium that had been attained. Moreover, Chinese opinion was not so important a factor as it has
since become, and far less attention was then paid to the
Chinese press, to anything written in Chinese. The habit-
ridden Chinese lower classes, the bulk of the population, nearly all of whom had been nurtured in Nationalist China, had

not picked up the habit of democracy as yet; they had not learned openly to criticize or challenge their masters; nor, on the other hand, had they any wish to be governed to death by a far too efficient team of foreign officials. They were as ambivalent in their attitudes as Europeans.

The crux of the matter is that, in the 1960s, corruption had neither been identified nor designated as a *major* social problem, only recognized as one of a large number of social problems affecting Hong Kong, even though legislation had been introduced or amended and various committees and public bodies had been set up to examine the issue. A fundamental weakness was that the Colony lacked the presence of a 'moral entrepreneur' (to use Howard Becker's term), an esteemed public figure, a moral agent, someone able to rally and mobilize the community to combat the evil. In the early 1970s, as we shall see, Sir Murray MacLehose admirably filled that role and succeeded in fixating, for a time, the minds of the public on the problem. A midget, perhaps, would not have been so effective. Sir Murray, taller than a Scottish caber, dominated the scene, and most of the public; he roused the population with his icy contempt for the corrupt, with his Covenanter zeal to clean up Hong Kong. Previous post-war governors —Sir Mark Young, Sir Alexander Grantham, Sir Robert Black, Sir David Trench, all decent men and competent administrators—lacked Sir Murray's particular mix or constellation of qualities. More than any governor, he appealed to the Chinese notion of 'righteousness', probity, to their respect for the incorrupt Mandarin. As a moral entrepreneur, Sir Murray was able to awake the conscience of Hong Kong and embark on his grand design, in 1974, to expunge corruption from Hong Kong.

The Star Ferry riots have been overshadowed in memory and in popular folklore by the tumultuous six months of the 1967 disturbances. But the riots marked a watershed in the history of post-war Hong Kong. In 1966, the problem of corruption emerged from its swaddling-clothes and was seen to be what it really was: a custom, a practice, that undermined the legitimacy of the colonial government and its claim to act, as it were, as a moral umpire within a metropolis given over to commerce and industry, trade and finance. The Hunger Striker's protest was a symbol of the future. It testified that youth was pushing to the fore, and would soon demand higher standards in public life.

4
THE ORIGINS OF THE ICAC:
THE CONTROL OF CORRUPTION

'We'll wipe out crime.
We'll put every cop on pension!'
From a Laurel and Hardy film, *A-Haunting We Will Go.*

IN previous chapters, a number of events covering the period 1842 to 1967 have been examined in detail or briefly commented upon. The problem of control has been mentioned frequently, *inter alia*, but has not been given any extended treatment. To this issue—control—we must now turn. Before outlining the steps taken from 1945 to 1974, when the ICAC was set up, to eliminate or reduce corruption it is necessary, first of all, to make some general comments on the historical events referred to in the preceding chapters.

The 1897 gambling house scandal gave rise to the Misdemeanours Punishment Ordinance of 1898, almost a carbon copy of English law, but Hong Kong's first piece of legislation to deal specifically with bribery and corruption. The government had learned by 1898 that both were more extensive than had been supposed, and this awakening or reaction led to increased penalties for the offence.

The great ARP scandal of 1941 had no immediate outcome; those who investigated this tenebrous affair were swept soon after into internment at Stanley, distressed former residents of the Peak. Top dogs, they became underdogs, reduced to the ranks. The Japanese temporarily supplanted the British as colonial administrators, so that new forms of corruption arose as modes of accommodation to changed, exiguous, and, finally, awful conditions. Corruption, in this special context, was an adaptive response; an illustration of the Darwinian thesis of the survival of the fittest (though not necessarily of the 'best'). When the British returned under Admiral Harcourt, on 30 August 1945, they unwittingly brought with them, like contaminating spores, new seeds of corruption. The need to control the economy—to introduce a wide range of economic measures—created a milieu in which corruption and the corrupt would continue to flourish.

British officials, such as Sir Mark Young, had tended to play down the fact of corruption in the colonies. In the 1920s and 1930s, colonialism had come increasingly under attack, dramatically so in India with Gandhi and the Congress Party. The inquisitive League of Nations, founded in 1920, caused further concern in official circles by constantly seeking information about conditions in colonial territories. Fabians, various socialist and liberal pressure groups, as well as the odd world crusader (someone enthusiastic to reform the entire universe), also performed a nuisance role by relentlessly asking questions about how possessions were really governed, for answers could not easily be obtained in official year-books. Trojan Horse critics, housed in the colonial service itself, such as George Orwell and Maurice Collis, were also shrewdly assessing the behaviour of those who governed subject populations. Before the Japanese day of reckoning came, in Hong Kong in late 1941, one might say that colonial officialdom had its back against the wall.

After 1945, colonial officials steadily lost their sense of mission; once proprietors, now they were caretakers. Post-war, they could depend far less on confidentiality; they could not easily conceal or disguise scandals or serious problems. The press—the media—would no longer allow them to do so, and what is termed 'investigative journalism' took root and spread. The events leading up to the so-called 'Godber affair' and the establishment of the ICAC should be viewed against this background. Administrators now perform, as it were, on a public stage, watched by a vast social audience; there is far less 'intimate' theatre.

Even if the Hong Kong government had attempted, in the inter-war period, to extirpate or reduce corruption, it would have found itself in an impossible position for there was no special unit to hand, armed with the necessary investigatory powers, able to do so. The control of corruption was then mostly in the hands of the police, a notoriously venal authority. In the immediate post-war period, the position was even more acute. Depleted and weakened by internment or by stringent conditions imposed on civilians, the police could not act vigorously against the menace; they had much else to do, in any case. The actual strength of the force in late 1947 was only 2,807; of the former 800-strong Indian (Moslem) contingent only 62 were serving at that time. Those Chinese constables recruited after the war, mainly Cantonese, were mostly of poor quality. Some had Triad affiliations and all had low educational qualifications. How could such a body of men deal expeditiously with the general problem, let alone corruption in its own ranks?

In July 1946, Pennefather-Evans (appointed Commissioner of Police in February 1941) suggested in a memorandum that a special 'Anti-Corruption Squad' should be created, with the aim of weeding out corrupt elements in the force (and presumably to investigate cases that occurred outside the confines of the police). His ideas were not taken up at that point, although they were adopted later. Perhaps the innovation was resisted in 1946 because it appeared unrealistic, since it was accepted that so many serving officers were tainted, or suspected to be so. On 2 August 1946, a discussion was initiated by four Unofficial members of the Executive Council, led by M.K. Lo (later Sir Man Kam Lo), on 'the extent to which corruption was prevalent amongst members of the public service and on the measures which might be taken to lessen or prevent corruption and punish offenders'. Pennefather-Evans' successor as Commissioner of Police, Duncan MacIntosh, was invited to attend the session. M.K. Lo, who originated the discussion, averred that 'corruption amongst members of the public service was more prevalent than ever before ... and said that allegations against the Police Force were very strong. He had even received rumours of corruption in the Education Department'. The comments made by MacIntosh are especially interesting. He stated that

> he had never seen such widespread corruption anywhere else before and blamed the attitude of the local populace, who were prepared to pay lavish bribes in order to save themselves trouble. He gave various instances of corruption which had been discovered in the Police Force; one man, he said, had been collecting $50 per head for recommending recruits; in another case an Assistant Superintendent had been handed $200 by a tenderer for police uniforms ... He said that there was much loose talk about corruption but that the general public afforded the Police little assistance in the matter.... He considered that senior subordinates were retained too long in key positions and were thus enabled to create deep-rooted 'rackets' which were extremely hard to expose. He said that he had no hope of quick results but advocated increases in pay which would remove the most common excuse for dishonesty.

These comments are taken verbatim from the minutes, but of course were not available at that date to the public. It is noteworthy that Duncan MacIntosh was well aware of the existence of 'corruption syndicates' ('rackets' as he called them), a matter that was to cause so many difficulties in the 1970s.

There were special circumstances in 1946, which have been referred to, that helped to amplify corrupt practices, such as stringent controls over imports and exports; licensing; shortages of all sorts; a prevalence of smuggling; the parlous state of trade, commerce, and industry; the ubiquity of crime; and the flocking back to the Colony of those who had left voluntarily or under compulsion during the war years. The main stimulus to deviate probably came, albeit unintentionally, from government regulation of much of the economy, a form of interference with market forces which usually promotes corruption and always encourages black-marketeering. Later, the crumbling of the Guomindang regime, between 1947 and 1949, caused a further flood of refugees and of the politically disinherited into Hong Kong. This inflow had a demoralizing effect in that it strengthened the need for these castaways to break the law, and had an equivalent influence on those who wanted to rise rapidly from the bottom of the social heap, from the lower depths (to use Gorki's evocative expression). Understandably, at that time there was much talk of corruption, as Unofficial members of the Executive and Legislative Councils, such as M.K. Lo, reported.

The 1948 Prevention of Corruption Ordinance was a product of the prevailing climate of opinion and of the concern to purify the public service. These were, to reiterate, the final years of dedicated colonialism; and the mood in England, after the defeat of the Axis Powers, was to expunge the ugly 1930s. This moral atmosphere affected those newly recruited into the colonial service, and some of its survivors. The granting of independence to India in 1947 was symptomatic of a new vision: an ideology of decolonialism. No one seriously believed it was possible to create a Hong Kong fit for heroes to live in; but there was nonetheless a degree of recognition that a better order should be established (the idea of local government was bruited for a time) and also an earnest desire to cleanse the territory of some of the social problems that had overwhelmed pre-war administrations.

The 1948 Ordinance incorporated the main provisions of the statute law of England dealing with bribery and corruption. It was also a symbolic action, a fixing of the battle lines, a statement from the government that it really meant business and had recovered from its daze. Obviously, this was perceived as a reformist measure. The *Hong Kong Annual Report* of 1948 declared in reference to the Ordinance:

An effect of the war which has been experienced in the Colony, as elsewhere in the world, has been an increase in corrupt practice. A strengthening and clarification of the law of the Colony became necessary and was effected by the enactment of the Prevention of Corruption Ordinance, 1948.

Later in that year, after the Ordinance became law, Pennefather-Evans' plan was taken up at last and a specialized police unit was established, located within the CID. Designated the Anti-Corruption Branch (ACB), it was handed the task of investigation and prosecution. In 1952 the unit was separated from the CID but retained its title. (It should be noted that in England corruption cases are still investigated by the CID like any other crime.) This apparent quasi-autonomy, granted in 1952, was in fact cosmetic in that, as before, officers were seconded for a time to the Branch and then returned to their units or formations. Nor did the change signify continuity, the creation of a corps of anti-corruption specialists, men who pursued a career solely in this highly complex professional field. However, from this embryo, implanted in 1948, was to grow the mighty ICAC, that future *Leviathan* so many would come to fear.

One side-effect of the Korean War (1950–3) was the creation of fresh opportunities for corruption, as Sir Alexander Grantham relates in *Via Ports* (1965), his autobiography. The embargo placed on strategic materials and other goods for China, then deemed an aggressor, led, Sir Alexander writes, 'to a great increase in smuggling out of the Colony and the bribery of revenue officers which was not easy to detect'. Smuggling had always been a traditional occupation in South China. It effloresced during times when controls weakened.

In caricature, the situation in the 1950s was like that of a dog attempting to catch its tail: it never does. The forces of law and order were in no position to stem the tide of corruption. Routinely the government reacted to accumulating reports of its prevalence by new or amended legislation, by the introduction of tighter regulations, or by the formation of advisory committees or monitoring bodies; sometimes by increasing the strength of the police. Each innovation or reform normally set off a chain reaction. It was a matter of stimulus and response. The corrupt and the incorrupt were thus involved together, dialectically. At times, the situation would best be described as one of unholy deadlock. These were the conditions, the necessary antecedent events, that gave rise to the symbolic crusade against corruption in the late 1960s.

The various commissioners of police were rather in the position of the Grand Duke Nicholas of Russia, the Commander-in-Chief, who, on meeting his commissariat staff for the first time, cautioned: 'Gentlemen, no stealing'. Commissioners would repeatedly exhort their men to be honest but lacked, not the authority or power, but the evidence, and sometimes the inclination, to do very much about venal elements in the force, protected as these were by brother officers, a point discussed in Chapter 3. The apparatus of control then was defective, out of date. The kingpins of corruption and the drug trade, as well as some senior police, were practically inviolate, like Mafia godfathers, despite the fact, for example, that the Narcotics Bureau had been merged with the ACB in 1954. (This merger had been agreed upon in government circles because it was well-known that corruption was closely tied to the narcotics traffic and smuggling, and of course to the ubiquitous Triads.)

These facts may put a gloss on the following developments. In 1956 the government set up a Standing Committee on Corruption under the chairmanship of a Principal Crown Counsel, picked by the Attorney-General. The other members were the Establishment Officer and the Director of the Anti-Corruption Branch. This small body met infrequently and it is not known what the Director advised, if anything. The Standing Committee soon became moribund as a factor in the fight against corruption. However, in 1960 it was revivified and strengthened in response to much talk of delinquent public servants. Everyone in the community knew that to pass a driving test the driving instructor must be offered a consideration—HK$400. Those who sought public housing or entry for their children into certain schools understood the important lubricating function of the gift to ease their way. The honeycombing of all areas of Hong Kong life by the corrupt was well advanced by the late 1950s.

The Standing Committee, after presenting its second report, was re-named the Advisory Committee on Corruption. It was now chaired by the Attorney-General himself, not his surrogate, while the other members were the Establishment Officer (as before), the Deputy Commissioner of Police, and three Unofficial members of the Executive Council. In Hong Kong eyes, this was a powerful body. Its new terms of reference were:

To consider and keep under review the extent of and problems presented by corruption in relation to the public service of Hong Kong, and to make recommendations from time to time.

The Standing Committee produced six reports in a very short period—from 5 August 1960 to 29 December 1961. These reports are valuable documents and many suggestions or recommendations contained therein were incorporated later in various government regulations, procedures and practices, and in the Prevention of Bribery Ordinance of 1971. As Sir Alastair Blair-Kerr concludes: 'There is no doubt that much was achieved by the Advisory Committee during the year 1961'. This body had no executive powers; as its title confirms, its role was purely *advisory*. No summary of the six reports will be given here but it should be stressed that the third—on the practice of giving and receiving presents—was particularly germane to the problems facing Hong Kong, to the peculiar characteristics of its society.

In their sixth and last report the Committee examined the delicate question of transferring the investigatory functions of the Anti-Corruption Branch to some outside or independent body. (In Singapore, before independence, the Corrupt Practices Investigation Bureau had been separated in 1952 from the police and placed directly under the Colonial Secretary.) The Commissioner of Police, invited to attend, argued persuasively before the Committee in favour of maintaining the status quo. 'We feel bound to accept', they concluded, 'the Commissioner's views on the matter'. One wonders why. Ironically, the Committee listed several convincing arguments in favour of divorce. Indeed, a reader is likely to conclude that separation was in the very best interests of the community.

Thus the report states:

There was a strong feeling among those who were heard by the Working Party on Public Co-operation that the Anti-Corruption Branch should not be part of the Police Force. It was stated that the public are reluctant to complain to the Police of whom they are afraid and there was danger in using police staff because they can put the techniques and knowledge which they so acquire to bad use when, as frequently happens, they are posted to other branches of the Force. We consider a further justification for this view is that nearly 50% of all complaints about corruption concern the Police Force itself.

The Commissioner's arguments centred on the fact, as he saw it, 'that since no specialized training is required for investigating corruption, an officer who has experience in Criminal Investigation should be fully effective soon after being appointed to the Branch'. If that were so, there was no need to develop a *corps d'élite*, either within or outside the police. This thesis surely falls to the ground if those officers transferred from the CID to the ACB were themselves corrupt or had been so at some stage of their career. In the great 'show trials' of the mid-1970s, many of those publicly unmasked as corrupt had served previously in the CID, or were still serving. It is sometimes cynically asserted that the best policemen are those recruited from the criminal classes, like François Vidocq (1775–1857), ex-convict, who became head of the French Sûreté and a celebrated thief-taker. He drew upon his extensive knowledge of the Parisian underworld to track down those suspected of crimes. But corrupt anti-corruption officers are likely to shield too many of the guilty, or be sluggish in investigating senior officers or members of the privileged élite. Bloodhounds of corruption, they also may have secrets they wish to hide, as discrediting to themselves. In retrospect, the Commissioner's defence of the status quo was weak, unconvincing, and inconclusive.

The Committee agreed with the Commissioner's views not, one imagines, simply to save his 'face' and that of the force he commanded, but because they felt that if the Committee took an opposite position this might further undermine confidence in the police. The 1956 riots had revealed how volatile a rootless population could be; the events of 1966 were to be a further demonstration of the fragility of law and order in an atomistic society. The police responded to the activities of the Advisory Committee on Corruption, towards the end of 1960, by creating a Target Committee. This was purely an internal police body, on which sat a number of senior policemen—the Deputy Commissioner of Police (Administration), the Director of Criminal Investigation, and the Senior Superintendent of the ACB (later, also, a senior man representing the Establishment Officer). The task of the Target Committee was to select cases for investigation out of a large pool of suspects—'targeting' as the police call this process—and also to evaluate results. The Advisory and Target Committees provide another example of stimulus and response, and bargaining, with tangible results for both, crusaders and police. The investigation of corruption was left in the hands of the police; on the other hand, the police now gave this offence a higher priority by setting up their own high-powered Target Committee. This sounded nice. The public read it as a signal that the force now really meant business.

The Advisory Committee declared in 1960:

From a preliminary study of the activities of the Anti-Corruption Branch of the Police Force, we are satisfied that it has possibly the most difficult task of any specialized branch of the Government service, and that its performance is not to be measured by the number of corruption charges brought successfully in Court. In this connexion we would like more publicity given to the results of cases investigated by this Branch. Everything possible should be done by Government to strengthen and assist the Branch.

If the ACB's performance was not to be measured by the number of successful prosecutions, then, clearly, the Committee viewed the ACB less as an investigative body than as a deterrent by its very presence. Later, this unit was to be criticized for spending too much time on the gathering of intelligence, such as the pattern of corrupt practices in selected areas of government service, as Sir Alastair states, and not enough on individual targets. As a result of a directive from the Target Committee, a directive inspired by Charles Sutcliffe, a change in emphasis came about in February 1972. In reality, the two objectives—investigation and prevention —can never be disassociated. This was accepted by the newborn ICAC in 1974, when it organized a trinity of departments—Operations, Corruption Prevention, and Community Relations (that is, investigation, prevention and education).

First introduced as a very small unit in 1948 (a man and a dog almost), the ACB had expanded step by step, each time under a more senior officer. The police had responded to increasing pressure from the government and the public by up-grading the ACB; but there had not always been a concomitant improvement in efficiency. Some critics have alleged that a by-product of this evolution had been greater corruption, for members of the ACB were in a favoured position to squeeze brother officers and members of the public. In this sense, the ACB, figuratively, was right at the centre of the spider's web.

It is not surprising to discover that as late as September 1973 Sir Alastair could write, 'however one looks at the matter, there are no signs, so far, that there has been any great break-through in the battle against corruption, despite the additional powers conferred by Cap. 201'. The latter referred to the Prevention of Bribery Ordinance of 1971, which contained some novel features and, theoretically, made the prosecution of the corrupt far easier than in the past. By now, 1973, the ACB had already been re-titled the Anti-Corruption Office and placed under a director, in fact an Assistant Commissioner of Police, above whom was only the Deputy Commissioner and the Commissioner. This was a response to the 1971 Ordinance.

The evolution of the ACB, which has been traced, can be interpreted as so many attempts made by the police to catch up with, or reflect, public opinion and the concern of the government. The ACB had not shown much enthusiasm for its tasks at times, until Charles Sutcliffe became Commissioner of Police on 19 April 1969. He was an officer who took corruption very seriously indeed. He was to change the picture radically by targeting some of his serving officers, notably Peter Fitzroy Godber of the Class of 1952, a vintage year for the corrupt, since it included Walter Boxall, Ernest Hunt, and Cecil Cunningham. All had joined the force in 1952 as sub-inspectors and all were to be imprisoned later. Since Godber's panic flight was one of the main factors in the creation of the ICAC, we should now present his story.

It is not impossible to decipher Godber's personality; he was no Yorkshire Ripper, no convoluted Kim Philby. Godber was quite normal. His deviant motivation is not difficult to unravel: he wanted a far, far better life than a policeman's salary could provide. Godber, one surmises, was affronted by nasty crimes—robbery, assault, and rape, for example—but was less perturbed by white-collar offences, the 'civilized' side of crime, such as corrupt practices, in which he indulged routinely. What he suffered from was a permanent condition of acute respectability: the yearning for a truly comfortable and middle-class existence back in the home country. He was a victim of what the French sociologist, Durkheim, calls 'the malady of infinite aspiration'.

Godber, properly speaking, was not a criminal activist, a man of action, like a housebreaker or pickpocket; he was a passive delinquent, a receiver. He accepted liberal hand-outs from those who organized the corruption syndicates. Most of his corrupt money came, upwards, from the Chinese station sergeants—the middle-management strata of the force. Station sergeants viewed policing as a business, and corruption as a police rate levied on sections of the public for the protection police offered the propertied classes. 'They also serve who only stand and wait' was Godber's motto.

Unlike Hunt, Godber was no big spender. He drove a very un-smart car, had a small circle of friends, entertained little. Hong Kong's night-spots did not know him. Godber led a remarkably quiet, subfusc, and discreet life. His sights were

93

always set on England, to which he was about to retire, to his home 'The Cottage', Iden Lock, near Rye, Sussex. Like so many civil servants, for whom Hong Kong is never home, he lived in a colonial limbo, in a European laager. While the average European civil servant wanted, to use Louis MacNeice's expression, to hang his hat on a pension, Godber wanted much more. His biography is thus a conventional one. Yet this highly conventional man was to become an element of Hong Kong's mythology, a Folk Devil, as notorious in Hong Kong as Landru in France and Dillinger in America.

Peter Godber was born in London in 1922. After war service, he joined the police and served for four and a half years as a constable in Hastings County Borough Police Force. In August 1952 he transferred to Hong Kong as a probationary sub-inspector (a designation that is no more). He rose to the rank of Assistant Superintendent in 1955, and to Chief Superintendent in 1969. He was posted, in December 1971, as Deputy District Police Commissioner, Kowloon (that is, second-in-command of the Kowloon District, where much vice is concentrated and Triads are very active). In the 1968 distribution of New Year's Honours he was awarded the Colonial Police Medal for Meritorious Service. Many police honours are like Boy Scout badges which go to the clean, the keen, the obedient, and the diligent. Godber deserved his gong since, as related before, he had shown great courage and persistence in very ugly times, the year 1967.

In late April 1973, however, the Commissioner of Police, Charles Sutcliffe, received private information that Godber was remitting large sums of money abroad. Who told the Commissioner about Godber's unexpected wealth is not known. Was it a banking official, or an envious colleague, or a jaundiced member of the public? We do not know: the Commissioner has not spoken. This snippet of information was passed down the hierarchy to the Deputy Commissioner, Christopher Dawson, chairman also of the Target Committee. Dawson then communicated the facts to the Director of the Anti-Corruption Office and instructed him to open a file on the suspect. As investigations proceeded, it soon became clear that Godber would not be able to offer a respectable explanation for the fortune he controlled. He could not have been charged, however, under Section 10 (1) (a) of the 1971 Ordinance, with maintaining 'a standard of living above that which is commensurate with his present or past emoluments'; for, as we have seen, Mr and Mrs Godber lived frugally, by expatriate standards.

The team from the Anti-Corruption Office had discovered, after an intense search into his financial affairs, that Godber's resources totalled over HK$4.3 million, which was nearly six times his total net salary from August 1952 to May 1973. (This estimate has been revised greatly upwards since his trial, but how much he is really worth remains a mystery.) In these closing months of his police career, it is understandable that Godber was becoming nervous about his freedom and the security of his assets. Hong Kong had changed markedly since the days when he was a probationary sub-inspector; the Colony now had a growing corps of local critics. Many expected more of the government. And Sir Murray MacLehose, a reformer and also a law-and-order man, was in the saddle and threatening the criminal classes, and the corrupt. In January 1972 Godber asked to retire early on the grounds of his wife's ill health and his own failing physical standards. He was given permission to proceed on retirement leave on 20 July 1973. Then he wrote again to the Commissioner requesting that his departure date be advanced to 30 June. He had the wind up. He was in a funk. He feared retribution. The good days were over. The Commissioner refused this latest request for he knew Godber was under investigation.

On 4 June 1973 a notice under Section 10(1) (b) of the 1971 Ordinance was served on Godber in Christopher Dawson's office. Godber fainted. This section reads that any person who, being or having been a Crown servant,

is in control of pecuniary resources or property disproportionate to his present or past official emoluments, shall, unless he gives a satisfactory explanation to the court as to how he was able to maintain such a standard of living or how such pecuniary resources or property came under his control, be guilty of an offence.

Godber was not arrested on the spot because it had been decided he should be given a week to 'make representations'. However, the game was up, as he well knew. Mrs Godber left Hong Kong on 7 June. He went the next day. Although his name had been put on the 'watch list' at Kai Tak Airport, he managed to evade security checks and slipped on board a Singapore Airlines flight, and so back to England. It was to be no escape to freedom.

Sir Alastair Blair-Kerr's first report gives a detailed account of this saga. After Godber's apparently puzzling departure and miraculous escape, rumours spread in Hong Kong that his vanishing had been 'fixed'. He was a man who knew too much; he had been encouraged and helped to leave by corrupt brother officers or by high-ranking officials who did not want nasty details about corruption to emerge. Sir Alastair concludes that there 'was not a scrap of evidence to suggest that any person assisted Godber'. This is highly plausible, for Godber was a distrustful, reserved, and solitary person, as secret deviants often are.

Sir Alastair includes in an appendix a copy of a letter sent by Godber, after his return to England, to a friend, another police officer. Referring to his resignation, he writes: 'If it is refused then they must please themselves but I am no longer—sadly—a policeman because it is still a good Force'. This sounds almost defiantly hypocritical, written by one who had brought so much discredit to that Force, one who was to have a permanent effect upon it by encouraging the establishment of what could be called a counter-police organization, the ICAC. But Godber's words, whether hypocritical or not, are an expression of his ambiguous values, and reflect, in a twisted form, the Hong Kong belief that what is good for business is good for the Colony. He did not see himself, one assumes, as a bent copper, as a villain or felon, and probably never has done. Ernest Hunt's excuse for his behaviour was, basically, that practically everyone in the police was on the make—so why not? We do not know how Godber would rationalize his activities—he has made no public statement, has given no lengthy interviews—but it is likely he sees himself on the side of respectable crime, white-collar crime, which in many ways is an extension, or perversion, of the themes of private enterprise and competitive capitalism: business is morally neutral.

Back at Iden Lock, he became a hunted and haunted man, pursued by the bloodhounds of the media. In 1941, Wing Commander Steele-Perkins had not had to suffer the indignity of being chased by television cameramen and inquisitive reporters: but Godber had to. His face became known to millions of viewers. He was seen driving a flashy car. His house looked nicely *bijou*, detached, and engardened. In Hong Kong, it was Godber's latest incarnation which startled the public. He had grown a Robinson Crusoe beard. This could hardly be disguise; perhaps a sign of emancipation. The Hong Kong government now took steps for the return of the runaway.

The government's most immediate reaction to Godber's disappearance was the appointment of Sir Alastair Blair-Kerr, a judge, as a one-man commission of inquiry. His two reports have been quoted from *passim*. Godber had left Hong Kong on 8 June 1973, secure in the knowledge that he could not be extradited from England under Section 10, for this offence does not exist in English law; Sir Alastair was made commissioner on the 13th and, with extraordinary speed, completed his first report (on the facts of Godber's evasion) by 13 July. His second report (a review of anti-corruption legislation and practice) was finished by 1 September. Before the publication of the latter, Godber's name had become a household word and a symbol for graft. A campaign to get Godber back to face trial spread swiftly, with student groups in the spearhead of the protest (such student action was a novelty in those days). This saga of a senior policeman who had cocked a snook at the community and had managed to exit safely with all his loot (sent on in advance like unaccompanied baggage) was widely reported and commented upon by the media. These revelations outraged some sections of the public; the man in the street, however, was perhaps less startled since he had grown accustomed to the rituals of squeeze; for him corruption was no mere abstraction. Sir Murray MacLehose, the Governor (1971–81), in his October 1973 annual review opined: 'I had been aware of suspicions of high-level graft as well as of a certainty of extensive low-level corruption'. He admitted that 'the suspicion of corruption on a more extensive scale was better grounded than I had personally realized'. Godber's activities had thus awakened and illuminated the Governor as to the seriousness of the problem. Godber had fortified his resolve to create an anti-corruption organization that would be independent of the police, a force which had sheltered Godber comfortably for so many years.

The decision to separate the Anti-Corruption Office from its parent body was not, in mid-1973, a foregone conclusion, despite the Governor's growing disillusionment with the way the problem of corruption had been handled both past and present. Sir Alastair had remained neutral in his second report, simply marshalling arguments for and against the proposition. The police, on their side, could present a good case in favour of the status quo. In 1968 the then Commissioner of Police, Edward Eates, had urged that his men should be given a chance—'a period of three to four years'—in which to clean up the mess. Eates criticized the weaknesses in the law (the 1948 Ordinance) but hardly referred to the moral calibre of the police. Eates was listened to sympathetically because of his deserved reputation as the man who contained the 1967 demonstrations. When the Prevention of Bribery Bill was tabled, in 1969 and 1970, a powerful lobby of Unofficials forcefully opposed the Attorney-General's intention that the ACB should continue to remain within the force. The debate ended in a compromise. The ACB was granted a period of three years in which to demonstrate its efficacy. Reorganized, strengthened, and re-named the Anti-Corruption Office, it was now more successful. The Target Committee was also re-

formed and now had a majority of members who were not
policemen. Results were better compared with the past. But
law-enforcers can always produce an upward trend in prosecutions, if they so desire, by switching manpower to the
investigation of a particular offence. Prosecutions for rape
increased notably in Hong Kong in the late 1970s because,
among other factors, the police paid more attention to this
crime; they responded to public concern and public pressure.
So-called trends in crime revealed by criminal statistics are
often (though not always or necessarily) an index or reflection
of police activity and energy—of targeting—just as the size of
a harvest is not determined totally by nature but by the size of
the labour force employed. No workers: no harvest. This is
true, it is obvious, of corruption. An upward trend in corruption cases was not unexpected in the early 1970s, for the Anti-
Corruption Office now employed more investigators.

Sutcliffe, a policeman of great integrity and, like Sir Robert
Mark of the Met, a reforming commissioner, believed the cor-
ner had been turned in 1973 and that the force could now
handle the problem of corruption better than any newly created organization (after all, *he* had unmasked Godber and had
initiated his investigation). His trenchant views are given in
Sir Alastair's second report in numbered sequence:

1. Corruption is a crime; and the investigation of crime is the task
   of officers trained in investigation work with court proceedings
   in mind. The investigation of crime is not within the province of
   lawyers and others.
2. There is no source of trained investigators in Hong Kong outside the Royal Hong Kong Police Force.
3. It is unlikely that police officers of ability would wish to transfer
   to an Anti-Corruption Bureau independent of the police because
   such a bureau would offer very limited career prospects. It is
   likely that any officers who would be willing to transfer from the
   police force would be officers of limited ability with little prospects of promotion in the force.
4. Apart from impairing their career prospects, officers of ability
   would find it distasteful to spend their working lives in an Anti-
   Corruption Bureau, independent or otherwise.

99

5. The recruitment of police officers from overseas would prove difficult and, in any case, would take time.
6. An independent Anti-Corruption Bureau would lose the vast knowledge and resources which the Hong Kong police can bring to bear against crime, including corruption, and the advice and counsel of the Commissioner, his Deputies, and the Director of Criminal Investigation.
7. There is no guarantee that corrupt elements would not soon infiltrate into an independent bureau. If that were to happen, it would be impossible for a small bureau to turn inwards upon itself in order to investigate itself, whereas it is a relatively simple matter for a vast organization like the Royal Hong Kong Police Force to investigate any part of itself. Corruption in an independent bureau would have to be investigated by the Royal Hong Kong Police Force.
8. A bureau staffed by police investigators but responsible to persons other than the Commissioner of Police and his officers would be nothing more than an emphatic vote of no confidence in the senior officers of the police force and would be strongly resented by the officers of the police force. The morale of the force is at stake. The result of any lowering of the morale of the Royal Hong Kong Police Force would be putting in jeopardy the peace, order and security of Hong Kong.

Sutcliffe's arguments reflected not only his own views but also those of his predecessors, such as Henry Heath and Edward Eates. They were nicely marshalled and well supported; and he did provide, on paper, a strong case for maintaining the status quo. On the other hand, with hindsight at least, it is not difficult to question Sutcliffe's theses. In England, for example, Sir Robert Mark, Commissioner of the Metropolitan Police from 1972 to 1976, largely rooted out corruption among the CID. Mark's battle to control his own detective force is described in his autobiography, *In the Office of Constable* (1978). He did succeed, for a time, in cleansing his CID and eliminating numerous crooked policemen. When he retired in 1976, much admired and honoured, the dubious practices he had once put down reappeared. These had become allegedly so flagrant that a special body of regional police officers was recruited to investigate conditions in the Met and code-named 'Operation Countryman'. When Sutcliffe retired (as he did in January 1974) would succeeding commissioners continue to feel as strongly about graft as he did? Would they continue to give priority to corruption in police ranks? No one has impugned the honesty or integrity of Sutcliffe's successors; but he was a special case. He had an *idée fixe* about graft which, it is said, went back to the early 1960s, to the time when he joined the Hong Kong police from Tanganyika and an attempt was made to frame him by some corrupt members of the force.

In normal times the Governor and his advisors might have been swayed by the police case. The times were not normal. On 17 October 1973, Sir Murray declared before the Legislative Council that 'the escape of Godber was a shocking experience for all of us'. He went on to argue that there was, in his opinion, a need for an independent anti-corruption unit. He stressed two points in support of this innovation:

I believe that it is quite wrong, in the special circumstances of Hong Kong, that the police, as a force, should carry the whole responsibility for action in this difficult and elusive field. I think the situation calls for an organization, led by men of high rank and status, which can devote its whole time to the eradication of this evil; [and]

A further and conclusive argument is that public confidence is very much involved. Clearly the public would have more confidence in a unit that was entirely independent, and separate from any department of the Government, including the police.

Later in his speech, the name of Jack (later Sir Jack) Cater was mentioned as the first man to head the new organization. It was clear from the text of his lengthy and most diplomatic speech that there had been much discussion in high government circles about the proposal, and that Sir Murray had imposed his will.

The Governor's role in the creation of the ICAC was so important that a brief biographical sketch should be interpolated. Governor after governor, committee after committee, had deferred to the police for a variety of reasons but principally because they feared a collapse of police morale if the control of corruption was handed over to an independent body. Sir Murray accepted that risk. Sir Ronald Holmes, then Secretary for Home Affairs, neatly sums up the pros and cons thus: 'The arguments for retaining [the Anti-Corruption Office] are largely organizational and the arguments for removing it are largely political and psychological'. Sir Murray's decision was both political and psychological; his eye was fixed on the public, his constituents.

Crawford Murray MacLehose, now Lord MacLehose, is a scion of the Scottish Lowlands bourgeoisie. He was born into a family associated with the Glasgow printers, R. MacLehose and Company, a firm that has printed many of T.S. Eliot's books for Faber, the London publishers. His family background is rather similar to that of Harold Macmillan, the former Conservative Prime Minister. Sir Murray was educated at Rugby in the 1930s. Although founded in 1567, this great school was revitalized by Thomas Arnold, headmaster 1828–42. Rugby, as we know it today, is thus really a product of the age of iron and steel, of early Victorian England and of Evangelicalism. It was transformed by Dr Arnold into an establishment notable for the stress it placed upon the development of character and the moral education of the adolescent British male. Possibly because of its Low Church flavour, the school always attracted a large contingent of Scots. They were encouraged to wear national dress at weekends—kilts on Sunday, as it were. Sir Murray was one of them.

After Rugby, Sir Murray went up to Balliol College, Oxford; then in 1939, hostilities broke out and he served throughout the war with the RNVR. In 1947, he joined the Foreign Service and was posted, as is usual, to various parts, including Beijing, and Hong Kong as Political Adviser in 1963. His occupational background and experience differed significantly, therefore, from other post-war governors, all of whom had been career colonial civil servants. Sir Murray came to Hong Kong in 1971, in this sense, as an outsider, as a chief administrator who did not conform to the traditional pattern. This background partially explains why he was not too overawed by hallowed bureaucratic procedures and government rigma-role. He distinguished himself, in these early days, in the public mind as a reformer, impatient at times (one imagines) with the way Hong Kong in the past had faced up to, or had attempted to solve, the many interlocking social problems that had taken root and were regarded too frequently by officials as incrustations which could never be removed.

Sir Murray's intimation on 17 October that the ICAC had been planned and would soon be operating, and that Jack Cater had been chosen to head it, was warmly applauded by the community. Sir Murray was extremely popular in 1973. The Senior Unofficial, Woo Pak-chuen, declared at the next meeting of the Legislative Council: 'There has never been before such vigorous leadership at top Government level. Never has so much been achieved in so short a time'. Even if we allow for a degree of civilized civility in Mr Woo's Churchillian comments, they remain an honest expression of the regard with which Sir Murray's actions were held. He had broken police control over the investigation of corruption.

5

THE INDEPENDENT COMMISSION AGAINST CORRUPTION

'Down these mean streets a man must go
who is not himself mean,
who is neither tarnished nor afraid.'
Raymond Chandler, *The Simple Art of Murder* (1950)

THE ICAC was formally established on 15 February 1974 with the enactment of the Independent Commission Against Corruption Ordinance of that year. The Commissioner was made directly responsible to the Governor; there was no supervening link between them. Their relationship, structurally, was necessarily close and intimate, although an Advisory Committee on Corruption was set up, at the same time, to comment upon major aspects of the Commission's work, including policy, finance, and related matters. Section 12 of the new legislation outlined the Commissioner's duties. These embraced not only the key tasks of investigation and prevention but also the pursuit of cloudier aims, such as (to use the legal draftsman's language) 'the education of the public against the evils of corruption and the enlisting and fostering of public support in combatting it'. Hence the Commission created three functional branches: Operations, Corruption Prevention and Community Relations, all serviced by a central administrative unit. The Commission was financed from a single expenditure vote in the Estimates but because of the importance of secrecy a degree of financial autonomy was granted it that was not to be found in other government departments. At first, priority was given, in terms of resources, to investigations (Operations) for public opinion demanded speedy results, a call inspired by the Godber affair.

CHAPTER FIVE

Those who eagerly greeted the new organization's unveiling obviously expected the Commissioner and his hand-picked staff to launch a crusade (what sociologists would term a 'moral crusade') against a deviant minority, a 'dark figure' indeed. What its total was no one knew, but that is a problem criminologists usually have to face with any offence. The public assumed that the Commissioner would now move vigorously against those who had been put beyond the moral boundaries of Hong Kong, outside the new society envisioned by Sir Murray MacLehose and his advisers. One is reminded here of the euphoria typically generated in America by the electoral success of reformist campaigners in urban politics, by their inspiriting promise to establish a 'clean' city administration. So it was to be in Hong Kong, in 1974. Euphoria was sustained by much idealism; but also by *schadenfreude*, by the pleasantly malicious feeling that the wicked at last would be punished or outlawed.

The notion of who in fact were the 'corrupt', in legal or sociological phraseology, was then only fuzzily construed in the public mind. For the man in the street, it implied, one would imagine, the devious behaviour of the bent policeman or the crooked minor official, one who used his official status to enhance his income. Well-wishers of the ICAC did not recognize that *total* support for the ICAC's actions would necessitate the acceptance of certain social costs, as well as another claim upon the Colony's revenues. As we shall see, enthusiasm began to flag within the business community once the ICAC's investigators moved closer to its preserves, an area of much moral ambiguity and sharp practice, where sailing close to the wind was common. But in February 1974 all was excitement; students, a troublesome group since 1967, were gleeful; and so, too, were truculent social critics, for Mrs Elliott now had competitors, had fuglemen and epigoni, many entrenched in places of learning. The media's men and women were generally supportive; and the average worker was certainly not displeased, although cynical, possibly, of the eventual outcome. We do not know how the dishonest reacted or responded, but some delinquents must have felt threatened, as Godber had in 1973, and a few might well have stopped breaking the law, at least pro tem, as too risky.

In brief, in 1974 reform was in the air; the Governor had loudly sounded the tocsin in his 1973 Annual Review and was to repeat the same message in 1974. Some traditionalist or conservative Chinese interpreted these events as a return to 'righteousness', a theme with many parallels in China's long history. Generally speaking, the Governor's energetic leadership encouraged high expectations of the future, of better things to come.

In these early days, Sir Murray and Jack Cater were compared, irreverently, to Batman and Robin of Gotham City, those intrepid American crime fighters. The tall lamplighter figure of the Governor, flanked by the slighter Cater, cast, as it were, a long protective shadow over the community. They were pictured as a team, a two-man team bent on stemming the rising tide of crime and corruption. Cater was certainly an excellent choice as the first man to head the innovative organization, although he lacked of course professional experience of crime investigation and crime prevention. After war service with the RAF, he became an early member of the Civil Affairs Unit, a group sent to Hong Kong in September 1945 to organize the interim British Military Administration. He then worked in the first civilian government—that of Sir Mark Young—set up in May 1946. He had become a cadet officer in the Hong Kong civil service. Hence he had been involved from the start in putting the shattered territory back on its feet. By 1974, Cater had acquired a wealth of experience as an administrator, having served in a large number of government departments. He was reputed to be conscientious and hard-working—in *Who's Who* he lists 'work' as a recreation—and a most competent official. He had other notable advantages: integrity, and the ability to speak straightforwardly to an audience, a talent not shared by all senior officials, some of whom appeared, like Mr Toad, to 'know all there is to be knowed'.

Men who inspire or lead crusades, it is an obvious point,

tend to be special people and to exhibit particular qualities. One may cite Peter the Hermit, Loyola, Wilberforce, and John Brown, or Zola, General de Gaulle, and Gandhi. They tend to be people with a marked degree of moral earnestness and conviction (fops, dandies, aesthetes, academics, cynics, the brilliant and the brittle, are more likely to sit quizzing the world from their windows). It would be some exaggeration to claim that Sir Murray and Jack Cater were a judicious mixture of Savonarola and Torquemada, of Calvin and John Knox; but the public, at least the British portion, could discern something of a Covenanter's spirit in their make-up, an urge to purify society of its iniquities, some index of which was to be found in the reported crime rates since 1967; in particular, by increases in commercial crime, juvenile delinquency, sexual offences and, of course, corruption cases, each upward trend documented for the public by the media, especially the press. Whether true, false, or simply fudged, these alarmist statistics were taken by most people to be a true reflection of the direction in which the Colony was moving. Sir Murray certainly believed there had been a declension, a belief illustrated by his June 1973 'Fight Violent Crime Campaign'.

The number of established posts in the ICAC was set at 682 in 1974; but actual strength was only 369, the great majority of whom—301—were in Operations. From the start the Commissioner was faced with the formidable task of recruitment, of selecting several hundred suitable staff and, in particular, experienced crime investigators. Initially he had inherited the personnel—181 police officers and 44 civilian employees—of the former police Anti-Corruption Office (ACO); these were, so to say, on loan temporarily from the force. This situation could not continue indefinitely since some policemen, exiled from their familiar surroundings, wanted to return to their old units as soon as possible; others did not feel entirely comfortable serving in a civilian-administered organization; and a few perhaps covertly hated the ICAC, stigmatized in their minds as a counter-police organ, whose actions were inimical to their own formations. It was, on the other hand, the ICAC's policy to distance itself from a police body tarnished in the eyes of the public for harbouring so many corrupt officers, past and present, and to demonstrate its independence and relative autonomy, a unique feature in that the ICAC was, as stated, the only government department responsible solely to the Governor. Nor did the ICAC wish in any way to encourage the view that it could be influenced by the Commissioner of Police. Understandably, there was in 1974 a considerable amount of tension between the new anti-corruption organization and the Royal Hong Kong Police Force; their relationship was a wary one. The ICAC was criticized at the time for relying too heavily upon police manpower (181 men serving with the ICAC). These animadversions were unfair and largely unfounded, as time would show. The critics revealed little understanding of police culture, of the nature of police work, and of what the American sociologist, Jerome Skolnick, calls the policeman's 'working personality'.

Modern police are members of a disciplined force; they work in a clearly defined hierarchical service; and they are trained, like those in the armed forces, to obey orders. The organization comes before the individual. This does not mean policemen always demonstrate a high degree of passionless intelligence in their occupational role, as Bentham demanded of his ideal bureaucrat, only that if a policeman is given a job to do he is likely to carry it out without excessive questioning, without much existentialist soul-searching about moral, social or political issues. Few Hamlets are to be found in any force; such types are discovered more often in the so-called 'caring professions', where a measure of guilt, anxiety, disquiet, or acute social consciousness, may act initially as a potent recruiting factor. The creed of the average officer may be summarized as one of protecting the public against wrong-doers and of maintaining law and order, the established fabric of society. The situation does not vary very much under any system of government, left or right. Thus the Hong Kong policeman could switch to the ICAC in 1974 without any great drop in efficiency or loss of work momentum. As Gerald

Harknett, an ICAC official, declared: 'If you move from the Police to the ICAC you must change sides' (that is to say, to continue to obey orders, not a difficult adjustment for a person initially trained in a highly disciplined force).

Whatever their moral scruples or qualms, police worked conscientiously to further the ICAC's aims, as the record shows. Critics were wrong to interpret the presence of police within the ICAC's ranks as a sinister portent. It must again be stressed that the ICAC inherited the ACO's assets. It took over from the eclipsed unit all its intelligence reports and investigation files, including a number that had reached fruition, such as Godber's case. Hunt had already been dealt with by the ACO and had been prosecuted successfully. This inheritance helped the fledgling ICAC to get off to a good start; and later, with the Godber trial (February 1975), to vastly impress an expectant public.

The ICAC obviously owed much to Charles Sutcliffe's pioneering attempts to reduce corruption within the police force. But it was the recruitment, from retirement in Malta, of Mr John (later Sir John) Prendergast that was to prove decisive. In October 1973, Sir Murray flew to Malta and persuaded him to accept appointment as Deputy Commissioner and Director of Operations of the planned ICAC. In December, he was in Hong Kong conferring with Jack Cater and other high-ranking officials. Even a telegraphic biography of John Vincent Prendergast should reveal that the ICAC was most fortunate in attracting such an experienced investigator. He was born in County Wexford, Ireland, in 1912, but his Anglo-Irish family left for London when the Irish Free State was declared. After meritorious war service, he worked in various British-administered territories—Palestine, the Gold Coast, the Canal Zone, Kenya, Cyprus, Hong Kong, Aden— as an intelligence officer or as a police official employed in the security field. Thus he spent six years in Hong Kong (1960–6) as Director of Special Branch, and met Sir Murray at that time. His deputy, Mr Gerald Harknett (currently Director of Operations), had also worked in Hong Kong's Special

Branch. The image, now deeply etched, of the ICAC as an efficient, ruthless, crime-fighting machine—an élite force— was largely created by John Prendergast and his aides.

At the outset, the ICAC had to rely upon a relatively small corps of experienced crime investigators and professionals borrowed from the force. In December 1974 they numbered 58, of whom 5 had retired before joining the ICAC. At the end of 1975, 26 Hong Kong police officers were still employed in the Operations Department. By that time most ACO staff had been dispensed with, although their value to the ICAC had been demonstrated. The Commissioner stated that his new organization had been established as a purely civilian organization. It seems probable that Cater had reacted, for he was sensitive to unfavourable publicity, to pressure from the public to minimize links between the ICAC and a suspect ACO and police force not yet recovered from the disgrace of the lingering Godber affair. The ICAC did not purge itself of its entire police element; there were conspicuous and important exceptions, and survivors, such as John Prendergast, the Director of Operations, Gerald Harknett, his deputy, and others whose integrity and incorruptibility were beyond doubt. The ICAC now had to seek another source for experienced investigation officers; so it turned to the United Kingdom, whose legal system and style of policing were substantially the same as Hong Kong's, and to a country whence many expatriate inspectors originated. Such persons had some advantages over local recruits. Like emigrants to a strange country, they arrived without strong attachments, commitments, or obligations to social networks of friends, colleagues, neighbours, or relatives (Hong Kong Chinese, like all Chinese, tend to be firmly enmeshed in a complex web of family and kinship relationships). Nine British police were recruited in 1974; thirty-four arrived the following year, mostly on secondment from one or other United Kingdom force. The Operations Department, always the largest of the three functional branches, has never evolved into a completely civilian-manned unit, and is not likely to. There are benefits that accrue to the ICAC from importing fresh blood, men from outside the system. But no one has determined how long it takes, as it were, to 'soften' or 'blandish' this imported variety of anti-corruption official. There is, however, no evidence to suggest that this matter has presented any real problem to the authorities. All new arrivals are given what is termed a 'conversion' course and their behaviour is monitored constantly. Those who falter in their duties do not last long, and so it must be. Despite being a civilian organization, the staff of the ICAC have been granted great police powers. In these early days the public were right to see the ICAC as a force set up to control the police.

Meanwhile, Godber, as related, had been harried back in England by press and television reporters as he flitted to and from his Iden Lock cottage. It was a kind of mid-life sabbatical, learning to survive as the hunted rather than the hunter. In his home country Hong Kong's black sheep thus acquired almost celebrity status. His reputed illicit wealth and his apparent invulnerability from the agents of the law gained him admirers. It is said every Englishman loves a lord; he also delights in someone who has successfully cocked a snook at the authorities (Ronald Biggs, the Train Robber, comes to mind). Godber had sought legal advice both in Hong Kong and England and knew full well that he could not be extradited for a Section 10 offence, an offence which did not exist under English, only Hong Kong, law. That explains his flight in June 1973. It had been a rush for sanctuary, for the apparently safe portals of England. Presumably, he had made up his mind to sit tight, in the hope that his pursuers would switch in time to more promising targets, as other delinquents caught the public's attention. The pressure on the Hong Kong government to get Godber back was intense—the student campaign, with its slogan 'Fight Corruption, Arrest Godber', has been referred to—and the ICAC dedicated much energy to this end.

On 29 April 1974, some two and a half months after the creation of the ICAC, Godber was charged in London with having accepted HK$25,000 from Superintendent Cheng Hon-kuen in return for arranging the appointment of Cheng to head the Wan Chai police division, a lucrative posting for any corrupt police officer, since Wan Chai was host to much entrenched vice, especially prostitution, drugs, and illegal gambling. The witnesses to Godber's alleged offence were given in the indictment as Cheng himself and Ernest Hunt, the latter once deeply involved in syndicated corruption, as he now admits. Through his solicitors, Godber fought tooth and nail to block extradition. He was charged, however, with offences of which English law is cognizant. On 2 November the Bow Street magistrates ordered that he be returned to Hong Kong. At once Godber applied for a writ of habeas corpus, but on 12 December this was rejected by the Divisional Court in London. He was then brought back to Hong Kong by ICAC officials on 7 January 1975. There was much jubilation in the Colony. He had been absent for eighteen months, but ten had been spent in a London gaol awaiting the resolution of extradition proceedings.

The trial itself, presided over by Mr Justice T.L. Yang, was unspectacular. Godber was charged with having accepted a bribe and with conspiracy and was found guilty on both counts. What did disturb some persons was a conviction based on the evidence of two self-confessed crooks, no better or worse than the defendant in the dock. But the court was prepared to accept their testimony as true. And so Godber was found guilty and sentenced, on 25 February 1975, to four years' imprisonment. The trial marked the completion of an investigation that had lasted over five years, and the end of an era. Corruption itself had not ceased, but the days of blatant, bare-faced, institutionalized corruption and the 'the firm within a firm' were over.

Lawyers and journalists were quick to seize upon the issue of the 'tainted witness', of the almost routine law enforcement practice of using a crook to catch a crook. The Editor of the *Hong Kong Law Journal* affirmed:

The man and woman on the Shaukiwan tram may be fairly, if not fully, satisfied with the result, but the methods adopted to land this prize are dubious, to say the least, and are unlikely to enhance their respect for the law or their confidence in certain public servants whose duty it is to uphold the law.

The Editor of the *Far Eastern Economic Review* commented:

Hong Kong has witnessed a man being found guilty on the evidence of two self-confessed crooks, evidence which was obtained by means of immunity deals. One witness, a Chinese police superintendent, got away scot-free, with even his pension rights intact. The other, a contemptible European police officer, had only spent eight months in jai. most of that time in air-conditioned comfort.

He concluded, in a satirical finale, that these facts 'did not reflect any reluctance on the part of the Hong Kong authorities to live on immoral earnings'.

In the eighteenth century, professional thief-takers obtained most of their convictions by persuading criminals to inform upon confederates. This applied especially in cases of robbery, housebreaking, burglary, and receiving. At that time, the 'tainted witness' was regarded as a necessary instrument of law enforcement, although the dangers inherent in the system were well known to the authorities. Sometimes, for example, a notorious criminal would plan a burglary, see that it was carried out, inform the Bow Street Runners about those involved, turn King's evidence, and then claim a reward. The informer had set up the crime. In modern times, the case of Derek (Bertie) Smalls is often cited. In the late 1960s there was a spate of bank robberies in London. When Bertie Smalls was interviewed by the police about these crimes, he turned Queen's evidence. In other words, he did a deal with the police. In April 1973 he gave evidence at the trial of a number of men, friends of his. As a result of his immunity from prosecution, Scotland Yard's Special Robbery Squad sent twenty bank robbers to prison for a total of over 300 years. This particular offence suddenly became less popular in the London area. And, one supposes, Bertie Smalls lived happily ever after, but at an unknown address.

Moralists and legal purists, especially academic lawyers who act as guardians of legal virtue, are critical of this long-established practice. The moralist is never pleased if a guilty party evades his just desserts and is particularly aggrieved if he is allowed to profit from his wrongdoing, as did Cheng and Hunt. Lawyers, on the whole, are always worried about the veracity of any testimony given by accomplices. A pragmatist is likely to share these concerns but to argue that so-called 'tainted witnesses' do *sometimes* act very much in the public interest and that it is up to the trial judge to assess the status of their evidence. It is certain, for example, that bank robberies would have continued in London after 1973 if Bertie Smalls had refused to co-operate with Scotland Yard. He did co-operate, for it was in his interest. As a result, he put many of his friends in prison. The bank robbers were professional criminals—their main occupation was thieving—and their activities had already caused death to innocent bystanders and injuries to others. There is, one must admit, no tidy solution to the problem that divides moralists and pragmatists. In Godber's case the prosecution believed it was acting in the public interest when it utilized the services of Cheng and Hunt, both of whom were known to have been corrupt (there is no dispute about that fact).

Godber's trial was a 'show trial', a word that derives from the Stalinist period, from the great political purges of 1936–8. These trials were designed, among other aims, to chart for the Soviet public the way Soviet society would be moving. In this sense, the trials were educational and propagandist. Godber's trial contained some of these elements, though latently. Up to that date—February 1975—he was the highest-ranking government servant since 1956 to have been prosecuted for corruption; he was an expatriate; and he was a policman. His conviction was meant to signify that no one was above the law and that the government was prepared to act harshly to put down corruption, wherever it appeared. The sentence passed on the runaway policeman—four years—was intended to be exemplary. Mr Justice Yang was not thinking in terms of individual deterrence when he sentenced Godber, for Godber was not likely ever again to find himself in a position where he could squeeze the public; nor was it an example of what penologists call an 'individualized measure', one designed to help or rehabilitate an offender. No one, needless to say, believed Godber should be placed on probation, put under the wise guidance of a social welfare officer. The trial, as the criminologist Frank Tannenbaum would say, was a 'dramatization of evil', a degradation ceremony.

In his 1975 Annual Report, the Commissioner stated that Godber's conviction was 'an important milestone in the advance of the Commission'. The preceding paragraphs have illumined, one hopes, the symbolic nature of the event. It is true that Godber's trial, despite some nice elements of dramaturgy, cannot be compared in scale or éclat with the Poulson affair; nor with the corruption trials that depleted Scotland Yard in the early 1970s; nor, again, with the great Lockheed scandal and its international reverberations (which touched Hong Kong also). The Godber saga, with its various progressions, must be placed firmly in a Hong Kong, not British or American, setting. It had a sharp impact on public opinion; it gave the ICAC, and the Operations Department in particular, a great boost; and it put the energetic Commissioner much in the limelight (be it noted that the ICAC has never flinched from publicity nor from publicizing itself). It also helped to further convince the Chinese, the vast bulk of the population, that Sir Murray was a genuine reformer, not a hidebound routineer, and that he would put the interests of the people in the forefront of his policies.

Godber was the community's scapegoat. He spent thirty-one months in prison and was released on 3 October 1977, on which day he returned, like an old campaigner, to Blighty. He then settled in Spain, in the village of Porsellanes, near Alicante.

Corruption is a species of crime without passion. Dr Edmond Locard, the French forensic scientist and author of *Manuel de technique policière* (fourth edition, 1948), is celebrated for his axiom that 'Every contact leaves a trace'. This is hardly true of consensual corruption, the satisfied customer type. The Operations Department, despite its excellent start, was still faced after the Godber trial with a formidable task, one which should not be underestimated even today. As with commercial crime, so many corruption cases may extend over a long span of time, may involve many investigations and investigators, numerous subsidiary inquiries, bypaths, and impasses: and the end result may yet be nugatory. Broadly speaking, in 1974 and 1975, the ICAC busied itself with pursuing flagrantly corrupt individuals (called 'personalities', a horrid vogue word borrowed from show business but a locution much loved by law-enforcement officers). In 1975, a small move was made against illegal commissions in the business world; and in 1976 an attack was launched against syndicated corruption. After 1977, the year of the so-called police mutiny and partial amnesty, the ICAC focused on the satisfied customer variant of corruption, a crime which normally leaves behind hardly a trace. These various campaigns will be explored in various chapters and an attempt will be made to assess their results, a daunting endeavour.

The campaign against syndicated corruption was adumbrated by the Commissioner as early as 1975. As he declared, somewhat apocalyptically, in his Annual Review:

1975 was a year of consolidation—of consolidation and of preparation for the titanic struggle which lies ahead. For our aim is to break the back of organized, syndicated corruption within the next year or two. 1976 and 1977 are going to be crucial and testing years both for the Commission and for the community of Hong Kong.

He went on to remark,

With increased staff, and ever increasing experience, the department is now in a position to take the offensive, using intelligence gathered from its own resources. The prime target will be syndicated corruption.

CHAPTER FIVE

Mr Gerald Harknett (Director of Operations in 1977) has defined a corruption syndicate as

a body of officers with a common interest in agreeing not to take action or take certain action which will produce a corrupt income. This generally involves covering up some form of illegal activity, whether it be trafficking in dangerous drugs, illegal gambling, prostitution and other vice, or breaches of procedures connected with immigration, housing construction projects, fire prevention, licensing, etc.

In other words, over time the habitual practice of corruption becomes institutionalized or structured; the action becomes routinized and even normative within a force. The pattern remains intact from year to year, but membership necessarily changes, as with any human grouping, such as a political party. It became widely known by 1976, after the completion of a number of investigations and trials, that every police division contained its own corruption syndicate, and that informal structures had developed within formal organizations ('a firm within a firm' in Scotland Yard parlance).

The pattern of syndicated corruption was illumined, notably, by the ICAC's inquiry into the ramifications of the so-called Yau Ma Tei Fruit Market drug syndicate. This prolonged investigation started in late 1976 when a Police Narcotics Bureau team arrested a number of drug traffickers in the area of the market. They also seized documents which convincingly demonstrated that organizers of the syndicate had been paying certain police officers—collectors—about $10,000 a day on a regular basis. These documents were then handed over to the ICAC for further action. The Commission brought the case to a successful conclusion in 1978, when fifteen policemen were convicted and imprisoned. A series of conspiracy trials, which focused on particular police divisions (such as Wong Tai Sin, Mong Kok, Bay View, and Tsim Sha Tsui), also helped to complete the picture. In effect, the police had been licensing vice for profit, distinguishing between acceptable and unacceptable law-breaking, according to their own peculiar criteria. Those who managed vice or gambling dens were not seriously incommoded; robbers, murderers, and other violent criminals normally were. Thus the police version of morality, or of the public weal, did not accord with that of the respectable citizen. A double standard operated. This was precisely the gravamen of the charge brought by the social critics in the 1950s and 1960s, but spurned then by the government as a ridiculous fiction.

The Hong Kong police, as a body, contains two main segments or layers: on the one hand there is the inspectorate and senior officers (superintendents and above), mostly British in the mid-1970s; on the other, there is the mass of the rank and file, then as now predominantly Chinese. This sharp division in status and salary is also found in the army, where the distinction between 'officers and gentlemen' and 'other ranks', or between commissioned and non-commissioned officers, has led to the evolution of two distinct communities or aggregations, with their particular cultures.

The ordinary Chinese constable or detective constable, a member of the uniformed or plain-clothes branches, did not as a rule hob-nob with his British superiors, with inspectors and senior officers, except of course when on the job. The man he looked up to, and was heavily dependent upon, was his sergeant, especially his station sergeant, a paternalistic or avuncular figure, a man usually older, more experienced, more imbued with police culture or influenced by police folklore, than himself. This relationship between constable and sergeant may be described as feudalistic; it was sustained by feudal elements of reciprocity, obligation, and loyalty. Sergeants, principally because of the strategic position they occupied in the structure, were natural middlemen and fixers, and a necessary link between higher and lower levels. Their power, both formal and informal, was then impressive. The rank and file needed their patronage; young European inspectors turned at times to them for advice and support; and senior policemen apprehended that sergeants were the cornerstone of the police edifice, and did not blithely meddle in their affairs. And, of course, when the police were publicly criticized, increasingly so from the mid-1950s on, the segments rapidly coalesced to present a very united front indeed, a manifestation of that extraordinary *esprit de corps* shown by nearly all police forces when thrown upon the defensive. Members of the Hong Kong public could not easily penetrate behind the formal face—the mask or façade—presented to them. When attacked, policemen tended tightly to close ranks. Thus corrupt sergeants, as we shall see, were given, though not intentionally, much protection by their organization's steely carapace. A commissioner of police, controlling a body of men referred to derisively as 'running dogs' by Chinese Nationalists and Communists, had always to show common cause with his men. In the words of the German novelist, Jean Paul: 'Er liebte jeden Hund, und wünschte von jeden Hund geliebt zu sein' ('He loves every dog and wants every dog to love him').

The true leaders of the rank and file, to repeat, were the sergeants or, more precisely, staff and station sergeants. In 1975, when the campaign against syndicated corruption was initiated, the Colony had been divided by police administrators into three land districts (Hong Kong Island, Kowloon, and the New Territories) and one marine district. Each land district was in turn subdivided into police divisions (Hong Kong Island and Kowloon had four each, the New Territories six). At that time, two staff sergeants (Class I) were to be found at each district headquarters, one from the uniformed branch, the other from the CID. Police divisions—the lower level—also had two staff sergeants (Class II). In the eyes of their Chinese colleagues, these senior and experienced officers formed an élite, the apex as it were of the purely Chinese police structure (although of course there were Chinese at inspector and higher levels).

Staff sergeants tended to meet informally and to share information, to think along the same lines. For them, policing was business. They formed, in the language of the political scientist, an 'interest group', defined by David Truman as 'a group of persons who share a similar attitude (interest) that makes certain claims upon other groups in a society'. They were alleged to be on good terms with Triad leaders and to be seen, at times, in their company, at restaurants and night-clubs. This practice of commensality is neither as sinister nor as reprehensible as first would appear. It is common for detective officers working in any force (the Metropolitan Police, for example) to cultivate some members of the criminal under-world or criminal fringe, full-time or part-time professionals, for the gathering of intelligence or for other proper reasons. In any case, nearly all police informers have criminal records or are engaged in some type of criminal activity. The benevolent Vicar of St. Cuthbert's or the jolly-boy doyen of the local YMCA are not likely to have sound knowledge of the criminal networks in their areas; but *habitués* of betting shops, gambling casinos, strip joints, drinking clubs, and other places where afternoon men or noctambules congregate, are prone to spot who has come into sudden riches, and to wonder why. Need-less to say, intimate relationships between policemen and crim-inals can, and often do, lead to collusion between them in crim-inal enterprise. He who sups with the devil, as the adage goes, needs a long spoon. And so it happened with the staff sergeants we have been discussing. The various conspiracy trials amply demonstrated that it was they who had played a key part in the organization and maintenance of corruption syndicates; and as a result of their diligence and business acu-men some had become millionaires, a remarkable example of self-help.

It was not difficult for syndicate bosses to recruit members. New arrivals at a station had money put in their lockers; if the cash was pocketed, it was taken as a sign of assent. The major-ity did participate, almost routinely, and took their weekly or monthly cut, a useful supplement to low official salaries. (One could perhaps think of this as a species of unofficial danger money, for in the course of their duties policemen often are injured.) The amount received varied according to rank and seniority; the average constable might receive, in the early 1970s, only about $20 to $50 a month; the big money went to the station sergeants and to senior officers. But they were all

'Assured that, no matter how much his rashness might be deplored, his integrity was unquestioned, the Englishman went off to India'. Wing Commander A.H.S. Steele-Perkins, Director of Air Raid Precautions, in Hong Kong, August 1941 (*South China Morning Post*)

戴麟趾滾出來!!
TRENCH! DARE YOU COME OUT!
議

The Cultural Revolution spills over into Hong Kong in May 1967. Inspired by the Little Red Book—'The Thoughts of Chairman Mao'—Communists demonstrate outside Government House (above and right); but the Governor, Sir David Trench, was playing golf at Fanling (*South China Morning Post*)

Chief Superintendent Peter Godber, 'the very first man to take action against the Communists in 1967', was honoured by the Queen in October 1972 with the Police Medal for meritorious service. Princess Alexandra performs the ceremony on behalf of the Queen (*China Mail photograph, Public Records Office of Hong Kong*)

Peter Godber, escorted by ICAC officers, is returned to Hong Kong. The ICAC had 'got their man', the most senior government official to be brought before the Hong Kong courts up to that time (*Associated Press*)

The Governor, Sir Murray MacLehose (above), and Jack Cater
(right), Commissioner of the ICAC, as a team known jocularly as
'Batman and Robin' for their implacable pursuit of the corrupt
(*Government Information Services*)

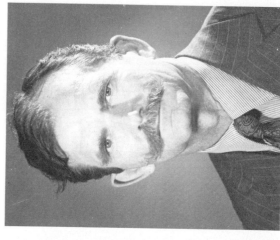

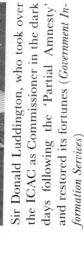

Sir Donald Luddington, who took over the ICAC as Commissioner in the dark days following the 'Partial Amnesty' and restored its fortunes (*Government Information Services*)

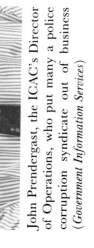

John Prendergast, the ICAC's Director of Operations, who put many a police corruption syndicate out of business (*Government Information Services*)

Peter Williams, appointed in 1980 as the third Commissioner of the ICAC (*Government Information Services*)

'Taffy' Hunt, the 'middle-aged juvenile', in happier, pre-arrest days
(*George Webber*)

'I have enough stashed away to live well for the rest of my life without lifting another finger'. 'Taffy' Hunt and his German wife, Ursula, arrive on the Costa del Sol, the favoured retreat of British villains 'in retirement' (*South China Morning Post*)

Shades of 1967! Police in Boundary Street demonstrate against
ICAC persecution (*South China Morning Post*)

Police at Colony Headquarters await the emergence of their delegates from a meeting with the Commissioner of Police, Brian Slevin, lampooned by them as the 'Invisible Man' (*South China Morning Post*)

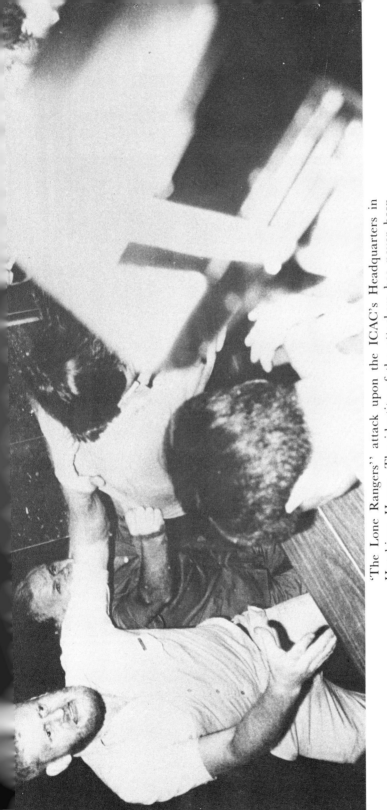

'The Lone Rangers'' attack upon the ICAC's Headquarters in Hutchison House. The identity of the attackers has never been established (*South China Morning Post*)

The ICAC puts its message across by poster; but the cynical believe that corruption continues 'to pay', and handsomely for some in Hong Kong (*Government Information Services*)

bound together, as it were, by a sense of collective guilt. Cheung Tak-sing and Lau Chong-chor, in their informative study of syndicated corruption, state that a police informant had told them that only one man, to his knowledge, had ever declined to join a syndicate. This very rum fellow was dubbed Ah Chi ('Bizarre' or 'Silly' in Cantonese) by his bemused colleagues. Ah Chi was a fervent Christian. He declared that God had urged him not to handle tainted money. The problem posed by Ah Chi was solved by assigning him to work in the radio room of an emergency unit, where he would hear no evil and see no evil.

Thus troublesome, difficult, unsound or uncooperative policemen, those who did not fit neatly into the corruption network, were normally transferred elsewhere, out of harm's way. The spirit of brotherhood, of camaraderie and mutual support, meant that even an honest policeman was reluctant to inform upon the obviously bent; he had no wish to further compromise the force, a body already under violent attack from civilians. This was, broadly speaking, the psychological situation before the ICAC was set up. After 1974, however, attitudes began slowly to change; some policemen were less disinclined to report incidents of corrupt behaviour.

The men who ran the big business—the key men with organizational ability, know-how, power and prestige—were not senior officers but the staff sergeants, later known as station sergeants (the title was changed in 1972). They have been referred to previously as an élite group, at least in the eyes of the Chinese rank and file. They formed an important reference group for the latter. It must have been obvious even to a tiro policeman that sergeants were men of substance, men of affairs, that they lived far above their official incomes. The spirit of emulation is a necessary social mechanism. The rank and file aspired to become like the captains and the kings they observed daily, like their sergeants.

In 1972, Mr Sutcliffe introduced a number of organizational reforms. Station sergeants were offered the chance of promotion to the inspectorate level, if they so wished; all corporals—

the rank was abolished—were upgraded to sergeants. The number of station sergeants per division was also increased from the former two to around eight to ten. The Commissioner, one infers, hoped by dilution to weaken the traditional powers of the old-time staff sergeants; he also diminished their position, in theory, by moving them back from the divisional to the subdivisional level, and placed each under the aegis of an inspector, a kind of official watcher. One should add that the elevation of so many non-commissioned officers was a device to promote a larger degree of localization and to improve recruitment. Mr Sutcliffe and his advisers were inspired by several motives.

There was much grumbling at this time about the changes. In fact, the power of the sergeant corps lingered on and was not seriously eroded. It is true that after 1972 their situation was more complex than before and that there were now more people contending for power in the syndicates. But, overall, the station sergeants remained the principal entrepreneurs of police corruption, although now in a more uncertain world. Adjustments and compromises had to be made before equilibrium was achieved. When the ICAC's drive started in late 1975, things were much as they had been before 1972, and colossal fortunes were still being made by the well-placed.

The person who managed or ran a corruption syndicate was usually described in the conspiracy and related trials of the mid-1970s as a 'caterer', a term which has become a catchword for these middle-management, corrupt Chinese police officers. Like any business manager or chief executive of a firm, he was responsible for profits and losses. His principal task was to maximize the syndicate's income; to see that it was maintained at a steady level. It was, to use engineers' language, a hydraulic problem: the flow had to be both steady and constant over time, if possible. The caterer also had to oversee the paying off of many policemen far higher than he in the hierarchy (Godber was a Chief Superintendent; Cecil Cunningham, convicted and imprisoned in 1976, Divisional Superintendent at the Bay View Police Station). It follows that the caterer needed special management skills. In nearly every case, before 1972, the position of caterer had been monopolized by the staff sergeants at the district and divisional levels and by barracks sergeants at the subdivisional level. Squeeze had to be collected regularly before it could be distributed, upwards and downwards within the police pyramid, with the élite getting the major share. A caterer thus had to recruit a number of collectors and runners as leg-men and strong-arm men; they could be compared to the urban desperadoes employed by the rack-renting slum landlord, Peter Rachman, in London in the 1960s. These collectors were either Chinese gangsters, with close links to Triad elements, or retired policemen, old professionals who knew their way almost blindfold through the maze of Hong Kong vice. In some of the smaller and less lucrative syndicates, those that derived their income from harassing hawkers or mini-bus drivers, the collectors were often patrolling constables. A few policemen went solo at times and indulged in a little private enterprise on their own, when the opportunity occurred.

Collectors and runners shielded the caterer—a working policeman with many official duties to perform—from direct exposure or contact. The caterer certainly administered the system in those days; but he could not, for obvious reasons, be seen too often in vice and other illegal establishments. Like the proverbial Sicilian Godfather, he had to keep up some sort of respectable front. The hallmark of the good caterer therefore was discretion and caution, a low and deceptive profile. He was a secret smiler, for all was right, he knew, with his world (at least, until the ominous year of 1974).

The structure of a large corruption syndicate, at district or divisional level, is given in the following diagram:

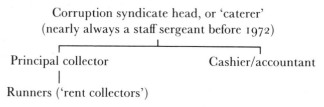

Corruption syndicate head, or 'caterer'
(nearly always a staff sergeant before 1972)

Principal collector   Cashier/accountant

Runners ('rent collectors')

Since the runners brought in a flow of money—the actual quantum determined by previous negotiation between 'squeezer' and 'squeezed'—to the principal collector, a large syndicate needed someone to act as bookkeeper, as with any business enterprise. The bookkeeper or cashier entered the various sums in his ledger, which was inspected from time to time by the caterer. At a later date, when the caterer was satisfied that the entries were correct, the arithmetic right, the record was destroyed. But the register of all those who contributed regularly to this illegal police fund was never destroyed but passed on to the caterer's successor, for policemen do not stay for ever in the same post. (Godber, who was never a caterer, appears to have compiled a private list of vice establishments, for such a document was found in the boot of his car.)

The ICAC's campaign had, by 1977, not only culminated in numerous prosecutions of corrupt police officers but had also led to a migration of retired staff sergeants, serving station and barracks sergeants, and other ranks, to many parts of the world. For example, Tsang Kai-wing, a retired detective sergeant, was convicted in March 1975 of a Section 10 offence but he eluded his persecutors and disappeared, for a time, into the great unknown. There were many similar flights in the ICAC's crusading years; surreptitious exits, often by boat; the clandestine passage of funds abroad; a vanishing into prepared boltholes; the placing of children in foreign schools or universities; and the sending of wives or mistresses out of Hong Kong, as pathfinders. Favourite sanctuaries were Taiwan and Canada. The United Kingdom was avoided (Godber's sad history had exposed its vulnerability); but even Amsterdam, not too far distant from London, has its little colony of absconding policemen, several in the restaurant business. Like peripatetic war criminals in South America, Hong Kong's fugitive policemen tend to change their addresses as their hunters get close. Latterly, many have given up the Western world as too unsafe and now cluster discreetly in Taiwan, where they are accepted as pillars of society. The

CHAPTER FIVE

ICAC, unlike the famed Mounties, does not always get its man.

The old ACO had shaken its pack of Hong Kong cards and out had fallen, face up, a pair of knaves—Godber and Hunt. The newly formed ICAC reshuffled the deck and disclosed a plenitude of knaves—station and staff sergeants and their numerous acolytes. The ICAC's unmasking of so many bent sergeants helped in demolishing most of the long-standing and deeply rooted corruption syndicates, whose pedigree went back to the great gambling scandal of 1897, and even to the early days of the Colony. Apart from the interregnum imposed by the Japanese Occupation, when money was in short supply, trade and commerce at a standstill, and the need to survive an intense and overriding motive, the police had always benefited from the local passion for gambling, in its many illegal forms. The end came for these syndicates, however, in the years 1976 and 1977, when the ICAC dismantled their previously resilient structures. In doing that, the ICAC practically brought life in the Royal Hong Kong Police Force to a stop. The force was dreadfully demoralized. The dramatic events of late 1977, the so-called police mutiny and amnesty, or 'counter-revolution' following 'revolution', will be discussed in the next chapter; and the problem of corruption in the private sector examined in a later chapter, for it demands separate treatment.

That large-scale corruption had been allowed to remain untouched for so long cannot be blamed entirely on the police. Trotsky, commenting on the Red Army he had created, concluded: 'The army is a copy of society and suffers from its diseases, usually at a higher temperature'. Trotsky's sociological observation can be usefully applied to the Hong Kong police, likewise a formal organization. The disease from which many of its officers suffered, although not necessarily at a higher temperature, was endemic in Hong Kong. It is usually called 'gross materialism'; or what Carlyle termed 'the worship of the Moneybag'. Corrupt policemen reflected the flaws in the society in which they served.

6
THE PARTIAL AMNESTY

'There was an old man of Hong Kong,
Who never did anything wrong;
He lay on his back, with his head in a sack,
That innocuous old man of Hong Kong.'

Edward Lear

THE ICAC had declared that 1976, its third year of operation, would be the 'crunch year' in its battle against syndicated corruption. It had certainly kept that promise. The Hong Kong courts would amply testify to the Commission's inquisitorial zeal and to its forensic triumphs, with a growing list of incarcerated policemen. In March of the following year, 1977, the Commission was busily investigating twenty-three large corruption syndicates, eighteen of which were police-operated. In July the Commissioner reported to the Governor that 'no major syndicates were known to exist'. The Commission had succeeded, at least for the time being, in substantially eradicating institutionalized corruption within the largest government department, the police. It is a commonplace that all social engineering implies costs and that the damage done by interfering with the normal or natural flow of social and economic life can only be assessed at a later date, not in advance. The government and the ICAC were to pay a heavy price for the suppression of so much traditional corruption.

The provisions of the Sexual Offences Act of 1967, which decriminalized some types of homosexual conduct in England and Wales, have not become law in Hong Kong, principally because of opposition from conservative or traditionalist Chinese groups. Thus consenting adults over the age of 21 are still at risk in Hong Kong if they engage in homosexual acts, even in the privacy of their own homes. This refusal to change Hong Kong law has led, among other matters, to one notorious scandal associated with the name of Inspector John MacLennan of the Royal Hong Kong Police Force. Surprisingly, the inquiry into Inspector MacLennan's death was to shed oblique light on the police mutiny of late 1977. MacLennan had been found dead in a locked bedroom on 15 January 1980 by a police party sent to arrest him on charges of homosexual misconduct. He had been shot five times. The number of bullet wounds convinced some interested parties that this must be homicide, not suicide. After much angry controversy and much official tergiversation, the Governor-in-Council set up a Commission of Inquiry under Mr Justice T.L. Yang to report upon the facts. The first public hearings were held on 24 July 1980; the last on 2 June 1981. The Inspector MacLennan inquiry was the longest and most expensive in the history of Hong Kong. The published report provides much odd information about how policy is formulated in the upper reaches of government.

The Commission and the public soon discovered that the MacLennan affair originated at the Yuen Long Police Station in August 1978, when a man telephoned the Duty Officer there and alleged that the Inspector had made homosexual advances to his son's friend. The informant was a certain Tsang Shing, a retired ex-station sergeant. Tsang Shing appeared twice before the Commission to give evidence. Mr Justice Yang had this to say of him:

I have no doubt ... that Tsang in fact harboured extreme hatred towards the Police. This was a result of his experience at the Independent Commission Against Corruption in May 1976 and what he considered to be the lack of support and assistance from his then superior about his complaints against the Independent Commission Against Corruption. His hatred was such that he resigned from the Force in August 1976. Later in 1978, Tsang was asked to move from his police quarters, as he had already resigned, and this further fuelled his hatred. But whatever his motive might have been in lodging the complaint on behalf of Lau, there is no evidence to suggest that his hatred prompted him to fabricate anything against MacLennan.

Tsang had been arrested in May 1976 by ICAC officers, kept incommunicado for forty-eight hours, and rigorously interrogated. He was one of the many policemen, in May 1976, who were questioned by the ICAC about corruption syndicates in the Wan Chai division. At that time, all nine station sergeants were arrested, together with fourteen of the other fifty sergeants. Soon after, the thirty-six remaining sergeants in the division experienced the same fate. With so many sergeants temporarily *hors de combat*, staff had to be transferred from other police divisions to fill the gaps. It was an unprecedented situation, unparalleled in scale even by the 1897 imbroglio. In mid-1976, the entire middle-management strata of the large Wan Chai police division was under investigation and, for a brief period, behind ICAC bars and face to face with its inquisitors. Tsang Shing was not the only police officer to feel outraged by his treatment and let down by his superiors, nearly all of whom were European.

The Commission's net was cast wide in 1976, and yet wider in 1977, as Cater kept his promise to crush syndicated corruption. The above events culminated in the Wan Chai conspiracy trial in which twelve police officers and three civilians were charged with conspiracy to pervert the course of justice and conspiracy to accept bribes. The Director of Operations, John Prendergast, stated in his 1976 review:

One witness gave a disturbing account of the ease with which corrupt officers posted from one duty to another joined syndicates already established in their new area, thus illustrating how these syndicates have an existence of their own regardless of the coming and going of individual members.

The morale of the police was seriously depressed by these and related events. The table in Appendix IV suggests that resignations of both commissioned officers and rank and file reached a peak in 1972, following (and, one infers, conditioned by) the enactment of the Prevention of Bribery Ordinance of 1971. Section 10 of this tough new measure, it will be recalled, had made it an offence to possess disproportionate assets or to maintain a disproportionately high standard of living. But resignations overall had declined by 1975. They shot up again in 1976, the year of the ICAC's drive against corruption syndicates. As the campaign accelerated, the police force as a whole felt boxed in, beleaguered, and betrayed, like a mercenary army abandoned by its leaders. The suicide of Senior Superintendent Jack English also caused much perturbation in police ranks: his death, in July 1976, symbolized the police predicament in an acute form. English had been seconded for two years to the ICAC and had only recently returned to his formation, as head of the Kowloon CID. Before he shot himself, he talked much about the deleterious effects the ICAC was having on police officers. He had become extremely worked up and emotional about the issue. In a farewell note, he complained about lack of leadership, about the aloofness of the Commissioner of Police, immured in his headquarters bunker, and of the force's sagging morale.

No policeman could accept with serenity the novel situation created by the Commission's existence. The police were now in competition with a rival organization, one which had the strong backing of both the government and the public. Traditionally, the Hong Kong police had been top dogs; they had overawed the lumpenproletariat and dominated the workers; they were given deference by the lower middle classes; avoided by the middle classes; but sometimes treated with scant respect by very rich Chinese or by the educated. Generally speaking, the police were feared; and the public's feelings about them were mixed and volatile, as in other countries. It was widely believed, if mistakenly, that the police could 'fix' anyone who got in their way (even Mrs Elliott, an educated Englishwoman, believed she had been the victim of a police plot or frame-up in 1966).

News about the mass arrest of the Wan Chai sergeants soon became known in the community. The sergeants' misadventures were much discussed in police messes, one surmises.

Their interrogation by investigators from a rival force must have bruised police egos and made some officers suppose they had lost much public face. The sergeants' humiliation and travail did not go down at all well with the rank and file, for they also felt threatened. The arrests infuriated and dismayed the entire Chinese police contingent. In 1976, and the following year, pressure was therefore building up; something had to give for there was no obvious safety-valve that could be utilized to regulate affairs, to reduce pressure.

The decline in police morale must also be related to a fall in corruption revenue, as life became more chancy, more problematic for those involved in syndicated and other forms of corruption. The ICAC was now, as it were, just a step behind, and fast catching up. Over time, many sergeants and senior officers had grown accustomed to a standard of living that their official salaries could not sustain. A number were big spenders—Hunt was of this class—well known in gambling casinos and on the racetrack, in Chinese ballrooms (where girls can be procured), and in numerous other places of revelry and recreation. Others had bought property, usually through a proxy, or had set themselves up as businessmen and entrepreneurs. The collapse of their corrupt world must have induced psychological malaise in some. No one, after all, except a masochist, saint or fool, takes kindly to life on a reduced income.

There is a well-known passage in *Theories of Surplus Value*, in which Marx discusses the role of the criminal in production relations. Part of it runs:

The criminal breaks the monotony and everyday security of bourgeois life. In this way he keeps it from stagnation, and gives rise to that uneasy tension and agility without which even the spur of competition would get blunted. Thus, he gives a stimulus to the production forces. Whilst crime takes a part of the superfluous population off the labour market and thus reduces competition amongst the labourers—up to a certain point, preventing wages from falling below the minimum—the struggle against crime absorbs another part of this population. Thus, the criminal comes in

CHAPTER SIX

as one of those natural 'counterweights' which bring about a correct
balance and open up a whole perspective of 'useful' occupations.

This excerpt from Marx, part of an extended polemic against
bourgeois moralists of the nineteenth century, was meant to
be ironical. Nonetheless, it does illumine the notion that law
enforcers, law breakers, and members of the work-force, are
aggregates in the same social, economic, and political
system—that each category is not autonomous. The analogy
is organic. In Hong Kong, there has always been a symbiotic
relationship between the police and the criminal or Triad
underworld (a matter discussed previously); each, paradoxically, is dependent upon the other. Broadly speaking, a
primary police function is the regulation of deviance and
of deviants; it is not, it should be strongly emphasized, the
eradication of the criminal classes or of all those whose behaviour deviates from accepted social standards. Such an
attempt would signify crazed Utopianism or deranged social
engineering. In a society where freedom is valued and private
life respected, the police, and other social agencies, are expected to establish some sort of order out of the anarchy of
competing, colliding, conflicting or deviating groups.

By the early 1970s, the police had largely succeeded in 'reg-
ulating' or stabilizing illegal markets, markets for the provision of sex, drugs and gambling, the popular demand for
which was so great in Hong Kong that black markets in these
areas had spontaneously arisen. However, this structure had
been mostly shattered in the mid-1970s by the ICAC. Its
equilibrium, to change metaphors, had been disturbed. Consequently, the police force's occupational environment had
altered. It can be argued that this major shift must have had a
strong influence on police morale. The old certainties had
vanished. Some established markets had been put out of business; others reported heavy losses.

Whilst the ICAC were busy eliminating police corruption,
the police themselves had responded strongly to the Governor's Fight Crime campaign by clamping down in 1973, and

following years, on vice establishments of all types. This drive had been firmly backed by Charles Sutcliffe and senior staff, and after 1974 by Brian Slevin, Sutcliffe's successor. In these years, it follows, the Hong Kong underworld also faced hard times, a sharp recession in its activities. As enterprise after enterprise was forced to close down—massage and music parlours, dance-halls and brothels, indecent exhibitions and blue cinemas—the income of the Triads, of corrupt policemen, and of the managers and operators of lubricious amusement and recreation centres, likewise declined. The disappearance, also at this time, of numerous gambling casinos and other gambling outlets had an even more drastic effect.

These events introduced much uncertainty into the world of commercial vice, an uncertainty which resonated throughout the police ranks. The Governor's clean-up had once again unhinged the established order, as had the ICAC's campaign. The great clamp-down on vice establishments increased disaffection among some police officers. They saw their traditional perks rapidly disappearing. The Governor had brought with him no zephyr wind but the winds of change.

Brian Slevin, in his 1973–4 annual report, stated:

Triads in Hong Kong represent organized crime. They are unlawful criminal societies involved in the systematic development, through use of criminal intimidation, of criminal monopolies. They are active in support of illegal gambling, prostitution, narcotics, loan shark operations and a variety of other extortion and protection rackets. Triads are suspected of being closely linked with syndicated corruption and are currently associated with much of Hong Kong's violent crime. A high percentage of wounding, assaults and gang fights can be traced to Triad attempts to create or maintain criminal monopolies.

He went on to relate that 'constant pressure against the Triads was being maintained'. Ironically, this signified pressure upon the police, upon the large corrupt segment of the force. By 1976–7 this pressure had become intense.

It would be useful, perhaps, to refer again to some sociological generalizations. One aspect of modernization is an increase in regulatory control, typically from some central source. This has been the European and American experience. It can be remarked upon in the history of most European states from the eighteenth century onwards, in Britain especially after 1906, and in the United States at the time of Roosevelt's New Deal (1933–9). In Hong Kong this process of regulation and central intervention quickened after 1945, noticeably so in the 1950s when the economic take-off (the advancement of regular growth) began. Hong Kong has experienced ever since a steady increase in regulatory legislation and in administrative law. This ineluctable development (for so it seems) has created new conditions for corruption. Thus the government's virtual monopoly of housing for the poor, to cite an example, means that those who allocate accommodation are monopolists: an unprincipled official may benefit from his distributional powers.

This important change, exemplified by an extension of supervision over larger areas of social and economic life, has given rise to an efflorescence of illegal markets, exploited in turn by Triads, bent policemen, venal officials, and by various sharp entrepreneurs. There is always a dyadic relationship between law-making and law-breaking, since the provision of new laws or the introduction of new rules and regulations also implies their infraction (by making the wearing of seat-belts mandatory this has happened). It also makes possible the non-enforcement, or selective enforcement, of such codes by police and other law enforcers. This is an obvious point, but it is mentioned to underline the fact that government itself 'manufactures' much of society's deviance. It has often been argued that if gambling and prostitution, both subject to much legislation, were decriminalized, then those who corruptly benefit from the prevailing conditions could no longer do so.

The Corruption Prevention Department (CPD) of the ICAC began functioning at the end of 1974. Its main task is to close loopholes opened for the corrupt by the routine working of government departments. It is not easy to measure the

CPD's impact and the Department has never sought publicity (its personnel have been referred to as 'backroom boys'). But we may claim that by late 1977 it was having some influence on the dishonest, in the sense that they were aware of its operations and were troubled by the knowledge that some loopholes were being plugged on the advice of CPD officers. This was another factor, although a relatively minor one, which suggested that the palmy days of the 1960s had gone forever. To survive, the corrupt had to become professionals. Not all could adapt to changing conditions.

The main factors that caused a declension in police morale have now been examined—the ICAC's heavy impact upon police organization, the demolition of numerous corruption syndicates, and, concurrently, the drooping income levels experienced by most venal policemen. Associated influences were, it has been suggested, diminishing returns from the management of vice establishments and other illicit enterprises, as well as the creeping recession, as the Fight Crime campaign raged, that afflicted the Triad underworld. It was further argued that destabilization of this underworld—the structured universe of organized crime—also affected the police force, since the two were interrelated, even commingled. But the principal cause was simply the existence, the brooding menace of the Commission, at whose helm then stood the dynamic Jack Cater, Hong Kong's Grand Inquisitor, that alarming energumen conjured up by Sir Murray MacLehose in February 1974. The immediate or precipitating reasons that gave rise to the police mutiny should therefore be viewed against this sociological background. With hindsight, it is easy to insist that some explosion was to be expected, because, to reiterate, the pressure—the tension—was too swiftly mounting in police circles, among law enforcers, whether straight or bent.

In the first three weeks of October 1977 some one hundred and forty police officers from three Kowloon divisions were arrested by the ICAC for alleged involvement in syndicated corruption. Those seized ranged from constable to superintendent. But it was the detention on 25 October of thirty-four men, including three British superintendents, which brought matters to a head. A number of policemen then met privately in Kowloon to examine ways of resisting the Commission. They decided to organize mass rallies so as to advertise claims of unfair treatment and harassment by the ICAC. When the meeting closed, five delegates visited the Senior Superintendent (Administration), Kowloon, and asked to see the Commissioner of Police. They were advised to put their request in writing, for that was the correct procedure. The following morning, the Kowloon police contingent was still simmering. About three hundred gathered in the Kowloon Police Headquarters canteen and drafted a nine-point letter for presentation to the reclusive Commissioner. The letter was handed in by the delegates, the five elected the previous day.

The letter of petition makes interesting and curious reading, viewed in the context of traditional police culture. The first point declared that a convicted narcotics dealer would give evidence against policemen involved in the Yau Ma Tei corruption investigation. In return for his help, the letter claimed, the narcotics dealer would receive a reduced sentence when his appeal was heard on 1 November. The letter spoke of this quid-pro-quo deal as 'moral corruption' and as 'highly prejudicial to the officers involved'. The second point stressed the mental strain imposed on officers by prolonged investigations, particularly when under interdiction. The third argued that *all* witnesses used against the police were either convicted criminals or persons involved in criminal activities. Such dubious individuals, the letter continued, were likely to respond to any inducement offered by the ICAC. Thus the Commission was 'perverting the course of justice'. The next two points emphasized the hardship caused to an officer and his family by early morning arrest—at 0700 hours—and by lengthy periods of detention following arrest. 'This is particularly burdensome on long serving officers who have shown their loyalty in many ways, including the 1967 riots'. The sixth argued that senior officers knew about corruption syndicates but took no action. Why should only junior officers be held responsible? The seventh averred that police were in contact with criminals, an inevitable feature of police work, and that it was highly probable that the underworld took revenge by making false allegations of corruption against junior officers, whereas senior officers were not so affected or incommoded. The eighth repudiated Cater's claim that police morale had not suffered as a result of the Commission's investigations. 'In fact, police morale is badly affected and strong leadership is necessary to raise it'. The final point urged the Commissioner of Police to show more concern for junior officers and to request the ICAC to review their operating procedures. It concluded: 'They should conduct their enquiries in a lawful and justifiable manner and not use oppressive tactics against police officers'.

The nine points were published in *Off Beat*, the police newspaper, and in the English and Chinese press and commented upon, for example, in the *Far Eastern Economic Review* and other journals. The nine points cut no ice with readers. Policemen appeared to be complaining about methods that were standard procedures in the force itself, such as early morning arrest (designed to catch a suspect in, and off his guard) and the use of 'tainted witnesses'. Lawyers, in particular, found these animadversions ludicrous. Those members of the public who had had close encounters with members of either the constabulary or detective branch were derisive. When did the police treat the man in the street with old-world courtesy, with Mandarin suavity, or with concern for his legal rights? But the petition did draw attention to a most worrying issue: the apparent lack of communication between junior and senior officers, and the loss of confidence by the former in those who administered the police. Even if some of the points listed were patently silly, the question of communication, up and down the police hierarchy, was a matter of great importance. In 1977, the ICAC may well have been undermining the police from without, but the commanders of the force were doing so from within.

CHAPTER SIX

When the petition reached the Commissioner, he at once appointed a senior officer to liaise with the delegates and to discuss with them the nine points. That same evening about two hundred and fifty members of the rank and file held a meeting at the Wong Tai Sin Police Married Quarters. This was, obviously, a mainly Chinese gathering. The following day—Thursday, 27 October—the delegates met the senior man appointed by the Commissioner and talked matters over. In the afternoon, the Commissioner hurriedly issued a note to all ranks. Some passages should be quoted:

I want you to know there is no lack of concern on my part over the matter of certain aspects of investigations into allegations of corruption in the Force. I realise too the strain that these investigations have placed not only on individuals but throughout the Force. I have sought to ensure that members of the Force are treated no differently from others similarly under ICAC enquiry. When need be, it has always been my policy to remonstrate whenever established procedures do not seem to have been followed. This I will continue to do ... We must guard against any encouragement to individuals or groups to take unilateral action outside the established channels for seeking redress in respect of imagined or real injustice. All ranks must be assured that any such instances of possible injustice will be given every consideration and action will be taken to remedy any unfairness or wrongdoing.

Tame, flaccid prose, police officialese, perhaps, but it is doubtful whether any amount of Churchillian rhetoric would have stayed agitation in police ranks. The Commissioner had lingered too long in his bunker: the battle was well under way. It had begun on Tuesday, 25 October, with the secret meeting in Kowloon of disaffected police officers.

On Thursday evening several thousand police officers and their families gathered at the Police Sports Association premises in Boundary Street, Kowloon. Agreement was then reached that off-duty policemen should be urged to assemble the next day at Colony Headquarters on Hong Kong Island. The following morning at around 9 a.m. about two thousand police congregated at Edinburgh Place, an open paved area adjacent to the Star Ferry Hong Kong concourse, an obvious meeting place for those disembarking from Kowloon. There they listened to a brief speech by a Chinese superintendent; then they moved off, shouting slogans, to Police Headquarters in Wan Chai. The scene was reminiscent of the Maoist street hubbubs of 1967. Their objective attained, the protesters massed in a car-park close to Caine House, the block which harboured the Commissioner and his senior staff. The five rank-and-file delegates entered the building. At last they faced Slevin (dubbed the 'Invisible Man' in some circles) in the flesh. For over an hour they talked. The most important issue was probably the proposal to establish a Junior Police Officers' Association, similar to those formed in earlier years for European and local inspectors respectively, and for superintendents. A so-called Junior Consultative Council did exist at that time (it had limited functions) but its members had not been approached about the problem of the growing restiveness in the lower stratum. Yet this council was, in 1977, the only formal communication channel between junior and senior staff. Traditionally, police administrators have always disapproved of unions. Any independent organization is seen as interfering with the established chain of command and of hierarchy in a disciplined service. In Britain, the initial attempt to create a national police union was thwarted by the police authorities; their negative response resulted in a series of police strikes, in 1918 and 1919. In Hong Kong, Slevin was forced in late 1977 to concede a wider degree of unionism than in the past.

When the delegates emerged from the Commissioner's sanctum, they informed the waiting assembly of what had transpired, that Slevin had agreed, in principle, to a rank-and-file association (which would necessitate amending the Police Ordinance). The two thousand-odd cheering police in the compound then scattered. But around noon a breakaway group marched on Hutchison House, their target the sixth floor of that building, which contained the ICAC Headquarters and its Operations Department. It was to be no lightning commando strike or SAS assault. An unruly, jostling, sweating mob of serving, retired, and dismissed police officers scrambled into lifts or up the stairs to debouch into the lobby that led to the Commission's offices. They found the doors closed; they broke a glass panel; the entrance doors were then unlocked; and the raiders swarmed into ICAC territory. A scuffle—a scrummage—then took place between police and ICAC teams. Five of the latter, outnumbered by their assailants, were injured. A staff member had already dialled 999. When a police patrol did arrive in response to the call, their turbulent colleagues had left. Differing accounts of the incident were given by the two law-enforcement agencies. The ICAC claimed one hundred intruders: the police put the figure at a modest forty and did not state that there had been cries outside Caine House for the Commissioner's resignation. Each side put a nice gloss on its story.

These events have been related in some detail in order to bring certain themes more sharply into focus. It is evident that the breaches of law and order and of police discipline enumerated above originated in Kowloon police divisions. Kowloon had (still has) much vice, was honeycombed with corruption syndicates, and suffered from a marked degree of police 'freelance' extortion. A high proportion of Kowloon policemen then benefited from graft. Thus those serving in the Kowloon Police District—Godber's and Hunt's old patch—were more at risk, in insurer's terms, from investigations than their colleagues in other areas. And in 1977 the Commission had targeted especially the Mong Kok and Yau Ma Tei divisions. The men behind the scene, those who master-minded the mass demonstration at Colony Headquarters, were nearly all members of the sergeant cadre, of the middle-management stratum. They were, to repeat, natural leaders of the rank and file; in late October they were the natural ringleaders, the manipulators who orchestrated the protest, aided by some former policemen, retired or dismissed officers. It is also clear that the Commissioner of Police, who then commanded over 18,000 men, was overwhelmed by the rush of events. His posture was inevitably defensive, like a chess player all of whose pieces are blocked. He could only react, feebly at times, to oppositional moves. Police organization was truly weak at that time. The head did not always control the body. And the department was further fractured by racial divisions, by the coexistence of distinct Cantonese and British police subcultures. Normally there was a high degree of accommodation between the two, but in times of crisis divergencies could appear. All these points were largely admitted in Slevin's 1977 Annual Review. As he wrote:

There can be no doubt that these events revealed certain weaknesses in communications and other factors arising, not least, from the rapid and very widespread expansion of the Force over recent years ... In summary, notwithstanding fairly formidable obstacles and growing pains experienced in the course of the year, the Force measured up well to its responsibilities, and significant steps have been taken to improve its effectiveness.

The sequel to the Hutchison House fracas may be briefly told. The police formed quite a high-powered team—nine CID officers under the direction of a Criminal Intelligence Bureau superintendent—to investigate the break-in at ICAC headquarters. The end result was the prosecution of only *one* person (a retired police sergeant), facetiously referred to in the local press as 'The Lone Raider'. At a Legislative Council meeting on 7 December 1977, the Attorney-General was asked to explain the government's remarkably liberal prosecution policy. He replied: 'The report submitted to me by the investigating officers contained, save in one case, no evidence at all as to the identity of those who participated in the events and no admissible evidence even as to who was present'. This greatly surprised the questioner since he knew the Commissioner of Police had sufficient evidence to initiate disciplinary action against eleven serving policemen. The decision to prosecute only one intruder, someone no longer in the force, was political. The government did not want a yet more fractious force, a completely alienated rank and file. And, in any case, police officers had closed ranks: no one was prepared to shop a brother officer. And so the matter ended. The attack on the ICAC headquarters remains a mystery, like the identity of Jack the Ripper.

An uneasy calm followed the 'battle' of Hutchison House. But the organizers behind the big demonstration at Colony Headquarters remained assiduously at work, now encouraged and emboldened by Slevin's acceptance of a rank-and-file association. On 31 October about one hundred police officers met in a canteen at Colony Headquarters. This was the first of a series of confabulations. There were numerous meetings in public and in secret to determine what tactics could be used to promote wider aims. The flashpoint came on 4 November when Slevin's considered reply to the nine-point petition was received by the delegates. Over a thousand police met behind closed doors for over three hours. At this extraordinary meeting hotheads had a field day. Spokesmen for the rebels declared the Commissioner's reply to be totally unacceptable. Their fighting words were loudly acclaimed. Some demanded industrial action, a police strike, to force the Commissioner to his knees. There was much cheering and jeering. It was obvious that junior and non-commissioned officers were quite out of control, that they had escaped from the strait-jacket of police discipline, a fact quickly brought to the attention of senior police, to Slevin and his deputy, Roy Henry.

The Governor from the start had been well briefed on the troubles in the force. On 28 October, for example, he had convened a meeting at Government House to discuss the incident at Hutchison House. This was only a few hours after he had received a report of the break-in. Present at this afternoon session were the Commissioner and Deputy Commissioner of Police, Jack Cater, the Attorney-General, and other senior officials. We do not know what was decided; probably they agreed upon a wait-and-see policy and hoped that things would simmer down, that the police—after letting off so much steam—would return somewhat sheepishly to their duty.

This, we know, they did not do. Instead, the number of malcontents grew daily. When intelligence of the packed, feverish meeting of 4 November reached the Governor it must have brought home to him the dangers that now threatened the community, the dread prospect that the forces of law and order would melt away, leaving the streets in the clutch of criminals and opportunists. (Did Sir Murray remember the New York black-out, caused by a power failure, in July of that year, when darkness immobilized the city's police and an orgy of looting resulted?) The Governor responded, the next day, by declaring a partial amnesty for the corrupt. It is no exaggeration to narrate that the news of this pardon stunned the public, for he had asserted on numerous occasions that the need for the ICAC was absolute and that the time had not yet arrived for any concessions. General Sir Douglas Haig, presenting trophies to an Aldershot cross-country team in 1913, congratulated its members with the words: 'You have run well. I hope you run as well in the presence of the enemy'. That seemed to be the gist, so the ICAC's Operations Department concluded, of Sir Murray's directive. He had sounded the retreat.

The Governor's directive of 5 November to the Commissioner of the ICAC is now generally referred to as the 'partial amnesty'. It stated that in future the ICAC would not normally act on complaints or evidence relating to offences committed before 1 January 1977 except in relation to persons who had already been interviewed (and allegations of an offence put to them), persons against whom warrants had been issued, and persons not in Hong Kong on 5 November. The phrase 'not normally act' was used to exclude from the amnesty offences considered so heinous that it would be unthinkable to refrain from action, but the Governor stressed that such cases would be rare and it was stipulated that he personally must be consulted first. A certificate under the hand of the Chief Secretary stating that the Governor considered an offence to come within the 'sufficiently heinous' category would be conclusive. There was, accordingly, no amnesty for such fugitive ex-policemen as Lui Lok (dubbed the 'hundred-million-dollar man' in the Chinese press), against whom a warrant of arrest had been issued in November 1976 on a Section 10 offence (disproportionate assets) and a writ filed by the Attorney-General to reclaim HK$9.93 million.

The legality of the Governor's directive has been questioned by Peter Wesley-Smith in the *Hong Kong Law Journal* and in the *Far Eastern Economic Review*. 'The Governor', he wrote, 'may determine priorities, and how best to organize the ICAC and to deploy its resources, but to go further and direct the Commissioner to act inconsistently with a duty imposed by the legislature is to go beyond his powers'. But the partial amnesty was belatedly given legal effect with the passing of an amendment to the ICAC Ordinance on 4 February 1978, which incorporated the substance of the Governor's directive to Jack Cater.

Police who had organized resistance to the ICAC were jubilant over the partial amnesty. Those excluded from the Governor's pardon were particularly active, behind the scenes, at this time. Both pressed for further concessions—a *complete* amnesty. No compromise or agreement was reached on 6 November at a meeting between senior police officers and representatives of the various associations (for superintendents, inspectors, and the rank and file). The militant tendency then declared that the police would march on Government House, if no favourable reply to their demands was received by 5 p.m. on 8 November. The moderate tendency were appalled by an ultimatum to the Governor, and stated they would not join the march. They were in the minority. No faction had demonstrated in strength outside Government House since 1967, when solemn ranks of Maoists stood outside its gates, chanting slogans from the Little Red Book. Government officials were not happy at the prospect of a revival of the practice, with police as actors this time.

Again Sir Murray acted swiftly. On 7 November, the day before the ultimatum ran out, he held a succession of meetings throughout the day with his advisers and top aides, including the Acting Commander of the British Forces. Civilian support was also quickly mobilized: over one hundred community leaders and prominent persons were brought together at a government-arranged press conference. At 5 p.m. he called an emergency sitting of the Legislative Council. Within twenty minutes, with the full support of the Unofficial members, an amendment to the Police Force Ordinance (Cap. 231) was pushed through. The hotheads in the police now faced check, and checkmate.

The amendment granted powers of summary dismissal to the Commissioner of Police. It was a potent weapon. Its promulgation stopped in its tracks the recalcitrant portion of the police. There was to be, now, no outright win for them. In a preamble, the Governor told Legislative Councillors that his directive of 5 November had been much discussed by the different police associations. 'Honourable members and the public', he went on, 'will be concerned to learn that informally it was suggested that it did not go far enough, that pressure should be maintained on the administration by demonstrations and progressive refusal of law enforcement until all current interviews, charges and court proceedings now in course were dropped'. Sir Murray continued, 'Concession to such demands under pressure would invite pressure on other issues; next it would be the suppression of the ICAC itself, possibly to have persons in prison released, and so on, until we had a situation in which the law was being administered in the interests of the corrupt'. The amendment, therefore, was badly needed.

News about this drastic change in the Police Ordinance must have leaked out, or been leaked out. The Governor reported that the Deputy Commissioner of Police and representatives of the various police associations had been meeting for most of the day and that agreement had been finally reached for a pledge of total loyalty to the Commissioner. He also confirmed that in future all grievances would be communicated through established constitutional channels. There would be no further public protest meetings or demonstrations. The officer responsible for these successful negotiations, Roy Henry, at that time a 'shadow Shogun', was to take over Brian

Slevin's post in 1979. He earned his spurs in these difficult, tense days.

Why Sir Murray amnestied a large number of police officers (and, one supposes, other civil servants, since his directive applied to all those working in the public sector) has never been explained satisfactorily. His action has been variously interpreted and has given rise to much speculation, of varying degrees of plausibility. Sir Murray has not given, as yet, a considered account of his sudden and unexpected change of mind, although he did admit to Legislative Councillors, on 7 November, that 'many were worried that it had been made at all, or that it went too far'. One difficulty is that we do not have access to confidential files and minutes and other memoranda. Government is not open in Hong Kong, in that it apes British rather than American practice. There is not much investigative journalism and no institutionalized opposition.

Inevitably, conspiracy theories have been advanced to account for the known facts. For example, some commentators have argued that Beijing put pressure on the Hong Kong government to compromise with the police, because the Chinese wanted no dislocation of the Hong Kong market and economy. Interference from Whitehall has also been taken as a decisive factor in explaining Sir Murray's volte-face. A sharp drop in the stock-market index in early November is advanced as a clue; for both Whitehall and the local administration were aware of how sensitive to social disturbances the economy was—hence an overriding need to mollify the forces of law and order. Raymond Yao, writing in the *Far Eastern Economic Review*, observed:

The Governor had no choice. The only alternative would have brought the British and Gurkha soldiers on to the streets—would have damaged Hong Kong's economic image. The colony's survival depends on its stability (the prerequisite for its economic well-being and business confidence) and it cannot afford to allow clients and investors to be scared off.

Yao's comments are sound, in that the state of the economy must have been given a prominent place in all deliberations.

What can be said, without demur, is that Sir Murray was forced to act quickly. He was not given much time in which to weigh the pros and cons of any course of action, to assess the possible consequences which would flow from any decision. The Hutchison House incident occurred on a Friday (28 October) and his directive was issued on a Saturday (5 November), one week later. During that brief period, disquieting rumours of further police recalcitrance and disaffection reached him: news of a possible police strike (already mooted in die-hard police circles) must have had a powerful impact on his thinking. He could not afford to waver. He was 'ike a general who sees his rear exposed, his position critical. There was little time for leisurely deliberation. He was fed, one imagines, conflicting or contradictory advice—from community leaders, the business fraternity, the Government Information Services, from his advisers and the Commissioner of Police. Did they argue with him, or go along with a reputedly autocratic Governor? P.G. Wodehouse informs us that 'A Nodder is something like a Yes-Man, only lower in the social scale. A Yes-Man's duty is to attend conferences and say "Yes". A Nodder's, as the name implies, is to nod'. Did his entourage include too many yes-men and nodders, too few men of iron prepared to tell the Governor that his judgment was at fault? We simply do not know. With hindsight, it is possible to conclude that his policy was wrong: but we have had more than a week in which to mull over the problem.

Another compelling pressure (although this would not have been known to the public at that time) might have been the threat of police leaking information about the sexually deviant habits of some prominent members of the community, including civil servants and members of the legal profession and judiciary. This hypothesis (for that is all it is) collected adherents at the time of the MacLennan Inquiry, and afterwards. It is an ingenious, even plausible thesis, but difficult to document or confirm. It runs on these lines: the police distinguish between what we may term 'mercantile corruption' and 'moral corruption'. Much routine corruption, as they see it, derives from protection afforded to the purveyors of illegal pleasures (gambling and prostitution, for example). But 'moral corruption' is a more serious or abhorrent offence, to which the criminal law testifies (life imprisonment is the maximum penalty for buggery in Hong Kong). Moral corruption is intrinsically wicked in that it implies infractions of the traditional moral code and corruption of the young. If the lives of corrupt policemen are to be investigated and made public, why not those who live in the twilight pederastic world?

Over the years the CID, as well as the Special Branch (a department of the police force) and the Security Branch in the Government Secretariat, had picked up random information, confirmed or unconfirmed, about practising homosexuals. This is routine work in Britain, and no doubt elsewhere, especially in sensitive areas of government where a civil servant potentially open to blackmail could pose a security risk. Even comparatively low-ranking police officers, such as Inspector John MacLennan, had access at times, we know, to some of these confidential lists of, or files on, suspected deviants; for the compilation, collation, summarizing, and storage of much run-of-the-mill intelligence data is usually undertaken by junior policemen: their seniors normally do not engage in clerical chores. It is obvious that dissemination of such discrediting information could, in theory, produce scandal, even a seismic shaking for some in high places. The proponents of this theory believe, then, that the possibility of leakage was discussed by both sides, and that policemen complained bitterly about a deviant minority, of a group of untouchables, who constantly broke the criminal law, but were immune from prosecution. The police had a point, a moral point, to make: they felt they had, unfairly, been made scapegoats in the past. There were others in the community, they averred, who had secrets to hide; but the latter had successfully concealed their true identity, and had escaped stigmatization. There was no equivalent of the ICAC—no Inquisition, no Star Chamber—especially to hound, interrogate, and pillory the sexually deviant. (As a pendant to this paragraph, it could be mentioned that during the early phase of the 1967 Maoist-inspired demonstrations, the Government Information Services (GIS) adopted a policy of discrediting some leaders and supporters of the Anti-Persecution Struggle Committee of All Circles. This tactic was disallowed once it was recognized that Maoist propagandists could publicize stories of the extremely bizarre behaviour of some well-known persons who backed the colonial government. A directive went out to GIS to 'cool it'. They did.)

This complex thesis is given a degree of verisimilitude by a number of established facts, but facts difficult to assess or interpret, such as the excessively strong police reaction to a case in August 1978 which involved an English lawyer and a number of under-aged Chinese boys. Again, during the early stages of the MacLennan saga, it was revealed that the new Attorney-General, John Griffiths, had been briefed in London about the Colony's homosexual scene before he took up appointment in June 1979. Hong Kong has many social problems, some uniquely its own, like most heavily urbanized territories; but few citizens would have regarded sexual deviance as one. Yet within a few weeks of his arrival, the new Attorney-General was showing a marked interest in the homosexual minority and examining confidential files held by the CID. Corrupt policemen and practising homosexuals were both outside the Colony's legal borders. It now appeared they would be given equal status. If this is so, what had provoked this equity? All we can conclude, with the paucity of data available, is that the problem might well have been brought to Sir Murray's attention in late 1977 and might well have played some small part in his decision to amnesty several hundred policemen and other public servants. The table in Appendix VII is suggestive of a change in prosecution policy at this time.

Sir Murray's actions have also been portrayed by his admirers as Machiavellian, as a mode of *reculer pour mieux sauter*. He won by giving way, like a judo expert. By amending the Police Force Ordinance he struck a stunning counter-blow.

This bowled over his opponents and gained him the victory. For after 8 November the police slowly settled down, and the Commissioner and Deputy Commissioner set about introducing necessary managerial and organizational reforms, helped in January 1978 by a three-man advisory team from Britain, led by J.W.D. Crane, an Inspector of Constabulary, who had been involved previously in investigating John Poulson's corrupt activities and John Stonehouse's extraordinary disappearance from public life. It is doubtful that Sir Murray was so marvellously clairvoyant: he was not to know that his partial amnesty would inspire the hotheads to make further demands. He had simply reacted to situations as they emerged; there is no reason to suppose he had developed any long-range strategy for police affairs. Everything had happened too quickly, too violently; and he was lucky to have found so soon a way out of the intricate maze of events.

Sir Murray's reaction did create puzzles for many Hong Kong residents. The effects of the partial amnesty should now be examined with reference to the Governor, the community, the ICAC, and the police. Readers complained that Sherlock Holmes was never quite the same after he had been pushed over the Falls of Reichenbach by Professor Moriarty. Sir Murray never totally recovered from the humiliation of having to accept unwarranted police demands. His most vehement critics (they emerged at this time) depicted him as a pot of shrivelled glue, as an administrator who had lost sight of his vision to cleanse Hong Kong of the corrupt. His gentler critics complained that much of his magic had volatized, for he had grasped the sword Excalibur and had let it drop. Much criticism was unfair and uninformed. Khrushchev had made a correct, a rational choice when he withdrew Russian missiles from Cuba in 1962; but his compatriots were dismayed by his action; and his political position came under attack. Sir Murray's strong leadership had always been much admired, particularly by the Chinese: but the partial amnesty was taken as weakness, as a fall from grace. A fallen idol, Sir Murray ceased to cast a long shadow.

In his 1978 Annual Report, the Commissioner of the ICAC wrote:

During the year there was a good deal of public concern about the possibility that the Commission was likely to be wound up. A sample survey undertaken early in the year indicated clearly that the events of November 1977 had shaken public confidence in the Government's determination to combat corruption. A number of later occurrences were interpreted as indicators of a general decline. Considerable effort had therefore to be devoted to reassuring both the Commission's staff and the public that Government had no intention of reducing its efforts to combat and steadily to eradicate corruption as a feature of life in Hong Kong and that there were no plans to reduce the efforts or the strength of the Commission. The Community Relations Department has had a hard year not only reassuring the public about the future of the ICAC but also trying to expand its influence on attitudes towards civic rights and duties within the community.

The community certainly needed much reassurance. The man in the street believed that the police had emerged, once again, as top dog; others that it was now dangerous to report cases of police squeeze or extortion. Complaints of corruption received by the ICAC in 1978 showed a drop of 27.4 per cent compared with 1977. There was a sharp decline in reports of police corruption for the same years, from 729 to 487. It is not unreasonable to conclude that the community had lost some faith in the integrity of the Commission and in the government's declared intention to root out corruption. Members of the public responded consequently by reporting less. The figures given in Appendix VI make this clear. It was, in caricature, as though the government had put up a notice outside its property, the ICAC, stating: 'No Admittance on Business'.

The partial amnesty was a watershed in the history of the ICAC. It led, temporarily, to a partial eclipse of the Operations Department, but an upgrading of its Community Relations Department—persuasion following force, as it were. The Commission's staff were well aware that the term 'partial amnesty' was deliberately chosen to blunt the impact of a policy which released large numbers of government servants from pending prosecution. Sir Donald Luddington, who took over from Jack Cater in July 1978, declared: '1978 was a year of re-dedication for the staff of the Commission. They had to accept the fact of the partial amnesty and get on with the business of eradicating active corruption'. Sir Murray, earlier, had rationalized that 'the resources of the powerful Operations Department are now free from delving into the past and able to concentrate on investigating and monitoring the present'. It was as though a vast criminal conspiracy, as in an Edgar Wallace thriller, had been uncovered by Scotland Yard and the Home Secretary had tamely instructed the Commissioner to forget about the matter and to search for other villains. Sir Murray's directive also killed the notion that the ICAC was truly independent; although it is fair to add that with the passage of time the partial amnesty has become increasingly irrelevant, since any corruption offence committed after 1 January 1977 is subject to investigation and prosecution. In any case, the ICAC should never be short of clients in a society that has much white-collar crime and much corruption. Nevertheless, the Commission suffered a severe blow in 1977, a loss of confidence. The Commissioner's Report for that year, not surprisingly, is suffused with melancholy. The ICAC, to adapt Nye Bevan's expression, on 27 October was like a Salvation Army forced to take to its heels on Judgment Day.

The Director of Operations, John Prendergast, stated that the immediate effect of the partial amnesty was the termination of eighty-three investigations into offences committed before 1 January 1977. These cases ranged from those involving single individuals to participating groups in corruption syndicates, the especial ICAC targets in 1976–7. Hence the Operations Department ended its fourth year with a much depleted case-load—only 203 investigations in hand—composed of exceptions to the amnesty and of cases opened since January. Much of the year's work, it follows, had been largely wasted; that was not good for morale. The

Commissioner and his dedicated staff had always displayed much *élan*; dispirited, they were to show less in 1978. They reacted like an army that is commanded to surrender on the verge of victory.

It is not easy to determine the after-effects of the various episodes that culminated in the partial amnesty and the amendment to the Police Force Ordinance, all three readings of which occurred in a single sitting. Paradoxically, the community probably benefited in the long run, for the Commissioner of Police and his close aides started to implement necessary reforms, weeded out some contaminating elements, and tightened force discipline. Moreover, the establishment of the Junior Police Officers' Association had a stabilizing effect, over time, and improved communication within the police body. Scandal is often an important agent of change. Many improvements in police efficiency and organization in America, Britain, and France, for example, have followed in the wake of celebrated scandals. A much-publicized scandal may break through the crust, the complacent shell of a bureaucratic organization, and may send its senior men scurrying into action. This happened in Chicago and New York in the early 1970s, when successful prosecutions of police extortion rings in the former, and the Knapp Commission exposures in the latter, led to important reforms. In Britain this occurred after the 1877 Turf Fraud scandal, and in the early 1970s when an outsider, Sir Robert Mark, took over the Metropolitan Police and partially cleansed its detective force; in Paris after the Stavisky scandal and the dismissal of the Prefect of Police, Jean Chiappe, in 1934. Reference has already been made to the Hong Kong gambling-house scandal of 1897, which led to a great purging of the force and a temporary reduction in police dishonesty. Scandal tends to bring together moralists, social reformers, and the civic-minded to demand improvements, a return to decency or better government.

Brian Slevin has been referred to in the text as 'aloof', for so he was portrayed by some policemen and by the press; but he had acquired a reputation as a good police administrator, and this talent he put to work in the post-amnesty period, ably seconded by his deputy, Roy Henry, who had brought the complex negotiations with disaffected members of the force to a successful climax on 7 November. Crane and his colleagues, known to a flippant press as the 'Three Wise Men from the West', were also involved in the post-mortem on the near-mutiny. They arrived on 18 January 1978, having been brought out at the express request of Sir Murray. Their terms of reference were to advise the Commissioner of Police on the organization and operation of his force 'with particular regard to discipline, staff management and morale, chain of command and channels of communication at all levels, sources and standards of recruitment, [and] relations with the Independent Commission Against Corruption'. They were also invited to advise Jack Cater on ICAC procedures, on methods which had come under attack in the original police petition. Raymond Yao pointed out, at that time, that

the abolition several years ago of the rank of staff sergeant—many of whom were admittedly corrupt—deprived the force of an important link between the man on the beat and the superintendent in his office. Perhaps a solution will be found in cutting down on administration, getting more senior officers out among their men.

It was plain that some restructuring of the force was necessary: it had expanded rapidly, from a strength of 12,000 in 1970 to over 18,000 at the end of 1977; and large-scale reorganization had been delayed by preoccupation with the various Fight Crime campaigns inspired by the Governor.

The Home Office advisory team left Hong Kong in late April. One result of their visit was the establishment of a Staff Relations Unit to oversee, among other matters, welfare in the force, the low level of which might well have contributed to the rank and file's growing discontent. The constabulary also benefited by the creation of a new status, that of senior constable, a reward for long service, for age is better appreciated in the East than the West. There is no need to document, nor to expatiate upon, all the changes and reforms introduced in

1978 and following years. But the Junior Police Officers' Association (JPOA) should be referred to again. It was set up ostensibly to look after the welfare and needs of those in lower grades. Over 13,000 took part in elections to appoint ninety-two unit representatives for the six police districts. The office-bearers for the various districts then jointly formed the JPOA executive committee. It soon became clear to all that the new committee had far wider aims than that of the general well-being of its members. It saw its function as also political; and its main adversary as the ICAC. It began to intervene to further curb the powers of the Commission, and took up the case of those police officers allegedly involved in the Yau Ma Tei Fruit Market drug syndicate.

In late 1976, a Police Narcotics Bureau team had arrested a number of drug traffickers in Yau Ma Tei. The police successfully prosecuted the principals on narcotics charges and then handed over their files to the ICAC, who in turn embarked on a massive operation to investigate all the ramifications of the case. It turned out to be the largest inquiry ever undertaken by them and terminated only in 1978. By the end of October 1977, the month of the police mutiny, 262 serving or former government officers and 13 civilians had been identified and suspected of involvement in the syndicate. Between January and late October, 118 police officers and 1 customs official had been arrested, questioned, and bailed; an additional 84 were interviewed but not arrested. The charges against the remaining 55 were dropped in November because of the partial amnesty. It was the fate of the unhappy 118 bailed policemen which concerned the JPOA. It is important to stress that the mass arrest of policemen allegedly involved in the Yau Ma Tei corruption syndicate was one of the factors that precipitated the attack on ICAC headquarters: the ICAC had leaned too hard upon the Kowloon police contingent.

Euphoria, and a degree of hubris, had been generated within the JPOA, as we know, by the partial amnesty, which was interpreted as a gesture of weakness and vacillation in the higher reaches of government. A number of police officers, 46 of the suspended 118, even refused to attend ICAC identity parades. At the same time, the JPOA's committee petitioned the Commissioner of Police, demanding that the ICAC relax its pressure on junior officers and switch to other targets. The Commissioner responded by threatening committee-men with disciplinary action if they did not cease from attacking the Commission. There were a number of other troubling incidents, which suggested that the near-mutiny was not yet at an end. On 9 March, sixty Yau Ma Tei interdicted officers set off from Kowloon to confront the Commissioner of Police at Colony Headquarters. They did not see him, but were met by Deputy Police Commissioner Richard Richardson of Special Branch, who curtly informed members of the group and JPOA officials that the matter of prosecutions rested with the Attorney-General.

The end of the story is quickly told. In early April, the government announced that the services of 119 Crown servants (118 working in the Yau Ma Tei police division) would be terminated in accordance with Colonial Regulation (CR) 55, which states that an officer holds office subject to the pleasure of the Crown. Under this regulation no reason need be given for compulsory retirement. This meant that those who had served for more than ten years would keep their pensions, and all would be granted six months' grace to remain in their quarters. This action apparently cut the Gordian knot, for it was not certain whether the ICAC had sufficient evidence for successful prosecution. The Crown had already failed in a case which involved ten police officers charged in connection with a Wong Tai Sin corruption syndicate. The government's decision to invoke CR55 was attacked by editorialists and members of the public as far too lenient and generous; but Henry Litton, QC, in the *Hong Kong Law Journal*, pointed out the anomaly of using a regulation invoked only in cases of espionage and disloyalty. It had never been utilized in this way by previous Hong Kong administrators.

The six-month sequence of events, originating in early October 1977, ended by mid-April 1978, a span of time roughly equal to that of the 1967 Maoist demonstrations (an odd parallel). After April, the force settled down, probably because it was no longer a primary target. The JPOA likewise relaxed, and returned to its proper task, that of looking after the interests of the rank and file, of those who composed the great majority of the police. It ceased to act like a militant trade union. It no longer supported notions of wild-cat strikes, direct action, or public protests. It now concentrated more on matters of pay, promotion, housing, or welfare in general. The use of CR55 and the ever-present threat of summary dismissal no doubt also dampened enthusiasm for confrontation with authority. The JPOA moved henceforth in orthodox bureaucratic grooves, most of the time.

The Hutchison House incident should be placed in a particular Hong Kong context. It was *opéra bouffe*, a midget contretemps. In historical terms, the fracas was on the scale of William Smith O'Brien's uprising in 1848, when Smith and a small band of supporters were routed by forty-six Irish constables in the widow McCormack's cabbage-patch. This slight skirmish lingers in Irish memories; similarly, the events of October 1977 continue to worry some Hong Kong citizens. That policemen should complain about the ICAC's investigatory techniques utilized to break up corruption syndicates, was likened by a local wag to 'Nazis protesting against fascism', a monstrous perversion, of course, of reality; but one that underlines the bizarrerie of the situation; for the police had always shown themselves to be pro-government and pro-Establishment, and had presented themselves in every crisis as a praetorian guard for the well-to-do. That policemen should suddenly demonstrate unreliability was a discovery that much disturbed the public, colonial administrators, and those who commanded the force.

In *Scandal and Reform* (1978), a study of four American police departments, Lawrence Sherman argues that a community may ultimately benefit from a notorious scandal, if response to it culminates in organizational and institutional reforms. Thus scandal need not demoralize a government agency or department; although it is certainly true that those in authority often fear that too much publicity will always lead to demoralization. 'Under certain conditions', Sherman writes, 'substantial police reform can follow a corruption scandal'. Such reforms would include the sifting of personnel, by the early or forced retirement of dubious officers, dismissal of those strongly suspected of dishonesty, and prosecution of the obviously guilty; as well as changes in leadership and command, and permanent improvements in organization, whether by innovation or restructuring.

It is now reasonably certain that the police mutiny and the partial amnesty did not have such deleterious effects as was once believed, for the Commissioner of Police and his aides started to introduce long-overdue changes and reforms. The re-focusing of ICAC operations, away from the police as a prime target, was beneficial. There was, and continues to be, much corruption in other government departments, especially those concerned with licensing, and in the private sector. It was time for both areas to be thoroughly investigated; moreover, the police now needed a breathing space, an armistice that would allow them to bury their dead, count their casualties, and re-equip themselves for further tasks. The Commissioner of Police had been caught for far too long in a cross-fire, between a belligerent ICAC and recalcitrant police officers.

The force weathered the crisis initiated by the controversial death of Inspector MacLennan, the subsequent Commission of Inquiry and its published report (1981). Although the last contained criticism of the actions of a few police officers, the force as a whole and its leadership were largely exonerated. The policy of paying greater attention to homosexual acts committed in private did not emanate from the police (although some were strongly in favour of it), but from Sir Murray MacLehose and the Attorney-General. Today (1984) the reputation of the Hong Kong police is high, locally and internationally, and it has excelled in the investigation of serious crimes. During 1982 the number of corruption reports against police fell by 7 per cent, from 735 in 1981 to 681 in 1982; the drop was balanced, however, by an increase in complaints against the private sector. Since 1974, corruption complaints against the police have fallen, overall, from 45 per cent of the total against all government departments to 26 per cent in 1982. These figures and percentages can be variously and differently interpreted; but, to put it another way, the tables in Appendices V and VI suggest that there has not been any marked upsurge, rather the contrary, despite steady population increase, an expansion in police manpower (from a strength of about 17,600 in 1977 to over 22,900 in 1982), and a severe recession in late years affecting all sections of the population, including police officers, who are in no way immune to the forces of inflation.

There is still police solo and free-lance corruption and small groups who engage in extortion on occasion; but the large organized corruption syndicates of yester-year seem to have vanished. The police are now more actively and effectually investigating corruption in their own organization than at any time; and relationships between police and ICAC officers have grown closer and even, according to informants, a shade warmer. The two law-enforcement agencies now exchange information and collaborate in a number of ways. Clearly much has altered since 1977. It is not absurd, then, to argue that these improvements owe something, inadvertently, to the 1977 crisis (the term police prefer). Scandal, a police scandal, as Sherman maintains, is not always a bad thing: it can be the agent of reform. There are copious historical examples that support this thesis. Whether these improvements will continue for long cannot be predicted, for evidence, alas, suggests that scandal and reform go in cycles.

7

THE ICAC EXTENDS ITS SCOPE

'Respected by all who did not know him'.
Suggested epitaph for Ernest Terah Hooley,
the great swindler.

A reader might conclude that inordinate attention has been
given to the problems of police corruption, as though it *was* the
main source of venal behaviour in Hong Kong, and complain
that this is patently false. The reason for highlighting the
police is that it accords, chronologically, with social perceptions. In the early 1970s, the public had come to believe that
most policemen were corrupt or easily corruptible. As members of the largest government department, they were more
frequently in contact with the population than any other
group of public servants; constables ('patrolmen' as Americans aptly call them), a uniformed force, were highly visible
in the streets as symbols of power and authority, and much
folklore had accrued around their occupation. It was, to
reiterate, the strong public reaction to Godber's surreptitious
exit from Hong Kong that gave rise to Sir Alastair Blair-
Kerr's two reports, which in turn were largely responsible for
the creation of the Commission. It follows, then, that the great
publicity which attended these events—the whole Godber
saga—inspired the government's campaign against the corrupt, master-minded by such moral reformers or moral entrepreneurs as Sir Murray. The concentration, so far, on
police corruption simply reflects the way the public has
viewed these matters. It is time, though, to examine some
other government departments and agencies, as well as the
private sector, and to present a more realistic account of the
extent and depth of the problem.

The table in Appendix VI suggests, but does not entirely confirm, that three government departments in particular, if we exclude the police, have encouraged most corruption complaints—Public Works (now Lands and Works), Urban Services, and Housing. The Public Works Department (PWD), because of the nature of its activities, has always been a prime site for corruption, from its origins in 1841, when a certain Mr Bird was appointed the first Clerk of Works. The 1902 Report on the Public Works Department, and its revelations of shady dealings, has been referred to. The 1907 Report on the Administration of the Building and Sanitary Regulations showed, yet again, the vulnerability of subordinate staff ('street-level bureaucrats', as Michael Lipsky calls them) to indulge in bribery, extortion, and general chicanery. The 1907 Report stated: 'We were forced to the conclusion that not only great irregularities but corruption and bribery were rampant in the Sanitary Department' (the Department animadverted upon became Urban Services in 1936, and has retained the designation). 'All inspectors want presents', the Report confirmed. 'All contractors give presents to the Inspectors', it further related. The 1907 situation is still present in Hong Kong; it has not been changed by the ICAC, though possibly corrupt practices have been made more covert, less blatant, for there has been re-channelling in recent years. The ceaseless struggle between the corrupt, on the one hand, and the incorrupt and their agents, on the other, has encouraged sophistication in the former.

The 1971 Report on Chong Hing Mansion revealed how difficult it was for the administration to regulate the construction industry and to see that the various provisions of the Buildings Ordinance (Cap. 123) were implemented. It also established, once again, that PWD officials were in a favoured position to benefit from close relationships with architects, builders, and developers. Sir Alastair Blair-Kerr commented in his second report that 'looking back over the years at various times there have been tremendous opportunities for corruption in the Public Works Department'. He also mentioned allegations that in the mid-1960s 'a number of very large corrupt payments were made to certain persons in return for their speeding up approval of certain building plans'. Although earlier inquiries into this murky area, in 1902 and 1907, produced much evidence of squeeze and extortion by government inspectors, today one is more likely to come across satisfied customer or consensual graft, from which each party to the transaction profits. Such corrupt practices normally do not come to light. They are low-risk crimes. There is a formal economy, delineated in economic textbooks; there is also a large 'hidden economy', operated by the dishonest, the devious, and the corrupt. The Chong Hing Mansion affair throws some light on the interconnections between the two, and on the lacuna between ideal and reality, between theory and practice.

The Chong Hing Mansion scandal, as it was later termed, originated in December 1955, when some premises were demolished in Queen's Road West. Approval was then given for a six-storey complex of buildings (known collectively as Chong Hing Mansion) to be erected on the site. Work started. Soon after, plans were amended to allow ten-storey structures. While construction progressed, PWD inspectors, both Chinese and European, regularly visited the site to see that work conformed to various government rules and regulations. The corps of PWD inspectors was then surely in need of a good oculist: although serious divergencies from the original plans were visibly obvious to all, since the buildings had been extended in both width and depth, no report of transgressions came back to headquarters. Thus no one in the top echelons of the PWD apparently knew of them. Then the arrival of an anonymous letter, in November 1956, alerted the authorities. Visits to the site by the building surveyor and other officials were made. Deviations were so extensive that a Cease Works Order was served on the developer, on 4 December 1956. This meant that he would not be given an occupation permit, and the building would remain empty. It was clear that the builder and his men must have been working from an alternative set of architectural drawings and civil engineering plans, unseen by the Building Authority.

The developer, Liu Po-shan, was a Chiu Chow (Teochiu) businessman and the owner of the Liu Chong Hing Bank, an enterprise set up by Liu in 1955. Understandably, he was aggrieved by the Cease Works Order and the added threat that he must demolish some unauthorized additions. On 26 August 1957 he wrote to the Governor, Sir Alexander Grantham, 'requesting the Public Works Department to issue an occupation permit'. It was a shrewd move. Sir Alexander was on very good terms with members of the Chinese business élite and entertained many of them at Government House. He and his American wife had done much in post-war Hong Kong to diminish racial barriers, especially in the area of social entertainment. Liu's petition was passed on to the Secretariat and in due course brought to the attention of the Building Authority, Allan Inglis. This particular official, as Inglis himself informs us in a published talk on the PWD, 'exercises control over the erection and modifications of all buildings and it is illegal to build or alter a building without the consent of the Building Authority'. Inglis knew that there had been serious contraventions of the Buildings Ordinance (completely revised in 1956). What should be done?

The plot, as it were, now thickens. When the Cease Works Order was imposed, in December 1956, Chong Hing Mansion was virtually completed, together with extensive deviations. The developer did not appear to be incommoded by the PWD's diktat to cease operations. He continued building. On 25 February 1957, a PWD official gave instructions that Chong Hing Mansion should be inspected weekly. Inspections continued until 27 May, then ceased. They were only resumed on 7 November, by which time many of the shops and flats were occupied. The Building Authority was then faced with a nasty *fait accompli*. To throw the inhabitants of Chong Hing Mansion on to the streets would provoke controversy and arouse the civic-minded and do-gooders.

During this crucial period, at a time when illegal construction continued and tenants were moving in with their goods and chattels, Liu Po-shan's new architect and his solicitors were negotiating with PWD officials and arguing that the fault lay with their department, since PWD inspectors had not reported deviations, as they were obliged to do. His solicitors made another adroit point: 'If there should be any further delay we cannot help but feel that public interest may turn into public criticism, in which the Public Works Department could not avoid being involved'. The PWD, one of the largest government departments, was now faced with the possibility of an embarrassing scandal, unless it kept quiet. It could be accused of gross negligence, lack of proper supervision, and even corruption. Officialdom does not seek public censure. Thus the Director of Public Works may well have been swayed by the arguments advanced by Liu Po-shan's agents.

In September 1957, the Director informed the Colonial Secretary that Chong Hing Mansion did not conform to the building plans originally approved by the PWD and that he was negotiating with the developer to have the deviations rectified. This letter was sent on 11 September. The day before, however, the Building Authority had indicated to Liu Po-shan's solicitors the conditions under which he was prepared to *permit* occupation. The Colonial Secretary was unaware of this previous, compromising correspondence. Indeed, on 1 October he instructed the Director: 'It is not intended that fait accompli in such matters should be accepted and if these buildings cannot be modified to meet building regulation standards in every way, their occupation must not be permitted'. Two days later, the Colonial Secretary was told about the letter that had been sent on the 10th to Liu Po-shan's solicitors. The Director then replied: 'I shall have to refer again to Crown Counsel to see if we *can* go back on my letter under reference'. The situation was delicate; the sensibilities of a number of persons could be hurt by too brutal a decision. The Colonial Secretary responded with a further memorandum, in which he declared: 'In the special circumstances of this case would you kindly proceed as originally intended' (that is, the occupation of Chong Hing Mansion would be condoned).

The developer had won his case. He undertook to comply with a number of conditions relating to modifications of the building complex's structure, as set out by the Building Authority. Curiously, these were not put in any legal form; no document referring to them was ever registered in the Land Office. More curiously, the Cease Works Order of 4 December 1956 was never revoked. The situation, to put it mildly, was anomalous.

Action was taken against some persons involved in this imbroglio. The authorized architect, who had been replaced by another, was brought before a disciplinary board and was suspended from practice for a period of five years. Complaints about the behaviour of PWD inspectors had been made by the new authorized architect to the Police Anti-Corruption Branch (ACB). He alleged that inspectors should have reported all deviations to their superiors in the PWD. The ACB decided that there was insufficient evidence to support criminal charges but that disciplinary proceedings against two should be taken. One resigned while on leave and did not return to the Colony; the other, who had left without permission, died soon after in foreign parts. No action was taken against the contractor (the 'Construction Department' of the Liu Chong Hing Bank). The 1971 Report on Chong Hing Mansion states: 'There were, therefore, three allegations of misbehaviour surrounded with a strong suspicion of corruption, all made by or on behalf of the developer who, if there was corruption, must necessarily have been the principal corrupting agent'. The Report did not pursue the matter, for in the meantime the developer had died, the events had happened over ten years before, and many of those involved were no longer living in Hong Kong.

With hindsight, one must conclude that the Chong Hing Mansion scandal contained elements, certainly strong suspicions, of malversation and malfeasance, of double-dealing, of extraordinary ineptitude within the PWD at that time. There was also the question of accountability. No one in high places was taken to task in 1958. The 1971 Report asseverated that 'the Building Authority acted rashly and inadvisedly and was in default in that he failed properly to exercise his statutory functions'. 'The Building Authority' was another incarnation of the Director of Public Works.

The story did not end in 1958; another chapter was to be added. In August 1968 and October 1969 residents complained about the state of the building, for cracks and crevices had started to appear. The government was forced to intervene. In December corrosion of the steel reinforcing structure was discovered, possibly caused by mixing cement with salt water. Chong Hing Mansion seemed likely to collapse, like a wormeaten barn. On 2 February 1971, fourteen years after construction, its occupants were forced to decamp. Controversy over how the owners and tenants of the shops and flats should be treated led to the setting up of a committee of inquiry, whose report has been referred to. The evacuees were later compensated for their losses, and the Liu Chong Hing Bank co-operated in the salvage work.

The government's defence was contained in a reply to a question asked in the Legislative Council on 24 February 1971. Sir Hugh Norman-Walker, the Colonial Secretary, stated: 'The decision to condone occupation in 1957 despite the fact that the building did not conform to the plans which had been approved was taken by one of my predecessors, after having obtained legal advice, in the light of the critical housing situation which existed at that time, and when there was no indication that the building would subsequently become dangerous'. It was not a convincing justification and was not, as we have seen, taken seriously by the Committee of Inquiry.

The Paul Lee Engineering Company scandal of 1974 resembles John Poulson's, for bankruptcy in each case disclosed evidence of corrupt practices to the official receiver or his agents. Paul Lee, born in Shanghai in 1920 and educated there at Ta Tung University, from which he received a degree in civil engineering, came to Hong Kong when the Communists took over in China. In 1962 he incorporated his pre-cast piling business as a private limited company. In November 1972, at the time of the great stock-market boom, the company went public. It was one of the largest civil engineering firms in Hong Kong, involved in numerous major projects, including roads and drainage works. Many of the Colony's flyovers were built by the company, as a registered government contractor. The events surrounding Paul Lee's bankruptcy and ruin need not concern us unduly. The Financial Secretary, then Sir Philip Haddon-Cave, appointed two inspectors to unravel the extraordinary complexities of the company's financial records. They published interim reports, in October 1974 and January 1975, which are not easy reading for the uninitiated; but broadly speaking, they established that the company was in deep water, that irregularities had occurred, and that much money had disappeared mysteriously, as into a black hole. On 30 January 1976, Paul Lee was sentenced to four years' imprisonment on charges of conspiracy to defraud shareholders and creditors by means of a false share prospectus and company reports and the fraudulent use of shareholders' money.

Earlier, Paul Lee had already been sentenced, together with accomplices, to a term of two and a half years' imprisonment for offering and giving bribes to PWD supervisors (both sentences were to run concurrently). What was revealed at this first trial is of great importance, and germane to the themes of this book.

During the probe into the dark side of the company's operations, the ICAC was alerted to its first case of syndicated corruption in the construction industry. As a consequence, Paul Lee and two of his assistants were charged with conspiracy to offer and pay bribes and, with a fourth person, with conspiracy to falsify accounts. One assistant pleaded guilty to the first charge and told the court how he distributed money, on his employer's behalf, regularly to PWD inspectors through the company's site representatives. These illegal fees were camouflaged in the accounts as 'entertainment' or as 'steak fees', a marvellous euphemism. Later, the payments were covered up by false invoices ostensibly made out for the hire of engineering equipment, such as cranes, from a firm run by one of the accused. James Duncan, a senior PWD highways engineer also pleaded guilty to a Section 3 offence, that of accepting an advantage. He was fined $12,000 and his services were subsequently terminated.

The habit of 'sweetening' PWD inspectors and other PWD staff was, the public learned (as it had long suspected), widespread. Over the years, the custom had developed into an institutionalized, almost conventional, practice, accepted in the construction industry as normal, as normal as the common cold. Presumably public tenders took these added costs into account, for accountants employed by large firms often budgeted for them. The ICAC's successful prosecution of Paul Lee and his assistants was a nice example of the fruits of serendipity. If his company had not fallen on hard times, from his inept financial manoeuvres, Paul Lee's conduct would have remained subterranean, hidden. 'We learn wisdom', Aesop's fable runs, 'by seeing the misfortunes of others'. The Commission's Prevention Department and the PWD directorate had their eyes firmly opened to this traditional form of corruption and each acted later, as we shall see, to inhibit its prevalence.

This species of graft needs little explanation: it is universal, banal, obvious. Construction firms engaged in major projects do not want constant interference from government busybodies, so they seek to neutralize them, and bribery is a convenient way. Building regulations are so numerous, so complex and convoluted, and in some areas so impractical (conceived, as it were, in a bureaucrat's dream-factory), that infractions are common. That, at least, was the situation in 1974. Time is money; speed is essential; fortunes are at risk; and so businessmen and entrepreneurs are often driven to break the law. Bribes are a small price to pay for a flow of uninterrupted work. The 1970 Knapp Commission, set up to investigate allegations of police corruption in New York, came to the same conclusions. New York police had a large regulatory role in the enforcement of many city ordinances and by-laws applying to building sites and transportation. This police supervisory role permitted much bribery, squeeze and extortion. Neither policemen nor PWD inspectors are angels: given opportunity, some are likely to succumb to corruption.

Gerald Harknett, ICAC Director of Operations, admitted in 1980 that it was not easy to determine the depth of corruption in the construction industry and PWD. He stated that 'a certain degree of arrogance probably existed among PWD officials who feel that their dishonest activities are harder to uncover since benefactor and beneficiary are both satisfied customers'. He then went on to say:

In most cases, information on such relationships comes from someone who is unhappy and complains. This is usually a small sub-contractor, who goes to the ICAC because he is broke and blames his financial troubles on the line of sub-contractors above him whom he has had to bribe to get his portion of the sub-contract in the first place.

These remarks suggest that the Commission is more likely to receive useful information during a period of economic recession, when a chain reaction normally sets in, with those at the base of the commercial and industrial pyramid, the smaller firms, under stress. A disgruntled businessman is then more inclined, one supposes, to give the game away. In so doing, he may reveal criminal connections between, say, contractors and PWD personnel, and thus open Pandora's Box, to the delight of ICAC investigators. In most cases, though, consensual graft never comes to light. This is also true of fornication, adultery, and homosexuality. If they are crimes (as they are in some places), they are usually victimless crimes. Who will report them? The Kennard trial threw further light on delinquencies committed by PWD staff, including very senior staff, and should also be discussed, because it supplies a prime example of the satisfied customer variety of corruption.

In April 1981 the much-publicized trial of Edward Trevor Kennard, the principal government building surveyor in the Buildings Ordinance Office of the PWD, opened at Victoria District Court. It was notable not only for further revelations of PWD corruption but also for its human interest, as journalists say, for there was a woman in the case, or rather in the wings. She was Kennard's one-time Chinese girl-friend. In Thurber's words: 'Let us ponder this basic fact about the human: ahead of every man, not behind him, is a woman'. This is what the public probably surmised when they read about Kennard's downfall in their newspapers, for it could be that he was the unwitting victim of the woman he claimed to love.

This successful investigation and prosecution was a great triumph for the Commission. The defendant was the most senior government official so charged. Till then, Chief Superintendent Peter Godber had held the record, from 1956. Because of the nature of the case and its complexities, the ICAC was forced to deploy a team of over fifty officers to delve into its ramifications; and investigations continued throughout 1980 and into 1981 when, in January, Kennard was charged at last, after eighteen months of questioning, with specific offences and a date was set for his trial.

Kennard, then aged 50, pleaded not guilty on 11 April 1981 to a charge brought under Section 10 of the Prevention of Bribery Ordinance (disproportionate assets) and to seven charges that he accepted $1.2 million from a real-estate consultant in 1978 and 1979 in respect of building projects, including the New World Centre. On the fourth day of the hearing, he changed his plea to guilty on a charge of being in control of cash and property to the value of $785,000, disproportionate to his official earnings. He was then sentenced to three years' imprisonment. Kennard lost his job and his pension, and was ordered to forfeit to the Crown the sum of $305,000.

Kennard's defence counsel told a sad, but conventional, tale of middle-aged infatuation. In 1974 he met a woman, Chau Yu-kit, then a trainee hotel waitress or bar girl. She had been married to a police constable, by whom she had three children, but they had separated. At the time of the trial, she had returned, however, to her husband. Prior to 1974, Chau Yu-kit had worked in a factory and earned (according to the press) about $120 a month; but between September 1974 and March 1980, her assets had increased from a mere $13,000 to almost $1 million, a quite remarkable example of thrift or ingenuity. Kennard, his counsel alleged, had largely contributed to the size of her fortune by his besotted generosity. The 'advantages' he received from businessmen went mostly to her and did not engorge his own bank account. When his wife learned of his love affair, she had returned to England with her two children, and he moved in with his Chinese mistress. As Chau Yu-kit was not charged with any offence, she did not give evidence, and in any case Kennard's pleading guilty made that unnecessary. Nevertheless, she cast a long shadow over the four days of the trial.

By April 1981, Chau Yu-kit had separated from Kennard and her legal position seemed invulnerable. This disturbed a *South China Morning Post* editorialist, who wrote:

During the proceedings it was revealed that he had befriended a woman whose assets had increased from $13,000 in September 1974, to almost $1 million in March last year, and it is with this sum that the public has a right to be concerned. What proportion of it was given by the accused is impossible to tell, though no doubt diligent inquiries by the ICAC could result in a fair estimate. Why was no attempt made to recover this amount? There is an evident loophole here which corrupt officers might exploit in future unless steps are taken to close it. For otherwise, by paying off sums of money to friends, the accused is virtually certain of withholding funds that rightly belong to the Crown. Whether the accused himself benefits or not is immaterial. The fact is the money was improperly gained and efforts should be made to recover it.

Kennard was released in April 1983, after serving two years of his sentence (in Hong Kong one-third of a sentence is remitted for good behaviour). Earlier in the year, the Attorney-General had taken out a writ to recover $895,000 for the Crown. Originally, Kennard had been charged with accepting $1.2 million in 'bribes and secret profits'. At the end of his trial, the judge had ordered him to forfeit the sum of $305,000, the amount held on his behalf in the safe of a real-estate consultant and architect. He was now being asked, in 1983, to return the rest of his illegal gains. But that, one imagines, will be difficult, since the bulk of his assets has been passed to another. We cannot predict what the outcome of the Attorney-General's action will be, but the decision to mulct Kennard is in line with the *South China Morning Post*'s editorial.

Two expatriate PWD officials, implicated in the same investigation, were convicted for soliciting complimentary tickets to, and accommodation in, Macau and fined $1,000 and $2,500 respectively. Afterwards, one resigned from the PWD; the other returned to his job in the Buildings Ordinance Office. An architect, mentioned in the preceding paragraph, was convicted on a charge of providing an all-expenses-paid trip to Las Vegas for Kennard, and sentenced to eighteen months' imprisonment. He appealed successfully against conviction and was released. This large-scale investigation into the Buildings Ordinance Office, the locus of much governmental corruption, was then wound up. That developers should choose Las Vegas, the Nevada town given over to gambling, as a place of entertainment for their treasured friends, is not unexpected. In the mid-1970s, these same tycoons had created the illusion, during the great property boom, that Hong Kong *was* one vast gambling casino.

The Commissioner's 1980 annual report stated that 'the investigation showed an unhealthy degree of socializing between senior Public Works Department staff and property developers and their representatives, during which the government servants were the recipients of lavish entertainment'. The 1981 annual report declared again that it 'showed an undesirably close relationship between members of the Buildings Ordinance Office and people involved in development and construction'. Developers, property tycoons, successful architects, and directors of large construction companies, are, needless to say, rich men; they are in a position to dazzle, to bemuse and enchant, to hypnotize others with their wealth, particularly a civil servant who is comfortably off, but not outrageously so. To get something for nothing, or for very little, is likely to thaw an official's rectitude (though not in all cases). Kennard, as the trial judge declared, 'was not corrupt in the positive sense that the disproportion (that is, between assets and income) arose because money was accepted as a consideration for neglecting or perverting his duties'. Developers, or their representatives and consultants, wish to keep on good terms with senior PWD staff so that they will not experience trouble from those with the official power to make their working lives difficult. Their provision of lavish entertainment is a mode of public relations, a way of becoming chummy with those with whom it is necessary to have dealings. But the dangers of accepting hospitality are obvious to the right-minded. *Timeo Danaos et dona ferentis* (I fear the Greeks even when they bring gifts), lines from Virgil's *Aeneid* might warn an official to keep a decent social distance from persons who are wont to seduce him, and weaken his resolution.

Mary Lee, writing in the *Far Eastern Economic Review*, commented on the apparent inconsistencies in sentencing offenders of the same type. Kennard's punishment was comparatively light, a result of plea bargaining (he pleaded guilty to only *one* charge, the first; the other seven were 'left on the file'). But in 1981, two China Motor Bus duty officers, who admitted soliciting and accepting advantages from ten fellow drivers, were given terms of four and a half and four years respectively. Yet Hong Kong courts do not appear always to regard corruption as a serious offence, if we examine the average tariff sentence meted out.

This would seem especially true when the defendant is a person of education or position, one who belongs to the upper social class, one who is of high status or who is rich. In most jurisdictions these distinctions are taken as aggravating factors—on the lines that one should know better!—but in Hong Kong they are too often accepted as mitigating factors, when brought to the attention of judge or jury by a smooth-tongued and sentimental counsel. Perhaps it is difficult to impose a stiff sentence on a person of one's own background or class. Yet in Britain, the former Police Commanders Wallace

CHAPTER SEVEN

Virgo and Kenneth Drury of the Met's Porn Squad (Dirty Squad) received in 1977 terms of imprisonment of twelve years and eight years respectively. Drury and his wife had enjoyed an all-expenses-paid holiday in Cyprus with James Humphreys, the Soho vice king, and his wife. Few in Britain complained about the severity of the sentence. The point is important: exemplary sentences underline a government's intention to strike at a particular offence; severe sentences dramatize a community's detestation of a crime. It may well be, of course, that the Hong Kong courts and community now believe that corrupt practices, so prevalent, so resistant to removal, are venial sins. If this is so, then the ICAC has failed so far in its task of educating the public, its leaders, and the élite.

The 1980 successful prosecution of Walter Boxall on charges of accepting illegal commissions (kickbacks) and of conspiracy to defraud his former employer, the Hong Kong Telephone Company, contains some interesting elements. Boxall, the company's property manager, whose name has been mentioned as one of the police force's Class of 1952, suddenly and without prior notice left the Colony in October 1978. He was on the verge of a nervous breakdown. No rational man would have believed that England then offered sanctuary to one suspected of graft. The following year he was extradited, without much difficulty, by the ICAC and brought back to face trial in Hong Kong. He was the second United Kingdom citizen to be so treated: Godber had been the first.

The Hong Kong Telephone Company is a franchised public company and is included in the schedule of public bodies given in the Prevention of Bribery Ordinance. The man in the street usually thinks of a public servant as a government employee or civil servant, but the term is defined in the Ordinance to include 'any employee or member of a public body'. Thus Boxall had been transformed by this legal fiction into a so-called public servant, although one feels he always saw himself as more of a businessman or entrepreneur than a bureaucrat. During the frenzied stock-market boom of 1972, a boom which affected all sections of Hong Kong society, Boxall, together with some friends, had established a limited company and, he claimed, this did very well. He also set up an offshore company, which would allow him (as English law then stood) to avoid payment of tax and death duties when he finally retired to Britain. And he put money into a boutique. Boxall's interest in the stock-market, in speculation, in making money, was shared by many expatriates and most Chinese, and was in no way a sinister portent. Speculation is the very stuff of Hong Kong life and gambling the preoccupation of both rich and poor. Boxall therefore was not exceptional in his drives and ambition. But the prosecution alleged that he used these companies as financial screens, as subterfuges that allowed him to launder the money that he corruptly obtained from his position as property manager to the rapidly expanding Hong Kong Telephone Company.

He was first interviewed by the ICAC in March 1977. His case was even discussed by the ICAC's Operations Review Committee and its members agreed that no further action should be taken. The ICAC's interest in his affairs should have alerted him to danger, to his precarious position: for the ICAC clearly had some intimations or reports of his dishonesty. Yet, according to the prosecution, he continued to break the law. In August 1978, it was alleged, he accepted $25,000 from a cleaning contractor: four of the conspiracy charges also related to the post-amnesty period. The Governor's amnesty, as we have seen, stated that the Commissioner of the ICAC would not take action against alleged or suspected offences committed before 1 January 1977, with the exception of people who had been interviewed by the ICAC before 5 November 1977, and to whom an allegation had been put that they had committed an offence. It would seem, then, that Boxall could not be charged with any offence committed before 1 January 1977: but in the indictment he was charged, with several others, with conspiracy to defraud the company between 1967 and 1978. The prosecuting counsel successfully argued that 'as an ordinance of pardon [the amnesty] was doomed to failure, despite what the governor said'. Counsel went on to argue that the amendment to the Ordinance—No. 3 of 1978—did not grant amnesty in that it could not stop either the police or private individuals from instituting investigations and bringing charges, which is what Peter Wesley-Smith had averred in the *Hong Kong Law Journal*. Boxall defended himself (he was aware how costly legal services are in Hong Kong) and argued well, but his account of his own actions was not accepted.

The trial had familiar features, as in so many corruption cases of this type. In early 1979, while Boxall was sweating it out in England and undergoing the process and the ordeal of extradition, an electrical contractor, a chief clerk, and an assistant manager of the Hong Kong Telephone Company were charged with conspiracy, together with the property manager, Walter Boxall, to defraud the company between 1967 and 1978 by manipulating to their advantage various contracts under the control of the company's property department. They pleaded guilty and the company employees received prison sentences of eighteen months and two years respectively. When Boxall's case came to trial, in May 1980, he was confronted with twelve charges of accepting kickbacks and five of conspiracy to defraud the company. He was convicted on all counts, on evidence provided by his co-conspirators. At the first trial, the cleaning contractor was granted immunity on condition he gave evidence at Boxall's trial and thus he became the chief prosecution witness. The use of tainted witnesses was once again commented on and criticized; but it was clear that Boxall had master-minded many of the corrupt transactions, and had done so for some time. It would be inexact to speak of syndicated corruption within the Hong Kong Telephone Company but there is some resemblance here to that form of corruption. It is also likely that other public utilities listed in the schedule have suffered from the same dishonest depredations, for those in control of the buying of equipment, stores, and supplies are in an enviable position to benefit from their position, in a society where commissions are common in business. And when firms tender for contracts there are always openings for the corrupt, needless to say.

Boxall was sentenced to varying terms of imprisonment, totalling four years. He did not appeal against conviction or sentence. Subsequently, the Hong Kong Telephone Company obtained a court order freezing his Hong Kong assets, which came to around $300,000. He had asserted that the court proceedings constituted a show trial and that he had been made a scapegoat, that the ICAC needed a big trial after its loss of face and of credibility following the amnesty. This seems unlikely, though one could argue he was just unlucky, for many had behaved like him and had remained anonymous, as they still do. It is a commonplace that only a biased sample of offenders ever appears in the courts. Therefore, in one sense, those charged with offences are always scapegoats for those who are neither charged nor prosecuted.

The investigations discussed above—the Chong Hing Mansion scandal, and the Paul Lee, Kennard, and Boxall cases—demonstrate the vulnerability of most government departments and public bodies to the activities of corrupt agents, whose motivation is greed, the commonplace desire to inflate income in an inflationary world. No government can entirely suppress the individual's drive to better his condition; even the puritanical Maoists did not achieve this end, for corruption continues to exist in Communist China despite the awful penalty—death—sometimes attached to the offence. However, governments can provide stronger or more appropriate deterrents. They can, if they choose, pay more attention to the crime and investigate it more rigorously. They may also reduce opportunities for wrongdoing by administrative reforms. The latter, to repeat, is the main task of the ICAC's Corruption Prevention Department. At an early date, this unit identified nine major characteristics of administration conducive to graft: policy weaknesses, inadequate instruction, inadequate supervision of personnel, unnecessary procedures and excessive discretion; and pinpointed the noxious effects of delays, of unenforced laws and regulations, and the ignorance of staff, and what it called 'position', presumably the abuse of status or rank.

In April 1976, the Director of Public Works claimed corruption was not widespread in his department and that only one PWD official had been sacked as a result of a successful ICAC case; but he hastened to add that his staff numbered over 14,000 and that such a large organization must provide opportunities for the dishonest. The Director was thus faced with the proverbial horns of a dilemma: if he bluntly agreed that corruption was rife, he would lower morale in his department and make many suspect; on the other hand, if he strongly disagreed, then he would be mocked by many in the know, for the public was well aware of the dodges and stratagems employed by some staff to supplement their official salaries, for squeeze was endemic at the lower levels. By this time, 1976, the PWD had established a small management unit to locate opportunities for graft. PWD staff then argued that the operation of this unit created delays, made staff nervous and cautious, and added costs to projects. Whether this unit had in fact reduced work efficiency is not easy to determine or measure: the problem is extraordinarily complex. If the ICAC has had a baneful effect on the machinery of government, and the work of the PWD in particular, then this is a hidden cost, the burden of which the public must ultimately bear; and, one should add, law enforcement is always expensive in a highly developed or complex society, where white-collar crime tends to come to the fore.

The ICAC has scrutinized the operation of nearly all government departments and public bodies and constantly updates its monitoring studies, copies of which are routinely sent to the senior officials concerned. The ICAC's main purpose is to discover where opportunities for corruption exist and to circumvent them, or to make corrupt practices easier to detect. The Commission's Corruption Prevention Department has, for example, invested much time in examining weaknesses in the structure and administration of the PWD and in the

Buildings Ordinance, an intricate hodgepodge of legislation. These various studies have centred on a number of key areas, such as the issuing of occupation permits, closure orders for dangerous buildings, the appointment of architectural and engineering consultants, the enforcement of legislation relating to unauthorized structures and alterations, and the illegal occupation of Crown land sites in urban areas. It has also looked into the problems generated by the application of the Buildings Ordinance to the New Territories. Hong Kong's rapid urbanization, as illustrated by the construction of new or satellite towns, has created, concomitantly, fresh opportunities for the dishonest—for PWD officials, developers, architects, technicians and experts, and for the many parasitic businessmen and local officials who hope to profit from change, innovation, and enterprise, just as John Poulson did in Britain in the 1960s.

The ICAC has been alerted to loopholes in the law, to new dodges, and to novel forms of corruption, often by its own investigations and prosecutions, whether successful or not. Paradoxically, even an abortive or failed prosecution may result in a further tightening up of flawed administrative procedures, practices, or rules. There is clearly some overlap between the work of the ICAC's Corruption Prevention Department and the probes initiated by the Director of Audit, also an independent agent, into government spending. The Director of Audit's annual report reads like investigative journalism at its best; it includes not only ripe examples of inefficiency and stupidity but, at times, convinces the reader that there is corruption in the background. One surmises that the Commissioner of the ICAC and his staff read it with great attention, as a pointer to grey areas in the civil service and its undertakings and, by extension, in public bodies and the private sector.

A partner in a firm of consulting civil and structural engineers claimed in October 1983 that the setting up of the ICAC had had a baneful effect upon the efficiency of the PWD (now Lands and Works); for after 1974 civil servants had adopted an apparently inflexible approach to the awarding of public works contracts. These now went to the lowest tender in order to avoid any suspicion of favouritism or corruption. Thus contractors were putting in bids at almost suicidal levels in order to gain work. Before 1974, he continued, government officials 'could reasonably give a decision based on engineering principles' without necessarily accepting the lowest bid. Nowadays 'they just can't give a decision as readily as they could or would in the private sector'. This situation had also worsened with the onset of the recession and the collapse of the property market. A new type of specialist had come into being: the 'claims adviser', an individual, knowledgeable about civil law, who advises his business clients on the ambiguities of contract specifications or other legal documents and spots legal loopholes contained in them. In some cases, the claims adviser works on a reward system by which he gets a percentage of the cash a contractor succeeds in extracting from the government. A successful claim improves the contractor's profit, low as it initially is. Thus legitimate business is sometimes transformed into speculation and litigation.

The consultant referred to suggested that in order to reduce claims, the PWD should rigorously screen all tenders and spend more time on the preparation of contracts. But he admitted that this would lead to a 'Catch 22' situation, since delay in finalizing a contract would slow down the pace of construction work, yet government departments were under great pressure to meet deadlines, such as the completion on time of public housing estates. The inexpert must find it difficult to decide on this issue: on the one hand, competition is presumed to be good—the more tenders the better in theory—for the public benefits from competition and the lower prices it ensures; on the other hand, the lowest bid might result in shoddy construction or, what is not uncommon, the company going bankrupt and leaving work unfinished. The issue is one of competing social priorities: should the elimination of corruption take precedence over, say, speed of construction or the needs of the business sector? The same problem emerges when we discuss the thorny question of the status of business commissions, to which we should now turn.

The Revd Justus Doolittle, a distinguished sinologue, writing in 1865 about Chinese commercial practice, stated that: 'The employment of gobetweens or middle persons between the two principals in the transaction of many kinds of business is one of the "peculiar institutions" of society as existing here, and probably all over the empire with local modifications'. 'The pay of these gobetweens', he continued, 'is usually five per cent on the sum of money given by the buyer to the seller. Of this percentage, the buyer pays three and the seller two parts, which on very large sums is a very handsome compensation for his trouble and responsibility'. Doolittle warned that this traditional, deep-seated custom was often open to abuse and that a buyer would sometimes be duped in regard to quality, and particularly with respect to price. He further commented: 'The seller is sometimes privy to deception practised by the gobetween, and comes to an understanding with him in regard to the manner of dividing between them the extra sum paid by the buyer, over and above what was readily demanded by the seller'.

The whole of China, it follows, then operated, as Sir Alastair Blair-Kerr was to allege of Hong Kong in 1973, on a commission basis. This practice was heavily institutionalized and perfectly legal. The go-between or middleman was an economic agent who helped to promote trade and commerce and acted as a necessary link between buyer and seller, bringing the two into apposition. The job of the go-between was, then, to find a purchaser for a seller and to negotiate an acceptable price; he performed the same role when called upon to act for a buyer. The go-between also saved a businessman from having to travel far in a country where, until modern times, communications were poor, and took over the task of verifying the bona fides of a buyer (or seller). He acted as a free-lance agent and was paid for his specialized knowledge.

Compradors provided, roughly speaking, the same services. A comprador (*mai-pan*) was the Chinese manager, sometimes called the Chinese business-manager, attached to a foreign firm. He served as a middleman in the company's dealings with Chinese, as an intermediary between foreign and Chinese merchants or businessmen, and, more grandly, as a commercial link between China and the West. Sir Robert Ho Tung (1862–1956), for example, was comprador to Jardine, Matheson & Co. from 1883 to 1900, during which period he carried on an extensive business on his own account, as did most compradors. In time, Sir Robert became one of the richest men in Hong Kong and his children and grandchildren have maintained a leading place in Hong Kong affairs.

The comprador's official salary constituted only a small part of his total income. Like the go-between mentioned above, he received commissions from buyers and sellers, from both Chinese and foreign businessmen. Typically, he obtained one to five per cent commission, with an average of two to three per cent, according to Hao Yen-p'ing, the author of a study of the compradorial system. But Hao also affirms that 'besides his salary, commission, and other legitimate income, he usually "squeezed" his employers', and that 'the comprador's main source of income came neither from salary, nor commission, but from "squeeze"'. The comprador's profession became less important in the twentieth century and the old-style comprador disappeared. After the First World War he tended to be taken into partnership with, or appointed a director of, the foreign firm. He changed, then, from an agent to a Chinese manager and oversaw for his company all Chinese contracts, especially those to do with labour. His interests now became fused with his parent firm. The compradorial system has vanished, but the legacy of commission-taking on all deals or business transactions lingers on. In Chinese eyes the practice is normal and moral, an aid to commerce and a stimulus to hard work.

In traditional China, go-betweens and middlemen, brokers and agents, intermediaries of all types, were well-known social types. Marriage-brokers, who had not totally disappeared, also played an important part in arranging Chinese customary marriages by seeking out suitable partners and by matching horoscopes. Lower in the scale were numerous fixers and touts, and even a class of persons, who, for a price, would act as substitutes for someone sentenced to imprisonment. These social types are not unknown, of course, in the West; but what should be stressed is that the use of go-betweens was probably more deeply entrenched and more extensive in China, and that few people in that vast country questioned the morality of such a custom. Go-betweens acted as a screen between buyer and seller and avoided direct confrontation between the two and no doubt helped some to save 'face' if a deal fell through, for the go-between could be blamed for any failure.

Section 4 of the 1948 Prevention of Corruption Ordinance made corrupt transactions with agents an offence. Section 4 (a) stated that it is an offence if:

any agent corruptly accepts or obtains, or agrees to accept or attempts to obtain, from any person, for himself or for any other person, any gift or consideration as an inducement or reward for doing or forbearing to do, or for having after the passing of this Ordinance done or forborne to do, any act in relation to his principal's affairs or business, or for showing or forbearing to show favour to his principal's affairs or business.

Section 4 (b) made it an offence for any person to give or offer any gift or consideration to any agent.

Section 9 (1) of the Prevention of Bribery Ordinance, 1971 (amended in 1974), states:

any agent who, without lawful authority or reasonable excuse, solicits or accepts any advantage as an inducement to or reward for or otherwise on account of his—
(a) doing or forbearing to do, or having done or forborne to do, any act in relation to his principal's affairs or business; or
(b) showing or forbearing to show, or having shown or forborne to show, favour or disfavour to any person in relation to his principal's affairs or business shall be guilty of an offence.

Section 9 thus draws a distinction between legal and illegal commissions. An 'advantage' changes its status once the principal (employer) is informed of the transaction and agrees to an employee's acceptance of a kickback. From 1948, therefore, the illegality of some types of commissions or rebates had been part of Hong Kong law: but the law was rarely, if ever, enforced in this tenebrous area and the notion of who was or was not a principal was not precisely tested in the courts. The term 'principal' was surrounded with ambiguities. In all likelihood, most businessmen and their employees were unaware that at times they broke the law, although all knew that embezzlement, another breach of trust, was a serious criminal offence, for such cases appeared routinely in the courts (but no cases of illegal commission). The establishment of the ICAC in 1974, together with the Governor's desire to purify the Colony's social and economic life ('moralization of the community'), did much to change the picture. Those engaged in commerce and industry were now at risk for the Commissioner, Jack Cater, decided in 1975 that the law should be enforced within the private sector. There could be no double standard, one for government servants, another for the rest of the population. Levelling was necessary.

The drive against illegal commissions (a custom much commented upon by Sir Alastair Blair-Kerr in his second report) was reviewed in the Commissioner's 1976 annual report when he wrote: 'At this stage we are not actively seeking out corruption in the private sector but, as required by law, the Commission responds to reports of corruption in that sector'. In his peroration he mentioned 'the Carter administration's approach to morality in business'. Here was an intimation of intention, a promise that the ICAC would be active in the private sector. In 1976 the ICAC moved, and a number of prosecutions of businessmen and their agents were given great publicity in the press. The next year, the Director of Operations notified the public that a substantial fall in reports involving illegal commissions (314 in 1977 compared with 427 in 1976) had occurred. 'This', he wrote, 'is felt to reflect an improvement in standards of honesty and business ethics, and, with the co-operation of the business community of Hong

Kong, it is hoped this improvement will continue'. There is, however, little evidence in support of the thesis that the downward trend has continued. In 1982 it was reversed, possibly as a result of uncertainty about the Colony's future, the continuing recession, and the stagnation of the property market. Hard times, one concludes, have increased the amount of white-collar crime, for the pursuit of what the American sociologist, R.K. Merton, calls 'money-success' has become more difficult to achieve.

The Gilman case was to send a frisson of horror through the ranks of the commercial classes and particularly touched those businessmen who had done so demonstrably well in free-and-easy post-war Hong Kong. The administration had always feared to alienate the business class, on whom the state of the economy largely depends, and rarely interfered in its internal affairs. Gilman and Company, one of the great hongs, was fined a total of $90,000 in May 1976 on six charges of offering advantages ('spotter fees' in Hong Kong parlance) contrary to Section 9 (2) of the Prevention of Bribery Ordinance. The company's import department manager was additionally charged with impeding the prosecution of an offender contrary to the Criminal Procedure Ordinance by destroying certain records and documents. Gilman admitted paying advantages ranging from $500 to $2,000 to six agents for proposing or negotiating business. The trial judge pointed out that the law, both in England and Hong Kong, has always held to be corrupt any gift given to another company's agent secretly, if the gift is paid as an inducement or as a reward in relation to the agent's performance of some duty in connection with his employer's affairs. He went on to say:

It will be just to bear in mind that the Court has been told that payments of this nature are a long-standing practice of some firms in the Colony, and it is only now, presumably because the ICAC is beginning to acquire adequate staff, that prosecutions are taking place. Thus a false sense of security has been engendered, and while this cannot excuse, it will be fair to take it into account in mitigation.

Gilman was thus a scapegoat in 1976 for the sins of all the other hongs and Chinese enterprises. There was much sympathy for the unfortunate company, since everyone knew it had been charged with offences prevalent in Hong Kong and not recognized within the community as criminal. An editorial in the *South China Morning Post* was headed 'Compradore ways die hard'. It summed up the issue nicely and tersely.

The Gilman case was followed, a week later, with the prosecution of Olivetti (Hong Kong) Ltd. on similar charges, of offering advantages contrary to Section 9 (2) (b). A third case which attracted much publicity and commentary at the time was related to Television Broadcasts Ltd (TVB). An assistant to the managing director of that company pleaded guilty to forty-nine charges arising from soliciting and accepting advantages from his company's advertising salesmen. He was sentenced to three years' imprisonment and was also ordered to return $49,000 to four TVB salesmen who had been asked by him to share their commissions. At a later date, the sales manager to the station was imprisoned on similar charges and another skipped bail and fled the Colony.

These cases certainly had a terrific impact upon the world of commerce. They led, as we shall see, to a campaign spearheaded by industrial and commercial organizations to change the law with regard to commissions and to persuade the ICAC to direct its operations away from the business community as a target. Concurrently, the ICAC launched its own counter-campaign to educate the public as to the dangers inherent in the commission system, despite its antiquity as a custom. In the Commission's 1976 annual report, the Director of Operations wrote:

The vast majority of these cases concerned bribes being paid by firms to obtain business and they became known as the 'illegal commission' cases. It has been held that investigations of such offences should be taken out of the hands of the ICAC as they are, if anything, a 'commercial crime'. The Oxford English Dictionary defines 'bribe' as 'money, etc., offered to procure action in favour of the giver'. This is exactly what many of the defenders of these 'illegal commissions' have been, or still are doing. Consequently, the offences in this area logically as well as by law should continue to be dealt with by the ICAC.

The ICAC's Community Relations Department was also busy at the same time in arranging much media publicity, and held round after round of discussions and briefings with the staff of business firms. It attempted to show that the law specifically recognized business commissions permitted by the recipient's principal or employer and that what the law prohibited was secret commissions or, in less euphemistic language, bribes. The attempt to differentiate between legal and illegal commissions mystified many businessmen, who simply wanted to return to the status quo ante, to the happy days of the uncomplicated past.

Let's legalize bribery and keep America prosperous. It is the sensible solution to a nasty problem. At present American business has to commit bribery to compete in Asian, European and Middle Eastern markets. At present this is a crime and, therefore, many businessmen are reluctant to do it. What a sad state of affairs! Is successful competition in the market-place a criminal deed?

So Russell Baker, the American columnist, commented in March 1976 on the great Lockheed scandal and its ramifications. Baker's ironic or sardonic conclusion—that bribery should be legalized in a free enterprise society—appears to have been taken seriously, about the same time, by the Colony's hardheaded businessmen. Soon after the Gilman prosecution, in April 1976, about fifty alarmed persons from the commercial and industrial sector held private meetings to mull over the implications of that case and its adjudication. Members of this newly formed pressure group then sat down with ICAC officials to review the position but were not able to wring any concessions from those implacable rigorists. A little later, representatives from various business associations appealed to UMELCO (Office of the Unofficial Members of the Executive and Legislative Councils). UMELCO offered to forward views of disaffected businessmen to government, but did little else; but UMELCO has never shown itself to be too critical of constituted authority.

In mid-July the Chinese Manufacturers' Association (CMA) took over and reorganized the nascent campaign. This body formulated three proposals: (a) that the practice of giving and receiving commissions, in particular those known commercially as 'spotter fees', should no longer be treated as criminal; (b) that members of the business community should advise the government on which types of commission did or did not benefit the economy; and (c) that those persons who in the past had proffered or accepted kickbacks should not now be prosecuted. Hence, in summary, the CMA and its allies wanted Section 9 either to be drastically amended or entirely repealed. They were also highly critical of Section 19 which declared that it was not a defence 'to show that any such advantage as is mentioned in this Ordinance is customary in any profession, trade, vocation or calling'. Section 24, which stated that 'the burden of proving a defence of lawful authority or reasonable excuse shall lie upon the accused', also came under attack. In general, the CMA argued that in most cases commissions (advantages) aided the Hong Kong economy; and, moreover, that the practice was a hallowed Chinese custom, and in no way immoral or criminal. As a pressure group, CMA spokesmen implied that Western legal notions did not accord with the reality of local conditions and beliefs. There was, in their eyes, a real clash between cultures, and the colonial administration should defer to the views of the great majority, to the dominant Chinese segment of the population, on which Hong Kong's stability and prosperity depended.

The Chief Secretary, to whom the CMA's petition was sent, did not accept these proposals. Then, following the successful prosecution, and imprisonment for ten days, of two proprietors of small businesses on charges of offering 'tea money' (tips) to installation workers from the Hong Kong Electric Company, the campaign gained support from the Chinese lower middle classes and the man in the street. The government, nevertheless, remained inflexible, and did not relent in any way. Indeed, on 11 November the Attorney-General intimated to the Legislative Council that the ICAC would continue to investigate Section 9 offences and that business-men could not expect to be treated any differently from civil servants. During this period, as mentioned, the Community Relations Department of the ICAC was busy orchestrating a counter-campaign to educate the public about the baneful effects of corruption on *all* sections of society. Stimulus was thus followed by response, action by reaction: both sides, the CMA and the ICAC, propagated conflicting moral accounts of Hong Kong enterprise. The culminating point came on 18 November when 700 representatives from 306 commercial, industrial, and civic organizations held a mass meeting to defend the age-old institution of the business commission, sacrosanct to Chinese. A memorandum was sent to the government, a document which did not differ from the previous three-point letter, except that the view was now advanced that irregularities or malpractices in the private sector should be investigated by the Police Commercial Crimes Office (CCO). This was probably a shrewd suggestion because the CCO was understaffed in 1976 compared with the Operations Department of the ICAC, which in that year had a strength of 486. The CCO specialized in unravelling allegations of fraud and embezzlement in public companies, business firms, and banks. Its main target was the devious white-collar criminal, but it was also concerned with tracking down those who counterfeited currency. The CCO, one imagines, would not have given illegal commissions great priority. It was after bigger game.

The quarrel over illegal commissions reveals some curious alignments and combinations. The great hongs, largely British-controlled or representing British interests, stepped quickly into line and accepted, without much demur, the new situation created by the ICAC's thrust into the private sector. The hongs did not support CMA insurgency, so to speak; they were part of the Establishment. Nor did the General Chamber of Commerce, which includes a large number of non-Chinese or European-run firms. On the other hand, groups which normally opposed each other, because they supported either Beijing or Taibei and were thus separated by an ideological divide, joined forces and now presented a united Chinese front. But in 1976 the Hong Kong government was not prepared to back down and would not allow the ICAC to lose public face. Behind the scenes there were numerous meetings; emollient words, one suspects, were uttered. CMA representatives, ICAC officers and officials from other government departments engaged in much confabulation. The CMA-led campaign did not last long and evaporated the following year. In 1977 there were far fewer prosecutions under Section 9 (1) and (2), a fall from 66 to a meagre 8. This suggests that a compromise had been arrived at. One imagines that the cessation of disturbing prosecutions reduced tension so that the business community felt less threatened. The stimulus to action, it follows, had been greatly weakened by early 1977. There was thus no need for further organized opposition and protest. The law was not changed in 1976. Section 9 remained inviolate, but was invoked less often. The Commission could bide its time.

This CMA-led campaign, emanating from discontent within the business world, tells us something about the community's expectations. When the ICAC was established in February 1974, most people believed the organization would concentrate on the sins of the police or on a few popularly stigmatized departments, such as Housing. After all, it was Godber who was largely instrumental in persuading Sir Murray that an independent anti-corruption body was badly needed in the Colony. The Governor's decision to create such a department was widely applauded, in 1973-4, by civic leaders. The police, to repeat, were not popular in Hong Kong (nor are they in many countries). Unlike the British, Chinese have no tradition of a professional police force or of the role of the constable as 'peace officer' rather than 'law officer' (a more punitive designation). In traditional China, *yamen*-runners were always disliked, and avoided as cruel, corrupt, and criminal. Under the Nationalist government (1927-49) the position did not improve markedly and the regime's police soon acquired a bad reputation for their treatment of dissenters and for arrogant behaviour. After 1949, Hong Kong's pro-Taiwan element caricatured local police as running dogs of the colonialists, as anti-national and anti-Nationalist. The Colony's Communist faction likewise derided them as lackeys of colonialism and imperialism, agents of the capitalist class, as counter-revolutionaries, the dregs of a dying social order. During the ebullient days of 1967, Nationalists changed sides and accepted the police as allies, and even commensals. But they reverted to contempt once the disturbances subsided. Hence, in 1974, the unmasking of venal policemen was regarded on all sides as a good thing. The setting up of the ICAC united, as it were, disparate elements and gave the colonial administration greater legitimacy. It was a popular move, Sir Murray's most popular innovation. He was also admired, at that time, as a 'law and order' man, a useful avatar for a populist leader.

As the ICAC expanded its operations in late 1975 and started to move into the private sector, this unexpected activity was regarded with apprehension and disquiet. The business élite, the most puissant pressure group in Hong Kong, has always believed that what is good for business is good for Hong Kong. The Commissioner, one assumes, did not realize in early 1976 that targeting the private sector would cause him and his aides so much trouble and unleash so much obloquy. All public bodies live by self-congratulation to some degree and, one imagines, the Commissioner sincerely thought the community was solidly behind his endeavours. But the community did not see matters in such black-and-white terms. They made distinctions between flagitious behaviour and, shall we say, 'respectable crime'; they accepted a double standard in social and economic life. The ICAC, then, was faced with its first crisis in late 1976, and survived it only by damping down investigation of the private sector. (The next year, as we know, it barely survived the police crisis and took time to convalesce from its wounds.)

The Commissioner, Jack Cater, may have misjudged the public mood in 1976 but he was correct in his analysis of the problems; whereas the arguments put forward by the CMA and its allies were self-serving, flawed, or bogus. It takes two to tango, as the saying goes: with the exception of extortion or squeeze (one partly dominating the other), corruption is normally an agreed-upon arrangement between two persons, a giver and a receiver, whereby each benefits, usually to the detriment of others. The only realistic way of raising the moral tone of Hong Kong, to improve business ethics and practices, to enhance honesty, was that taken by Jack Cater—to penalize *both* participants in a corrupt transaction and not to admit any distinction between those working in the public and private sectors, for there is always a possibility of cross-infection.

That Section 9 offences declined in volume after the end of 1976 has been mentioned. There were only 8 prosecutions in 1977, 11 in 1978, 25 the following year. But an upward trend became clearly visible in 1980, with 51 cases. The truce with the business community had surely ended. The ICAC had bided its time; but it had intervened again. This upward trend has been linked, by the Commissioner himself, with Hong Kong's continuing recession and with the downturn in the property market, which became marked in the last quarter of 1981. The 1976 campaign waged against illegal commissions was, it is now certain, largely symbolic or declaratory, as was the Godber trial. The selection of Gilman and Company, one of the great European hongs, as culprit, victim, and scapegoat, brought the issue before the general public in a suitably dramatic form. The *South China Morning Post*, Hong Kong's leading English-language newspaper, devoted two editorials to the prosecution. The trial also had an educational function. After April 1976 no Hong Kong businessman could truly argue that he was not cognizant of the law. This prosecution spelled out for those who could not read, or did not know, what was inscribed on the tablets of the law.

The ICAC has always claimed, at least in public statements, that it simply responds to reports of corruption; that it is not 'proactive', as Americans say, but reactive. It does not, it maintains, seek out infractions of the law. This suggests that it refuses to discriminate among cases but waits like a shop-keeper for customers to turn up. All are treated equally, in rotation. This is certainly not how police forces commonly work, as we know from sociological studies of police organiza-tions. In any decision to arrest or prosecute, many factors are involved: the process is neither automatic nor inflexible.

CID investigations and those conducted by the Commis-sion's Operations Department are much alike. Both must arrange priorities; each must discriminate when faced with a large case-load. Since manpower is never unlimited, minor of-fences may be downgraded or not pursued rigorously. It fol-lows that in all law-enforcement agencies there is a degree of selectivity. The ICAC, in order to deflect criticism of its policy to outlaw certain types of standard but illegal commissions, argued that it only responded to corruption complaints but did not initiate them. The Commissioner hence declared in his report for 1976:

At this stage we are not actively seeking corruption in the private sector but, as required by law, the Commission responds to reports of corruption in that sector. In such cases, the investigation is car-ried out with equal determination and energy as is investigation of a report concerning corruption in the public service. Less than 1% of the Operations department establishment is at present engaged on private sector corruption. Even so, in 1976 there were 96 prosecu-tions for offences connected solely with this sector. It was encourag-ing to note the support of many companies in respect of better ethics in business and the very real efforts being made by many others during the year to ensure that they complied with the law.

The Commissioner's words were meant to disarm the pub-lic, but they are not entirely convincing, for they appear to be contradicted by the existence of an Operations Target Committee, whose terms of reference include advising the Commissioner 'on which complaints of bribery shall be investigated and on the priority to be given to them'. This duty was later re-worded to read: 'To receive from the Commissioner reports on action taken by the Commission in the investigation of offences within its jurisdiction and to advise the Commissioner which complaints should no longer be pursued'. In each case, in the original and revised versions, there is a suggestion of selectivity and discrimination. This is not surprising. We do not know what goes on when this Committee meets the Commissioner but one imagines that at times the targeting of particular corruption offences is discussed, and priorities arranged. If this is so, then the ICAC is both proactive and reactive in its investigations. It behaves like any other law-enforcement agency or organization, as it must do necessarily.

8
CONCLUSION

'Those who do not learn from history
are condemned to repeat it.'

George Santayana

THE ICAC has been in existence for over a decade. In February 1974 this new government department received the community's approbation; some, mostly levellers at heart, greeted its birth with enormous enthusiasm. Yet at times sections of a fickle public have responded to its activities with marked hostility, as in 1976. It suffered another setback the following year but, bruised, rebounded. The ICAC appears to be a permanent structure, though one cannot predict what shape it will take after 1997 when the Colony will revert to Chinese jurisdiction. At present, the Commission continues to elicit mixed feelings and fitful ambivalence.

It is possible to chronicle the fortunes of the ICAC by selecting extracts from the Commissioner's annual reports and to use these as convenient pointers; but its private history, its true or secret history, remains buried and is not easy to excavate. One may only pick up some clues by following the faint footprints its agents leave behind. The main reason why it is difficult precisely to chart the evolution of the territory's second law-enforcement agency is the secrecy that must surround its operations. This would be true, also, of an intelligence service, such as the British M.I. 5, whose story is only now being filled in; and it is unlikely that the jigsaw will ever be completed.

The Commission receives a flow of extremely sensitive and confidential information, reports, and allegations. Some, one

concludes, must throw light on the turpitudes and machina-
tions of members of Hong Kong's élite—'top people' in
journalese—especially millionaire businessmen and very
senior civil servants. At this high and delicate level, political
considerations cannot be completely disregarded; they must
be weighed in the balance, for in Hong Kong's highly stratified society the few are sometimes more equal than the rest.
The decision to open a file on someone, to investigate or to
prosecute, is never straightforward or clear-cut. The public is
rarely, if ever, told why a particular person or 'personality'
has been targeted and another not; nor is the rationale behind
the Commission's priorities always entirely clear to the
layman.

Each Commissioner, in turn, has encouraged the view that
his organization merely reacts to reports of corruption, that he
does not comb the streets for suspects; and one frequently
hears the parrot phrase that all are equal under the law. The
Commission, like any large public body, engages on occasion
in disinformation and misinformation, and so do other government departments, for this is a practice common to all
bureaucracies. (It was not Orwell but the bureaucrat who in-
vented 'Newspeak'.) Only part of the ICAC is open to inspection; the greater part remains submerged, submarine.

The same comments would apply to its rival body. Two
histories or studies of the Hong Kong police, one by Colin
Crisswell and Mike Watson, the other by Kevin Sinclair,
more or less evade the crucial question of how policy is made
at the top—is it even rational?—and the problem of the tensions that must exist in a mixed-race, hierarchical formation.
The façade is nicely described: but the interior is neglected. It
must be admitted that the authors would in any case confront
formidable obstacles in attempting to solve these mysteries or
in throwing light on some shadowy areas. Those involved in
security or law enforcement are normally tight-lipped about
their professional activities; rarely are they chatterboxes,
except perhaps within their own perimeters. They exhibit a
persona, a public face outside. And that is true, in the main,

also of the ICAC and its officers. Police and ICAC, although they rarely admit it, share in a common culture, a subculture.

Hence an historian or sociologist is faced with unremitting problems. Criminologists have been accused, and fairly accused, of raising more problems than they solve. But some attempt must be made in this concluding chapter to arrive at an assessment, a balanced one it is hoped, of the ICAC's ten years of service to the community. Both splendours and miseries should be recorded, for every Achilles has his heel, and failure, ironically, is more interesting than success.

In the preceding chapters two issues in particular were keynoted: first, the question of why in the 1950s and 1960s the government paid so little attention to corruption, an obvious fact of daily life; and second, why in the early 1970s there was such a great flare-up of interest in the subject. The answer given to the former was relatively simple: corruption was not recognized as a serious social problem: it had not assumed that status among the public or in the hearts and minds of those who governed. Senior officials of course agreed it was a problem of sorts and felt obliged at times to look at the matter, as in 1960 and 1961.

R.K. Merton writes that Royal Commissions of Inquiry in Britain came into their own in the nineteenth century as favoured instruments leading to major advances in social legislation, such as the Factory Acts. The work of Royal Commissions was praised even by the acerbic Marx, who lauded commissioners as 'free from partisanship and respect of persons'. Yet recommendations from such bodies need not be acted upon since their members are given investigatory but not legislative powers. Even if proposals are accepted in principle, there may be a considerable delay in implementation, as in England with the second part of the Wolfenden Report of 1957. The setting up of a body to inquire into the facets of a complex social problem may also be used as a device to delay change or to put some contentious issue temporarily into limbo, into cold storage. Again a government may just tread water, mark time, by declaring that a matter of public concern is under consideration and that one must await the outcome. On the other hand, if there is rioting in the streets or a dramatic fall in the value of the currency, or a taxi strike (in Hong Kong at least), then the government may act with surprising speed. There is, it follows, a vast gulf between thinking about a problem and doing something about it. That was the situation, broadly speaking, before 1969–70. The various reports of standing and advisory committees on corruption were excellent and well thought out: but the government then saw no pressing need to confront the problem head on. A community must be strongly motivated to accept change, the climate of opinion must be positive, the *Zeitgeist* favourable. By the end of the 1960s a dislocation in thought and perception obviously had occurred.

Biologists use the concept of homeostasis to depict the way an organism maintains stability despite conflicts in its physical environment. The term suggests that a living organism is a self-regulating or self-adjusting mechanism: in hot weather, for example, the body loses moisture in order to maintain a standard temperature. There is, in other words, a tendency towards a relatively stable equilibrium between interdependent elements. The idea has been applied analogically to social systems by the Harvard biochemist, L.J. Henderson, in his book, *Pareto's General Sociology* (1935).

Thus in the 1950s and 1960s the primary concern of the Hong Kong government was to maintain social stability, or equilibrium, and the economy was taken as the key to achieving that end. The speeches and *obiter dicta* of Sir John Cowperthwaite, Financial Secretary 1961–71, corroborate that he interpreted stability in a narrow economic context: he was certainly no friend of the Welfare State. (Alvin Rabushka, in *Value for Money: The Hong Kong Budgetary Process*, makes plain the dominance exercised by Sir John, a man with the mind of a brilliant accountant, in government councils.) Any unusual innovation could, potentially, disturb the meshing of interdependent elements in the economy and society. To launch an anti-corruption crusade on a large scale might, then, have perilous consequences and lead to a flight of entrepreneurs and capital to Taiwan, Singapore, or other places.

In those days Hong Kong was still typically a colony. Since 1975 the government has preferred to use the more neutral term 'Territory' in all official publications except where 'Colony' is a legal requirement. This change in appellation is not entirely cosmetic, for if Hong Kong society has changed, so too has the government, following the Star Ferry Riots of 1966 and the disquieting 1967 confrontation with Maoists, who poured into the streets daily to challenge the government's legitimacy and to invoke a vastly different social order, one in which the common man was (in theory) an equal or a master. By the 1970s the notion of equilibrium had therefore acquired new connotations. The 'social' was now perceived as equally important as the 'economic', a point grasped by Sir Murray MacLehose, when he became Governor in 1972.

The second issue—why corruption emerged as a major social problem in the early 1970s—is more complex. The symbolic interactionist perspective in sociology is concerned primarily with plotting the connections between communication, meaning, symbolism, and action. The interactionist sociologist has, therefore, paid particular attention to the origin, context, and development of moral or symbolic crusades, such as the rise of the prohibition movement or the outlawing of marijuana in America, or the child-saving crusade in Britain. A campaign is always the inspiration and work of a minority, of those who wish to impose their own moral version of society on the majority. Crusades and campaigns do not flourish in a social vacuum—that is obvious—but are linked with politics and political processes and, in particular, with interest groups. In *Outsiders*, Howard S. Becker remarks:

Rules are the products of someone's initiative and we can think of the people who exhibit such enterprise as *moral entrepreneurs* ... The prototype of the rule creator ... is the crusading reformer. He is interested in the content of rules. The existing rules do not satisfy him because there is one evil which profoundly disturbs him ... The prohibitionist serves as an excellent example, as does the person who wants to do away with gambling.

Without pushing the analogy too far, it is not implausible to depict Sir Murray MacLehose as closer to Becker's moral entrepreneur than to the cynic or the world-weary. Sir Murray, especially in his early gubernatorial years, was a man of action, someone who had very clear views on what ought to be done. No one could caricature him as an official who moved on fixed tracks staidly towards his pension: for Sir Murray was prepared to take risks, and by setting up the ICAC he did take a large leap into the dark.

Sir Murray's role in these matters has been discussed in Chapter 4. By February 1974 he had obtained the strong support of many in the community and much backing from students, a social group listened to more readily in the East than in Britain. In twentieth-century China student participation in politics has been notable, as in the May Fourth Movement, a mass response to Japan's unwarranted Twenty-one Demands of 1915, a landmark in modern Chinese history, and in the May Thirtieth Movement of 1925. Hong Kong students, however, had shown little interest in local or international affairs and politics until the 1967 demonstrations, in whose wake a measure of student radicalism developed, influenced not only by the Maoist legacy but by student unrest in America, Europe, and Japan. The student-inspired 'Bring Back Godber' campaign of 1973–4 was taken as a disturbing portent, one imagines, by paternalistic administrators, who liked to lead but not to be led. The establishment of the ICAC did not, at first, encounter much open opposition. It was not divisive but unifying or integrative. Countervailing forces took time to evolve. They had been submerged momentarily by euphoria.

It is unarguable that Godber provided the *efficient* cause (the producing cause in Aristotelian logic) for the creation of the ICAC; but he was not the *necessary* cause for that institution's existence. At the time of his trial, the public was repeatedly informed that Godber was the most senior government official to be charged with corruption (presumably in the entire history of Hong Kong). Yet in fact he ranked only as chief superintendent, one of thirteen, with a monthly salary of $7,200. Above him—far above him—was the Commissioner (Charles Sutcliffe), two deputy commissioners (Brian Slevin and Christopher Dawson), two senior assistant commissioners, eight assistant commissioners, and an administrative officer. Godber, then, was not too important a prize. Although not a departmental head, he was nonetheless a symbol, a symbol representing corruption in the abstract, corruption personified. And, to repeat, he was both expatriate and policeman, attributes which nicely satisfied Chinese feelings of *schadenfreude*. Dissatisfaction tended to crystallize around his name. The Watergate Scandal, on the other hand, unmasked some very important people indeed, including, incredibly, the President himself. Thus Hong Kong's Godber Scandal must be kept in reasonable perspective: he was really rather small fry. In the circumstances, though, the catch was important. Godber's trial dramatized the issue of corruption and highlighted a social problem that needed mitigating, and at the same time supplied great publicity for the infant Commission.

The underlying causes of the eruption of interest in corruption, a topic then given extensive coverage by the media, must remain problematical; but in Chapters 3 and 4 it was argued that the events of 1967–8 had unhinged Hong Kong, had panicked some individuals, though not the government. Residents had sought sanctuary abroad, fearing a sudden Communist take-over of the Colony; others had sent children overseas (Canada was especially favoured). At the same time, there was a sharp fall in the price of property and in rents, always a warning signal, a sign of uncertainty in Hong Kong. When conditions partially improved—for Maoist elements had vacated the streets, no longer swarmed forth to demonstrate from China-owned stores and premises, and had ceased leaving home-made bombs on pavements and roads to disrupt traffic—the population remained still tense and edgy, as after a nasty visit to the dentist.

CHAPTER EIGHT

The twelve months' series of incidents, which resulted in a number of deaths, tapered off slowly, but continued to exacerbate nerves. Following these events, there was an increase in overt criticism of the government, particularly from younger people, and an efflorescence of radical magazines and journals, mostly Chinese. Student unions also veered to the Left, but that was almost a world-wide phenomenon in the late 1960s. One could plausibly claim that Hong Kong had become a more difficult place to govern than at any time since 1945, when the Union Jack was raised again. (The 1920s had also been a troublesome period for colonial administrators because of strikes and left-wing agitation.) A surprising number of people now were openly critical, truculent, and rancorous. This apparent contracting out from a colonial ethos may also be related to rising expectations, for real wages had risen steadily, and the population was increasingly literate, according to the 1961 and succeeding censuses.

Sir Murray and his supporters believed that corruption had proliferated in *both* volume and scale. Yet no one appears to have looked closely at the evidence. The community accepted Sir Murray's viewpoint as definitive. Even the Blair-Kerr reports did not explore the question of magnitude. It is possible, then, that a mere crime-reporting wave might have misled the public, or that the media might have inspired the anti-corruption crusade. It seems unquestionable, though, that over the years corrupt practices had increased in volume— why should they have diminished?—for population growth had been steady, with some marked jumps. The total population went up from 3.1 to 3.9 million between 1961 and 1971, and to over 4 million in 1973.

The question of scale is more mysterious. Commenting on the situation in the early 1950s, Sir Alexander Grantham wrote: 'Corruption was as great a problem as ever', and went on to state that 'most corruption is petty'. The point has been made several times that corruption is likely to expand with rapid economic growth and, paradoxically, with recession: prosperity and depression, boom and slump, appear conspicuously to affect its volume and/or scale. The best we can say is that corruption was endemic in the immediate post-war period (nurtured by shortages, government regulations, and economic chaos) and in the three years preceding the Korean War, an era of reconstruction, consolidation, and rebuilding. Much corruption was simply traditional squeeze; a lot was routine police extortion. One suspects (as Blair-Kerr did) that it was rife within the PWD, for control over that large organization had never been sufficiently stringent.

Chinese contractors were notoriously venal, masters of graft, as we know from various commissions of inquiry going back to the turn of the century. But given the nature of their work, they had at times to engage in bribery to survive in a cut-throat business environment.

What we can plausibly argue is that many had come to believe that the corrupt, like a contagion, had infiltrated all sectors of society and the economy. A gloomy few deponed that there was a pandemic of corruption. History—it is a commonplace—reshapes social perceptions: in Hong Kong they had altered to a marked extent by the 1970s. But we still cannot decisively conclude that there was *more* corruption. Like Monsieur Jourdain, surprised to find he had been speaking prose all his life, some citizens, one feels, had discovered what had always been true, that Hong Kong was almost as corrupt as the Philippines.

The police pose special problems, however. They have always been stereotyped, unfairly for many officers, as corrupt or peccant, certainly by the man in the street. But we really do not know how far up the hierarchy corruption reached. Did it ever lap the tip of the pyramid? Did it go far, far beyond Godber, the man who established an official tidemark, a scum line? Information in the mid-1970s, emanating from trials of corruption-syndicate members, suggests that police graft had increased in both volume and scale after 1967, for Maoists had succeeded for a time in turning Hong Kong into a lawless zone, like the American Badlands of the past, with opportunists and villains profiting from relaxed levels of law enforce-

CHAPTER EIGHT

ment. The mushrooming of vice establishments was one sign of reduced policing. Drug traffickers also led less risky lives; and gamblers found a greater range of illegal outlets for their obsession.

From 1967 to around 1974 there was probably a sharp increase in police corruption, typified by the figures of Godber and Hunt among expatriate, and Lui Lok among Chinese, police officers. But how did the rate of police corruption compare in these years with rates for government departments that also had close relations with the public, such as Housing, Immigration, Commerce and Industry, and Urban Services? In these organizations corruption had long been institutionalized, and routinized at the base. The point is important, though unanswerable, because policemen were stigmatized at the Commission's birth as the principal plague-carriers. There is no reason to believe they were any more dishonest, proportionately, than workers in other government departments. The majority of police, above all the Chinese contingent, came from the same social milieux, the same social class or income groups, as the bulk of the civil service: they were not recruited from a pariah group, from the lower depths of society.

Too often, then, police are depicted in bleak monochrome, in black-and-white terms, when in fact they differ not at all from most of the population. It is worth reiterating that police corruption is but a small segment of a far wider problem, that of crime and white-collar crime in general, and that Hong Kong tolerated corruption for decades, as Chapters 2 and 3 seek to establish. No doubt at times policemen are also victims of slow horses and fast women and redeem themselves by a little graft. Graham Greene's *The Heart of the Matter* (1948), a novel which centres on the self-destruction of Henry Scobie, deputy commissioner of police in a wartime West African colony, develops another theme: that of a man who initially breaks the law from the most human of motives, friendship and compassion. There is a scale of moral culpability, of which judges take cognizance in sentencing; but not all police officers convicted of offences against the Prevention of Bribery Ordinance should be placed automatically at the extreme negative pole. Police should not always be surveyed *en masse*.

It was argued in Chapter 4 that the community's reaction to police corruption did provide a powerful impetus toward the creation of the ICAC, but that this was contributory rather than fundamental. The Commission, a department independent of the civil service by the terms of its charter, was not established principally to eradicate police graft (a Utopian task). This was a problem which could be handled, in theory, by the police force itself, as is the British custom. What is obvious, one hopes, is that in 1973–4 police corruption was in the foreground, clearly visible. It had become a matter of public debate. The searchlight of obloquy, of moral indignation, played largely on it, as on a huge dirigible illuminated by glare, by a probing light that left other important targets in shadow. Hong Kong was then honeycombed with corruption, indisputably so at the lower levels, and much of this internal rot went unnoticed. The business community was mostly immune from inspection, as it still is, to some degree, today. The white-collar classes benefited from a double standard: their delinquencies were treated with greater leniency. The point, a straightforward one, suggests that other factors should be sought to explain the extraordinary concentration on the issue of corruption as a *major* social problem. But, as under a magnifying glass, the police did provide in 1973 a fine focus for discontent.

Were citizens stimulated by a real change of heart, similar to religious conversion or mass hysteria, by spasms of doubt concerning the moral dimensions of their society? Such an elusive and fuzzy concept as an 'awakening conscience', so Victorian in flavour, cannot be measured, although it is true that historians do chart those social movements labelled moral panics, as well as revolutions in taste, sensibility, and morals. However, this thesis, one which assumes that an attitudinal shift happened in the late 1960s or early 1970s, is too vague to advance as a plausible explanation of the march of events. If such a change has occurred, how does one account for the high levels of crime in the succeeding period, for there has been no steady abatement in wrongdoing, as revealed in criminal statistics? The weakness of this thesis is, then, that it lacks a political framework: it is impressionistic.

The thesis proposed by the writer is that political factors were primary and decisive in the establishment of the ICAC and that the public's marked interest in corruption owed more to political considerations than excited interest in law and order. Administrators found the 1960s a difficult period; they were challenged from many sides; they were confronted by what was termed a 'generation gap' (much remarked upon in the *Report of the Commission of Inquiry into the Kowloon Disturbances 1966*), a problem that surfaced, with remarkable synchronization, in most industrial or industrializing countries at this time. Demands for improved social services or more social welfare were frequently heard, despite Sir John Cowperthwaite's dislike of overspending in this area. Another discovery was juvenile delinquency, regarded as a modern disease, the herpes of the time. This concern is well reflected in the 1965 *Report on Causes of Violence Committed by Young Persons*. The 1960s were thus a period in Hong Kong's history when social problems started to emerge, one after the other, to the stupefaction at times of government officials, whose normal response was to set up an advisory committee or working party to investigate them. In this decade Hong Kong at last entered the modern world and made great strides economically. But the stresses and strains of uneven economic and social development soon became evident. All these problems were compounded, moreover, by population increase.

The Chinese concept of the Mandate of Heaven, which developed historically into the well-known 'right of rebellion', is an important factor in the Confucian pattern of Chinese history. Professor J.K. Fairbank describes the later version in these words:

It emphasized the good conduct or virtue of the ruler as the ethical sanction for preserving his dynasty. Bad conduct on his part destroyed the sanction, Heaven withdrew its Mandate, and the people were justified in deposing the dynasty, if they could. Consequently any successful rebellion was justified and a new rule sanctioned, by the very fact of its success.

The Chinese, it follows, believed in government by moral prestige: a ruler was not expected to condone immoral (non-Confucian) behaviour among officials, whose members were mostly degree-holders and usually recruited from the gentry class. The Censorate, instituted under the Han, had also been set up to check abuses within the civil service and to monitor the behaviour of officials. There was thus a strong *moral* or *moralistic* element in Chinese notions of good administration, an element that has never taken so prominent a place in European ideas of good government, where a system of rational bureaucracy (to use Max Weber's typification) has been more emphasized.

The implications of this theme have been adumbrated in Chapter 3 and need little further gloss. What one may suggest is that in the early 1970s senior officials felt that their mandate to govern (in essence a moral claim) was now heavily under attack, and more so than at any time since the 1920s. Traditionalists, especially older Chinese, a group still influenced by Confucian tenets, also worried about the colonial government's performance, for it had allowed the wicked, the morally corrupt to flourish. Cynicism was spreading; disquiet too. In many Chinese eyes, the administrators' clocks had stopped in December 1941; they had not been rewound. A small but very vocal radical group—an odd amalgam of Maoists, Trotskyites, anarchists, and other 'trouble-makers', whose mouthpiece was the satirical *70s Bi-weekly* (published between 1970–3, in Chinese)—used the issue of corruption as a stick with which to beat the Establishment, following in the footsteps of others in the region antipathetic to right-wing, colonial, or neo-colonialist regimes. In brief, the legitimacy of the Hong Kong government was being questioned. There was a need, many then thought, to move away from a largely passive mode of governing to a system that would allow greater

CHAPTER EIGHT

control over the economy and society, so that administrators would be better placed to deal with acute social problems, such as crime and corruption.

If this analysis is correct, it has important consequences for the ICAC, because it suggests that the creation of that institution was largely political in intent (so, too, though to a lesser degree, was the Fight Violent Crime campaign launched in June 1973 to persuade the public to co-operate with the police and to report crime). The subjects chosen for special articles in the *Hong Kong Annual Report*, a government publication, are revelatory: in 1972 the key essay was 'A Better Tomorrow'; 'The Community: A Growing Awareness' the following year; and 'A Social Commitment' in 1974. These were signs of recuperated officialdom: the sleeper had awakened, not languid but full of pep. Sir Murray was attempting, by gingering up various government departments, to restore public confidence in the colonial administration, much shaken in previous years by its inability to control the quality of Hong Kong life and to penetrate all segments of society.

There are a number of organizations or agencies that monitor aspects of crime and deviance and are involved, in one way or another, in law-enforcement work. These include the police (to whom would be given primacy), Customs and Excise, Inland Revenue, and the Security Branch; and to a lesser degree, Immigration, the Narcotics Division, and the Legal Department. To these must now be added the ICAC, whose investigative arm, the Operations Department, in 1983 employed over 700 staff, an impressive figure. Together they provide an apparatus of control over the life and work of the community, buttressed by the law. Marxists, with their special perspective on society, would describe this as a mechanism of oppression and repression; a network of control designed by the State to impose its own pattern of social order. Conservatives would argue that deviance is a fact of life, part of the human condition, and must be regulated in the interests of all. In shorthand, deviance results in control; control in deviance. There is no need to arbitrate between these contrasting perspectives. They are both true. What is incontrovertible is that the ICAC is but *one* unit in this structure and cannot be analysed in isolation from it, for the parts are interconnected. This suggests, surely, that there are necessary limits on the ICAC's growth, for if it grew immoderately there would be repercussions throughout the system, and, consequently, disequilibrium. Thus the ICAC will never be able to eliminate corruption (a point touched upon in preceding chapters) but only, and only at auspicious times, to reduce it to levels acceptable to the community. The police, also, are rarely able seriously to reduce crime, despite at times considerable increases in manpower. Even saturation-policing of an area may only temporarily reduce crime. When the police depart, deviants return, like rabbits after a hunter has left.

If we question the power or ability of the ICAC to reduce corruption significantly (and this is a proposition that does not suggest the Commission should be discredited or disbanded), what follows? What follows, surely, is that no one has seriously believed, apart from the midwives of the new department, that the ICAC could remove corrupt practices from all areas of Hong Kong life, without changing the Colony's social framework. To attempt to do so would necessitate a vast and tight apparatus of control, as in Marxist states like East Germany, Albania, or North Vietnam; and it is an axiom, stated before, that control leads to deviance; not even a Communist government has succeeded in throttling all types of private enterprise, one deviant characteristic of which is corruption. The expense occasioned would be dismaying, in any case. The annual cost of the ICAC has risen from about HK$16 million in 1974–5 to nearly HK$132 million in 1984–5; and this cost to the community must be placed, in review, against other necessary government expenditure. Moreover, at some stage diminishing returns will start ineluctably to operate.

The ICAC was established, it has been argued, basically for political reasons; or, to put it another way, as a partial solu-

CHAPTER EIGHT

tion to a number of difficult problems that the government then faced in the early 1970s. Sir Murray, at that time, needed to show that he, and the administration he headed, was moving in the path of 'righteousness', a Confucian or Neo-Confucian concept that has obvious moral or moralistic popular reverberations; it was certainly a notion that could be apprehended by most traditionalist or educated Chinese, for whom democracy, and its associated demagogy, were foreign developments or imports. The idea of the good or virtuous ruler, on the other hand, is a key element in Chinese historiography. The Hong Kong civil service has always been populated, at its higher levels, by expatriates, a legacy from the days of colonialism and imperialism; and the legacy remains, like the debate over the use of the Chinese language, a delicate and sensitive issue. It was extremely important, it follows, for Sir Murray to convince the majority of the people he ruled that the government could deal effectively with social problems, most of which had surfaced in the 1960s, the period of Hong Kong's take-off into economic growth, from which there was no going back.

It is possible to survey the ICAC from various levels. One may focus upon it as a government department, or organization, contained within a larger bureaucratic structure; refocusing, one may examine it as a special type of law-enforcement agency or intelligence-gathering unit, of which one finds numerous examples in advanced industrial societies, such as the United States; and, narrowing the perspective, one may treat the ICAC principally as a counter-police organ, or watch-dog over the police force, with which it is linked dialectically. Each focus suggests different questions and problems. But what has been stressed in the text, above all, is the symbolic or emblematic character of the Commission, an institution now over ten years old, and in good health.

The ICAC typifies authority; it makes plain by its presence that corruption will no longer be tolerated to the degree it once was; and it maps out the moral boundaries of Hong Kong society, helped in this task by the law courts and other minatory institutions. No one can now truthfully assert that the government is unaware of, or indifferent to, graft, for the very existence of the ICAC must largely contradict any such assertion. Fancifully, the ICAC provides an extra eye, or revolving lens, for 'Big Brother', the *Leviathan* we call the State.

Even if the number of investigations initiated by the ICAC declines, compared with previous years, or the Operations Department is cut back, the ICAC would still remain a symbol for moral enterprise and government intention. It would continue to prescribe how one should behave in the market-place, the business world, the civil service, or in any occupation.

Compared with the police, the ICAC has a clear advantage in that it can concentrate on a relatively narrow spectrum of criminal activity, since the investigations it undertakes relate almost entirely to a limited number of criminal offences, those defined in three special Hong Kong laws—the Prevention of Bribery Ordinance (Cap. 201), the Corrupt and Illegal Practices Ordinance (Cap. 288), and the ICAC Ordinance (Cap. 204). The police, on the other hand, traditional specialists in all forms of crime and deviance, have a far wider role: they are invested with omnicompetent functions and deal with almost the whole spectrum of law-breaking, from petty to serious crime, including sexual offences. Thus, so to speak, one segment of the chain of crime and deviance in Hong Kong has been handed over to the Commission for special attention. The restricted focus given the ICAC has permitted that organization to build up spectacular expertise in a narrow field, and has allowed it to maintain a high success rate in major investigations, which are often of peculiar complexity. But crime, even bribery and corruption cases, should not be viewed too restrictedly; for much crime and corruption may fall under the rubric of white-collar crime, a category of growing importance to criminologists, who now distinguish between the former and conventional crime, such as robbery or burglary.

It was the distinguished American criminologist, E.H. Sutherland, who popularized the term in 1939 in a presiden-

CHAPTER EIGHT

tial address to the American Sociological Society. He was not referring to the delinquencies of the well-to-do as such, but to the problem of crime in modern business practice, to what is sometimes called corporate crime. Briefly, Sutherland pointed out that criminal statistics summarize the criminality of the lower classes but mostly exclude that of the upper, which remains largely hidden. White-collar crime manifests itself, he argued, primarily in breaches of trust and in misrepresentation; in tax evasion, monopolistic practices, the rigging of markets, the misuse of insider knowledge, and the bribery of public officials to secure desirable contracts or to obtain particular benefits. The cynical Al Capone dubbed these common practices the 'legitimate rackets'.

Sutherland's formulation has given rise, ever since 1939, to much controversy and a spate of articles and books. Paul Tappan, for example, a lawyer sociologist, saw the concept of white-collar crime, then a relative novelty, as a term of propaganda and as political in extension, because by implication it tends to discredit those in positions of power or authority. If we undermine confidence in the pillars of society, then we may help to fan waves of cynicism or restiveness across the population. There is no need to elaborate on this spiky debate but simply to suggest that the notion of a particular category of crime has relevance for the ICAC's work. Most corruption— the point has been made repeatedly—is low-level extortion, and much is petty; but at higher or grander levels high-ranking officials or entrepreneurs may be involved, such as company promoters, financiers, industrialists, developers, property tycoons, and members of the professional classes, people who are normally respected for their abilities, acumen, education, wealth or position. They are the successful ones: they are exemplars of Hong Kong's work ethic. At this level, then, it is difficult, analytically, to separate corruption offences from business malpractice in general, for the two are interrelated.

There is no obvious cut-off point between certain offences investigated by the ICAC and the circumambient or overlapping area of white-collar crime. Businessmen seeking a profit

211

are apt on occasion to infringe the law; but recourse to corruption is only one device that may be chosen from a repertoire of illegal stratagems, as Sutherland affirmed. It follows that you cannot make a heavy impact upon corruption in the private sector without attempting also to moralize commercial life and to elevate business ethics. No one would suggest that this is other than an uphill and long-term task; but the professions have mostly succeeded in establishing codes of practice and in disciplining their members; the norms by which they should be governed are now quite explicit, although often contravened, as with fee-splitting among doctors. All governments must involve themselves, to some degree, in the reduction of moral anarchy, which flourishes when controls weaken. Today, in those countries where private enterprise is institutionalized, chambers of commerce or similar bodies seek to make their members adhere to higher standards of conduct and conform to more socially acceptable economic practices. Generally speaking, the public sector in Hong Kong has been better regulated than the private (one may cite the general order relating to the acceptance of gifts by government servants); but the law, with its normative function in social life, has lagged behind, as it usually does, in protecting the citizen from dishonest business concerns such as travel agencies, and finance, investment, and deposit-taking companies.

A number of organizations or bodies were created in the 1970s as watch-dogs for the community, of which the ICAC is probably the best-known. They exemplify, once again, the interchange between processes of deviance and control. The Securities Commission, mooted in 1973, now monitors certain financial transactions and investigates cases of insider-trading in securities. The Consumer Council, established in 1974, is a statutory body whose task is to promote the interests of consumers and to protect buyers of retail goods or services. The Director of Audit, who is not a civil servant and has complete autonomy, provides each year a critique of selected elements of government spending (usually overspending) and may pinpoint by his animadversions examples of dishonesty, corruption, negligence, or sheer ineptitude, but it is not his job to initiate investigations. The police have their own Commercial Crimes Bureau, which has been upgraded in recent years. This unit deals with various types of fraud, an offence defined as obtaining property by deception (however, the Theft Ordinance, 1970, has tended to narrow the legal distinction between fraud and theft). There are other monitoring, investigatory, or protective organizations, and there certainly will be more as economic enterprise expands, becomes more complex, intricate, and sophisticated, and larger in scale. The need to protect a vulnerable public, to defend consumers and investors, will grow correspondingly.

White-collar crime has been called—satirically one supposes—'respectable crime', for its perpetrators do not look like stereotypical villains or desperadoes but behave and dress like the generality of the business or commercial classes. But it is in this area—the private sector—that the ICAC is likely in the future to find the majority of its cases, for it has largely eliminated syndicated corruption (no come-back has been reported), eradicated to a degree illegal commissions, and closed numerous loopholes for corruption in government departments, although not too successfully with Lands and Works (formerly the PWD). Yet it is doubtful whether it has made any significant dent in the world of big business, or affected the Freemasonry of the business élite.

Hong Kong is not in the throes of a terminal sickness but the territory's future is uncertain and few people believe in the bland words of diplomats and politicians. Hong Kong's future is cloudy. The nervous worry that the economy will decline into chronic invalidism, but no one can predict what will happen after 1997, when sovereignty reverts to China. The atmosphere generated by doubt, by the sense of an end to continuity and a known way of life, is conducive to higher levels of crime and corruption. The ICAC is not likely to run out of clients.

One must conclude that crime in general, and corruption in particular, will probably steadily increase as Hong Kong moves towards 1997—a doomsday date for many middle- and upper-class Chinese—even if there are regular cyclical movements in the property market (the historical experience) or in industry. The desire to get rich quickly, by legal or illegal means, since wealth acquired in any way provides insurance against the future, will surely grow more intense: money must act to facilitate emigration to a favoured land, such as Australia, Canada, or the United States, or to allow a person to send his children overseas for education or as pathfinders. What this suggests is that the private sector is likely to provide the ICAC with more cases than at present. If the Commission is forced to invest a larger part of its resources in the investigation of dishonest members of the business world, it will have got its priorities right at last, and no doubt satisfy the moralist, though not necessarily an economist. The point has been made before that you cannot bracket off police corruption or graft in any government department or public body from the larger public sector; any separation is only conceptual. The volume and scale of corruption in a country is mainly determined by its general tone or standards and by the attitudes or values of its citizens. And it is a sociological commonplace that social order is maintained mostly by informal controls stemming from public opinion, that great regulator of behaviour and conduct. Before the late 1960s, few in high or in low places bothered much about white-collar crime, of which corruption is an insidious component: the end justified the means in the sphere of business enterprise, an axiom that both hawker and tycoon would subscribe to even now.

The point was made several times in previous chapters that Sir Murray MacLehose sought to cleanse Hong Kong and to moralize—that seems the most appropriate word—civic life, and to transform Hong Kong from a relatively atomized society into a real community, defined by sociologists as a group of people with common expectations, shared values, and agreed-upon ways of doing things. The various campaigns he either promoted or supported were taken as evidence of this aim, and of his reformer's zeal and liberal-socialist ideals, transferred and adapted to a colonial setting. At first his impact was great, above all on the Chinese population. But did he succeed in changing the face of Hong Kong, so lined with sin? One of the normal consequences of 'revivalism' is that enthusiasm exhausts itself, and others; and those converted to a new way of life are prone in time to lapse. A number of opposition or countervailing forces have been described, such as the 1997 political issue, but also the recession, first strongly experienced in late 1981 and early 1982 when the property market started to collapse. It is likely, then, that Sir Murray's impact has weakened because the pattern of political, social, and economic forces has shifted position since 1974. The caravan, as it were, has moved on and is now traversing more dangerous terrain, bandit country. This implies, it has been argued, that private-sector corruption is likely to grow in magnitude and that a larger proportion of those who wish to survive current events will break the law; normal social controls over behaviour are likely to lessen. Economists define an entrepreneur as one who assumes the risks of a business or enterprise; corrupt practices, need one say, are essays in risk-taking. One may liken the present situation to Germany in the 1920s when inflation, the fall in the value of the mark, and political uncertainty caused a great rise in commercial crime.

Each year the Commissioner of the ICAC publishes an annual report, as do heads of other government departments. The first ICAC annual report appeared of course in 1975. The format has changed little; there are always the sections on the work of the Operations, Corruption Prevention, and Community Relations Departments. Each commissioner has reported 'trends', at times, and usually warns readers of the direction or form corruption is taking. This is sometimes misleading. A trend is simply a tendency; but trends, which are not social laws, are reversible—they may change abruptly from year to year. An historical trend, such as a rise in real wages, will take time to manifest itself; it is revealed only in the long term. Fortuitous circumstances, the influence of external factors, policy decisions, and operational changes may all affect the flow, or types, of cases encountered from year to year. In this way, the ICAC creates its own statistics, as do the police. So one should be extremely careful in postulating trends and in predicting future tendencies. Nevertheless, it is plausible to suggest higher levels of corruption in the immediate future, although the ICAC must influence the magnitude of any increase. We may compare the Commission to a breaking mechanism that retards but cannot totally stop a piece of moving machinery. It is a regulator, like all law-enforcement agencies. We should not expect the Commission to be as efficient as a vacuum cleaner, and sweep up all of Hong Kong's filth.

It is now time to present the Commission's scoring-card for the past ten years. Since 15 February 1974 the Operations Department has brought more than 3,000 prosecutions, with a successful prosecution rate of 70 per cent; the Prevention Department, a less well-known unit, has completed 804 studies relating to government departments and public bodies; and the Community Relations Department has inspired around 74,000 public functions and organized about 32,000 special activities. The Commission has disseminated the message, and other slogans, that corruption does not pay to almost all members of the community and its propaganda is presented, suitably packaged by skilled media men, in newspapers and on TV. This great publicity campaign must have made an impact, although constant iteration of various themes might tend to lessen their potency over the years, for that is what citizens of socialist countries sometimes report of their own state propaganda, just as the expounding of the Decalogue on Sundays has sent many a schoolboy to untroubled sleep. But we cannot measure the effect of such repeated messages on the unconscious, for information can be conveyed even to a sleeper, as psychologists confirm. Nevertheless, most people must be aware of the social problem of corruption and know that it is prohibited and that penalties are severe.

A large number of complaints were registered in the first two years of the Commission's life—a 'floodgate' effect as people rushed to report misdeeds—and for comparative purposes the Commission has regarded these years as abnormal. But since 1976 there has been an upward reporting trend, only interrupted temporarily by reaction to the 1977 partial amnesty. More importantly, there has been a steady increase in the number of corruption reports by persons who identify themselves, and hence a fall in anonymous reports. The former have risen from thirty-four to sixty-three per cent of the total. This may be taken as a sign of public confidence in the Commission's work and of knowledge that it treats all complaints with discretion and does not leak the names of those who supply information. It is reasonable to assume that the public respects the Commission, some indication of which is the fact that people constantly complain to the Commission, as if to an ombudsman, about matters unconnected with bribery and corruption.

In March 1984, twenty-eight former Hong Kong police officers then overseas were wanted by the ICAC on warrant and sixteen were wanted without warrant. Of the latter, three were classified as deserters by the force. The Godber saga had not ended: like soap opera, it seems to go on for ever. Some $300,000 in a Hong Kong account has been seized by the Inland Revenue Department but efforts are still being made to possess Godber's house at Rye, occupied by tenants. It appears that his exact whereabouts is not known to the Commission, although rumour has it that he still lives in Spain, the haven of numerous crooks (it was a favourite haunt of the London bank robbers referred to), of fraudsmen, tax-dodgers, runaway spouses, and gypsy types. Ernest Hunt, also a denizen of this lotus-land, has not published his revelations. But the Taiwan-based contingent of absconding Hong Kong police officers were disturbed, reports claimed, by the Nationalist government's decision to deport a number of wanted criminals. On 11 April 1984 five men were returned and were arrested at Kai Tak Airport; others soon after. 'Where to go?' must be in the minds of certain former Hong Kong policemen now resident in Taiwan. Bolt-hole after bolt-hole has been blocked over the years.

There are elements of the ICAC's work usually not keynoted. The setting up of that organization, in the form of an independent civil service department responsible solely to the Governor, was a notable experiment, a remarkable innovation. In a society not directed by dogma or governed by doctrinaire obsessions, social experiments are of especial importance, and of great value to a democratic society that wishes to advance. The ICAC is, in essence, an example of a 'piecemeal experiment', as Sir Karl Popper would call it. We learn from doing, and we learn from our mistakes. Anticorruption organizations, those separated from a police force, are to be found in a number of countries. Singapore's Corrupt Practices Investigation Bureau dates from 1952; the Malaysian Anti-Corruption Agency from 1967. There are similar bodies in Sri Lanka and Tanzania, but not in Britain and the white Commonwealth countries, although Australia has evinced some interest in the matter. But the leading agency today—the pace-maker in this highly specialized field—is Hong Kong's ICAC, the largest, most efficient, and most successful of them all. This is a result of the quality of its leadership over the years, the type of person it has been able to select, recruit, train, and keep, or even employ temporarily, and the strong support provided by the government. An organization—it is a trite comment—is only as good as its personnel. From the start the ICAC was designed as an élite formation—its members are better paid than those occupying roughly equivalent positions in the civil service. It has maintained that reputation for a decade. It may be compared with the American FBI, whose reputation was made in the 1930s by its G-men (government men) and by its director, Edgar Hoover; but unlike the FBI, the ICAC has not been accused of political bias.

Criticism has largely centred on the ICAC's draconian powers, those granted by the Independent Commission Against Corruption Ordinance, 1974, and succeeding amendments. The Commission may seize under a magistrate's order a suspect's passport, examine his bank accounts and safe-deposit boxes, and hold and inspect all business and private documents. Furthermore, a suspect may be required to provide statutory declarations or statements in writing enumerating his properties, expenditures and liabilities, or any money or properties transferred from Hong Kong, by him or on his behalf. He may not dispose of his assets during an investigation, even if they are held in the name of a third party. Thus a suspect's biography can be scrutinized in fine detail. To an outsider, this process appears formidably inquisitorial and reminiscent of French criminal law procedure or the legal habits of Communist countries.

Investigating officers also have full powers of arrest without warrant; and those arrested may be detained in the offices—cells—of the Commission for up to a maximum period of forty-eight hours for the purpose of further inquiries. The Commission in effect operates its own lock-up, employs trained guards, and organizes a custodial regime. To be confronted across a table by the bitter or brutal, quizzing or sarcastic eyes of a trained investigating officer is not as comforting as a visit to one's psychiatrist or confessor; and to be taken from one's home, held incommunicado, and implacably interrogated is not a happy experience.

In 1974 the government thought it essential for the Commission to be given wide and stringent powers; it was accepted that mild measures would not discourage the corrupt. There is little evidence that the Commission's agents have abused these powers to any large degree, although over-enthusiastic officers have infringed the letter and spirit of the law at times. The law courts do act as watch-dogs for the community; and the Commissioner does take note of criticism, for he is involved in delicate public relations work, promoting the anti-corruption cause. The situation is not an ideal one, for stigma may be attached to anyone, however innocent, questioned by the Commission; but this must not be exaggerated. It is often the guilty who are most outraged, even when they escape their just desserts. This does not suggest that the end justifies the means, but that the ICAC has developed into a formidable instrument for righting wrongs, by unmasking the corrupt; and that this particular outcome does not dismay the public.

Some attempts have been made to estimate the economic cost of corruption. Leo Goodstadt, for example, has argued that 'corruption in Hong Kong is essentially a form of taxation or licence fee paid to some person in authority for immunity from the law's intervention'. He computed that, in 1973, the figure for corruption was around five per cent of net profits assessed for tax (or one-third of the standard tax rate), which amounted to US$68.83 million. It is however the public who finally absorb these costs, for they are passed on to consumers, just as a rise in the international price of oil is likely to force up the cost of living for all. But the social costs are probably far more important and severe, because if high levels of corruption are left unchecked, cynicism, opportunism, and general dishonesty are likely to amplify: taking short cuts becomes a habit. Again a government's legitimacy, its mandate, may be challenged. This, it has been argued, was what happened in Hong Kong in the late 1960s and early 1970s. Stable political institutions do not permit rampant corruption. Revolutionaries of all types, and dissenters from both the Left and the Right, have used accusations of corrupt officialdom and of a corrupt society to dismantle established regimes: one may cite numerous examples from Asia's post-war history to underline this point.

Finally, corruption cannot be brought down to an acceptable level unless the government widens the ambit of its control over business operations and pays more attention to white-collar crime and to phantom capitalists, to those almost anonymous entrepreneurs who promote vast enterprises or take-overs and succeed too often in fleecing the public. There is a marked difference between 'capitalism' and 'unbridled capitalism'. The ICAC's task would be greatly helped if this distinction was more insisted upon by those who govern. In the end, it is mostly a matter of standards of conduct in public life, a question explored in Alan Doig's *Corruption and Misconduct* (1984), where the author shows that Britain's Poulson

CHAPTER EIGHT

affair was merely the tip of an iceberg and that malpractice is greater than most people assume. There is no reason to suppose that the United Kingdom and Hong Kong vary in this respect. The ICAC has not eradicated bribery and corruption; but it is safe to state that without the Commission they would be at higher levels. This is a negative summing-up. Much will depend upon whether the Hong Kong government becomes a more adroit ringmaster.

APPENDIX I

Duties of the Commissioner

THE duties of the Commissioner, as described in Section 12 of the Independent Commission Against Corruption Ordinance, are as follows:

It shall be the duty of the Commissioner, on behalf of the Governor, to

(a) receive and consider complaints alleging corrupt practices and investigate such of those complaints as he considers practicable;

(b) investigate any alleged or suspected offences under this Ordinance, the Prevention of Bribery Ordinance or the Corrupt and Illegal Practices Ordinance and any alleged or suspected conspiracy to commit an offence under the Prevention of Bribery Ordinance and any alleged or suspected offence of blackmail committed by a Crown servant by or through the misuse of office;

(c) investigate any conduct of a Crown servant which, in the opinion of the Commissioner, is connected with or conducive to corrupt practices and to report thereon to the Governor;

(d) examine the practices and procedures of government departments and public bodies, in order to facilitate the discovery of corrupt practices and to secure the revision of methods of work or procedures which, in the opinion of the Commissioner, may be conducive to corrupt practices;

(e) instruct, advise and assist any person, on the latter's request, on ways in which corrupt practices may be eliminated by such person;

(f) advise heads of government departments or of public bodies of changes in practices or procedures compatible with the effective discharge of the duties of such departments or public bodies which the Commissioner thinks necessary to reduce the likelihood of the occurrence of corrupt practices;

(g) educate the public against the evils of corruption; and

(h) enlist and foster public support in combatting corruption.

APPENDIX II

Commissioners of Police (1959–84)

Henry Heath, April 1959–December 1966
Edward Tyrer, December 1966–July 1967
Edward Eates, July 1967–April 1969
Charles Sutcliffe, April 1969–January 1974
Brian Slevin, January 1974–March 1979
Roy Henry, March 1979–

Commissioners of the ICAC

Jack Cater, February 1974–July 1978
Sir Donald Luddington, July 1978–October 1980
Peter Williams, October 1980–

APPENDIX III

The Staffing Position of the ICAC

	1974	1975	1976	1977	1978	1979	1980	1981	1982
Establishment	682	905	940	965	1,121	1,088	1,099	1,138	1,172
Strength	369	652	763	903	957	925	974	1,005	1,087
Administration	35	48	46	56	62	86	89	95	109
Operations	255	429	486	569	580	568	600	615	668
Prevention	51	64	81	77	80	59	60	60	59
Community Relations	28	111	150	201	235	212	225	235	251

Source: Annual Reports of the ICAC.

APPENDIX IV

Police Resignations and Dismissals

	Commissioned Officers		Non-commissioned Officers	
Year	Resignations	Dismissals	Resignations	Dismissals
1970–1	34	0	475	34
1971–2	34	1	698	75
1972–3	18	0	461	81
1973–4	28	3	455	93
1974–5	34	6	170	61
1976	54	9	285	65
1977	53	8	350	61
1978	38	5	350	60
1979	26	2	450	58
1980	25	2	406	88
1981	27	4	475	91
1982	21	3	398	63

Source: Annual Reports of the Commissioner of Police.

APPENDIX V

Targets of Corruption Reports

Year	Police	%	Other Government Departments	%	Public*	%	Total
1974	1,443	45	1,308	41	438	14	3,189
1975	1,492	47	1,177	37	510	16	3,179
1976	1,119	46	767	32	547	22	2,433
1977	729	43	547	32	424	25	1,700
1978	487	39	404	33	343	28	1,234
1979	635	38	551	33	479	29	1,665
1980	523	29	626	37	613	34	1,762
1981	735	33	798	33	787	34	2,320
1982	681	26	731	35	917	39	2,329

Note: *The private sector and public bodies listed in the schedule to the Prevention of Bribery Ordinance, 1970.

Source: Annual Reports of the ICAC.

APPENDIX VI

Complaints Received Relating to Certain Government Departments

	1974	1975	1976	1977	1978	1979	1980	1981	1982
Fire Services	51	49	28	34	21	19	15	31	25
Housing	226	209	136	66	44	64	104	190	164
Immigration	98	70	58	35	28	56	37	69	39
Medical and Health	53	73	44	35	15	8	15	21	33
NTA	72	79	64	40	38	59	62	84	73
Prisons	98	66	33	19	20	26	36	49	23
Public Works	96	169	85	74	59	91	72	89	92
Royal Hong Kong Police Force	1,443	1,492	1,119	729	487	635	523	735	681
Transport	48	26	24	11	18	35	31	31	27
Urban Services	188	207	135	96	65	79	148	123	142
Private sector	410	393	471	378	301	398	534	695	828
Public bodies	28	117	76	46	42	81	79	92	89

Note: In 1982 the Prisons Department was renamed Correctional Services, the NTA (New Territories Administration) became the City & New Territories Administration, and the Public Works Department is now called Lands and Works.

Source: Annual Reports of the ICAC.

227

APPENDIX VII

The Number of Reported Unnatural Offences, 1971–82*

Year	No. of Cases Reported	No. of Persons Prosecuted
1971	7	3
1972	2	1
1973	14	7
1974	21	13
1975	17	13
1976	40	35
1977	27	14
1978	44	40
1979	52	42
1980	80	70
1981	63	54
1982	31	18

Note: *These figures refer mostly to homosexual offences; but it should be noted that the totals include a vague category termed 'Other Miscellaneous': two in 1979, one in 1980, and nine in 1981. There were no reported cases of bestiality.

Source: The Royal Hong Kong Police Force.

APPENDIX VIII

Expatriates Serving in the ICAC's Operations Department

Year	Chinese Strength	Expatriate Strength	On Secondment from United Kingdom Forces	Retired from United Kingdom Forces
1974	*	*	*	*
1975	*	*	*	*
1976	*	*	*	*
1977	449	120	52	27
1978	460	106	42	27
1979	472	96	39	18
1980	422	87	44	17
1981	440	83	42	17
1982	464	98	54	21

Note: *The ICAC discounted figures for 1974–6 because of the 'floodgate' effect.

Source: Annual Reports of the ICAC.

APPENDIX IX

The Strength in the Two Major Grades without a 100 per cent Localization Policy 1979/80–1983/4

Police Inspectors and Above

Year (as at 1 April)	Local Officers	Overseas Officers	Total	Local Officers as a % of Total
1979	989	891	1,880	52.6
1980	1,082	875	1,957	55.3
1981	1,183	845	2,028	58.3
1982	1,283	877	2,160	59.4
1983	1,363	919	2,282	59.7

Administrative Service

Year (as at 1 April)	Local Officers	Overseas Officers	Total	Local Officers as a % of Total
1979	103	124	227	45.4
1980	132	135	267	49.4
1981	156	150	306	51.0
1982	170	159	329	51.7
1983	199	176	375	53.1

Source: Civil Service Personnel Statistics, 1983.

APPENDIX X

The Annual Cost of the ICAC

Year	HK$
1974–5	16,108,152
1975–6	24,150,596
1976–7	34,026,748
1977–8	44,107,010
1978–9	49,168,184
1979–80	54,319,053
1980–1	74,942,672
1981–2	89,945,866
1982–3	108,935,747

Source: An Introduction to the Independent Commission Against Corruption (Hong Kong, ICAC, 1983).

BIBLIOGRAPHY

Books and Articles

Abueva, José Veloso, 'The contribution of nepotism, spoils and graft to political development', *East-West Center Review*, Vol. 3, 1966, pp. 45–54.

Allason, Rupert, *The Branch, History of the Metropolitan Police Special Branch, 1883–1983* (London, Secker & Warburg, 1983).

Allen, Frederick Lewis, *Only Yesterday: An Informal History of the Nineteen-Twenties* (New York, Harper and Brothers, 1931).

Ascoli, David, *The Queen's Peace: The Origins and Development of the Metropolitan Police, 1829–1970* (London, Hamish Hamilton, 1979).

Astor, Gerald, *The New York Cops, An Informal History* (New York, Scribners, 1971).

Aylmer, G.E., *The King's Servants: The Civil Service of Charles I, 1625–1642* (London, Routledge & Kegan Paul, 1961).

Ball, J., Chester, L., and Perrott, R., *Cops and Robbers: An Investigation into Armed Bank Robbery* (London, André Deutsch, 1978).

Banton, Michael, *The Policeman in the Community* (London, Tavistock Publications, 1964).

Barber, Noel, *The Fall of Shanghai* (New York, Coward, McCann & Geoghegan, 1979).

Bayley, David H., 'The effects of corruption in a developing nation', *Western Political Quarterly*, Vol. 19, 1966, pp. 719–32.

Becker, Howard J., *Outsiders: Studies in the Sociology of Deviance* (New York, The Free Press, 1963).

Beigel, Herbert, and Beigel, Allan, *Beneath the Badge: A Story of Police Corruption* (New York, Harper and Row, 1977).

BIBLIOGRAPHY

Bent, Alan Edward, *The Politics of Law Enforcement* (Lexington, Mass., D.C. Heath, 1974).

Borniche, Roger, *Flic Story* (Paris, Fayard, 1973).

Brown, Michael K., *Working the Street: Police Discretion and the Dilemmas of Reform* (New York, Russell Sage Foundation, 1981).

Browne, Douglas G., *The Rise of Scotland Yard: A History of the Metropolitan Police* (London, Harrap, 1956).

Burnham, David, *The Role of the Media in Controlling Corruption* (New York, John Jay Press, 1976).

Cameron, Nigel, *Hong Kong: The Cultured Pearl* (Hong Kong, Oxford University Press, 1978).

Cantlie, James, *Hong Kong* (London, Kegan Paul, 1899).

Carlyle, Thomas, 'Latter-Day Pamphlets', in *Collected Works* (London, Chapman & Hall, 1857), Vol. 13.

Chambliss, William J., *On The Take: From Petty Crooks to Presidents* (Bloomington, Indiana University Press, 1978).

Chang Chung-li, *The Chinese Gentry: Studies on Their Role in Nineteenth-Century Chinese Society* (Seattle, Wash., University of Washington Press, 1955).

———— *Income of the Chinese Gentry* (Seattle, Wash., University of Washington Press, 1962).

Cheung Tak-sing and Lau Chong Chor, 'A Profile of Syndicate Corruption in the Police Force', in Rance Lee (ed.), *Corruption and Its Control in Hong Kong* (Hong Kong, The Chinese University Press, 1981).

Ch'ü T'ung-tsu, *Local Government in China under the Ch'ing* (Cambridge, Mass., Harvard University Press, 1962).

Cooper, John, *Colony in Conflict: The Hong Kong Disturbances, May 1967–January 1968* (Hong Kong, Swindon Book Company, 1970).

Cox, B., Shirley, J., and Short, M., *The Fall of Scotland Yard* (Harmondsworth, Middlesex, Penguin Books, 1977).

Cressey, Donald R., *Criminal Organization: Its Elementary Forms* (London, Heinemann, 1972).

Crisswell, Colin, and Watson, Mike, *The Royal Hong Kong Police, 1841–1945* (Hong Kong, Macmillan, 1982).

Critchley, T.A., *A History of Police in England and Wales* (Montclair, NJ, Patterson-Smith, 1972, second edition).

Cullen, Tom, *Maundy Gregory: Purveyor of Honours* (London, The Bodley Head, 1974).

Curvin, Robert, and Porter, Bruce, *Blackout Looting! New York City, July 13, 1977* (New York, Gardner Press, 1979).

Davenport, Andrew, 'Hong Kong: a scandal unfolds', *Far Eastern Economic Review*, 18 April 1975.

Davies, Derek, 'Inherent dangers', *Far Eastern Economic Review*, 29 October 1973.

Davies, Derek, and Goodstadt, Leo, 'The Fixers', *Far Eastern Economic Review*, 12 November 1973.

_____ 'Graft: almost a way of life', *Far Eastern Economic Review*, 6 September 1974.

_____ 'Crawling out of the woodwork', *Far Eastern Economic Review*, 7 March 1975.

Dilnot, George, *The Trial of the Detectives* (London, Geoffrey Bles, 1928).

Doig, Alan, *Corruption and Misconduct in Contemporary British Politics* (Harmondsworth, Middlesex, Penguin Books, 1984).

Doolittle, Revd Justus, *Social Life of the Chinese, A Daguerrotype of Daily Life in China* (London, Sampson, Low, Son and Marston, 1868).

Douglas, Jack D., and Johnson, John M. (eds.), *Official Deviance: Readings in Malfeasance, Misfeasance, and Other Forms of Corruption* (Philadelphia, J.B. Lippincott Company, 1977).

Downey, Bernard, 'The Godber affair', *Hong Kong Law Journal*, Vol. 5, 1975, pp. 129–33.

_____ 'Combatting corruption', *Hong Kong Law Journal*, Vol. 6, 1976, pp. 27–66.

Droge, Edward, *The Patrolman: A Cop's Story* (New York, New American Library, 1973).

Durkheim, Émile, *L'éducation morale* (Paris, Félix Alcan, 1925).

Eitel, E.J., *Europe in China* (Hong Kong, Kelly and Walsh, 1895; reprinted by Oxford University Press, 1983).

BIBLIOGRAPHY

Elliott, Elsie, *Crusade for Justice: An Autobiography* (Hong Kong, Heinemann Asia, 1981).

Endacott, G.B., *A History of Hong Kong* (London, Oxford University Press, 1958).

Endacott, G.B., and Birch, Alan, *Hong Kong Eclipse* (Hong Kong, Oxford University Press, 1978).

Fairbank, J.K., *The United States and China* (Cambridge, Mass., Harvard University Press, 1958).

Ferris, Paul, *The Detective: A Tale of Corruption in High Places*(London, Weidenfeld and Nicolson, 1976).

Fitzwalter, Raymond, and Taylor, David, *Web of Corruption: The Story of John Poulson and T. Dan Smith* (London, Granada, 1981).

Fogelson, Robert M., *Big-City Police* (Cambridge, Mass., Harvard University Press, 1977).

Gardiner, John A., *The Politics of Corruption: Organized Crime in an American City* (New York, Russell Sage, 1970).

Gittins, Jean, *Stanley: Behind Barbed Wire* (Hong Kong, Hong Kong University Press, 1982).

Goodstadt, Leo, 'Squeeze me please', *Far Eastern Economic Review*, 25 June 1970.

_____ 'Apart at the seams', *Far Eastern Economic Review*, 27 February 1971.

_____ 'Blighty's so nice in the summer', *Far Eastern Economic Review*, 18 June 1973.

_____ 'Rude awakening', *Far Eastern Economic Review*, 22 October 1973.

_____ 'Clearing the fence', *Far Eastern Economic Review*, 12 November 1973.

Goodstadt, Leo, and Li, Andrew, 'The Iron Rice Bowl—Hong Kong Law Regarding the Crown's Relationship with its Servants', *Hong Kong Law Journal*, Vol. 4, 1974, pp. 22–40.

Grantham, Sir Alexander, *Via Ports, from Hong Kong to Hong Kong* (Hong Kong, Hong Kong University Press, 1965).

Greene, Graham, *The Heart of the Matter* (London, William Heinemann, 1948).

Guilleminault, G., and Singer-Lecocq, Y., *La France des gogos: trois siècles de scandales financiers* (Paris, Fayard, 1975).

Haffner, Christopher, *The Craft in the East* (Hong Kong, District Grand Lodge of Hong Kong and the Far East, 1977).

Hall, Stuart, *et al.*, *Policing the Crisis: Mugging, the State, and Law and Order* (London, Macmillan, 1978).

Hao Yen-p'ing, *The Comprador in Nineteenth-Century China: Bridge Between East and West* (Cambridge, Mass., Harvard University Press, 1970).

Heidenheimer, Arnold J. (ed.), *Political Corruption: Readings in Comparative Analysis* (New York, Holt, Rinehart and Winston, 1970).

Henderson, L.J., *Pareto's General Sociology* (Cambridge, Mass., Harvard University Press, 1935).

Henry, Stuart, *The Hidden Economy: The Context and Control of Borderline Crime* (Oxford, Martin Robertson, 1978).

Hooley, Ernest Terah, *Hooley's Confessions* (London, Simpkin, Marshall, 1925).

Howe, Christopher (ed.), *Shanghai: Revolution and Development in an Asian City* (Cambridge, Cambridge University Press, 1981).

Howson, Gerald, *Thieftaker General* (London, Methuen, 1971).

Hsiao Kung-chuan, *Rural China, Imperial Control in the Nineteenth Century* (Seattle, Wash., University of Washington Press, 1960).

Hucker, Charles O., *The Censorial System of Ming China* (Stanford, Calif., Stanford University Press, 1966).

Huessler, Robert, *Yesterday's Rulers: The Making of the British Colonial Service* (Syracuse, NY, Syracuse University Press).

Inglis, Allan, 'Public Works Department', in *The Government and the People* (Hong Kong, Government Press, 1962).

Jeffries, Sir Charles, *The Colonial Police* (London, Max Parrish, 1952).

Juris, H.A., and Feuille, P., *Police Unionism* (Lexington, Mass., D.C. Heath, 1973).

BIBLIOGRAPHY

Key, V.O., Jr., *The Techniques of Political Graft in the United States* (Chicago, University of Chicago Libraries, 1936).

Kracke, E.A., Jr., *Civil Service in Early Sung China, 960-1067* (Cambridge, Mass., Harvard University Press, 1953).

Lee, Mary, 'Countryman and colonialists', *Far Eastern Economic Review*, 2 May 1980.

_____ 'Work suspended', *Far Eastern Economic Review*, 21 August 1981.

Lee, Rance P.L. (ed.), *Corruption and Its Control in Hong Kong: Situations Up to the Late Seventies* (Hong Kong, The Chinese University Press, 1981).

Leff, Nathaniel H., 'Economic development through bureaucratic corruption', *American Behavioral Scientist*, Vol. 8, 1964, pp. 8–14.

Leys, Colin, 'What is the problem about corruption?', *Journal of Modern African Studies*, Vol. 3, 1965, pp. 215–30.

Lipsky, Michael, *Street-Level Bureaucracy: Dilemmas of the Individual in Public Services* (New York, Russell Sage Foundation, 1980).

Litton, Henry, 'Editorial: Colonial Regulation 55: the fragile rice-bowl', *Hong Kong Law Journal*, Vol. 8, 1978, pp. 137–44.

Locard, Edmond, *Manuel de technique policière* (Paris, Payot, 1948, fourth edition).

Lorenz, Paul, *L'Affaire Stavisky* (Paris, Presses de la Cité, 1974).

Lyons, Richard L., 'The Boston Police Strike of 1919', *The New England Quarterly*, June 1947, pp. 147–68.

Mangold, T., 'Tigers and Flies', *The Listener*, 16 January 1975.

Mark, Sir Robert, *In the Office of Constable* (London, Collins, 1978).

Marsh, Robert M., 'Bureaucratic constraints on nepotism in the Ch'ing period', *Journal of Asian Studies*, Vol.19, 1960, pp. 117–33.

_____ 'The venality of provincial office in China and in comparative perspective', *Comparative Studies in Society and History*, Vol. 4, 1962, pp. 454–66.

Marsman, Jan Hendrik, *I Escaped from Hong Kong* (New York, Reynal and Hitchcock, 1942).

Mauss, Marcel, *The Gift: Forms and Functions of Exchange in Archaic Societies* (London, Cohen and West, 1954).

McKitrick, Eric L., 'The Study of Corruption', *Political Science Quarterly*, Vol. 72, 1957, pp. 502–14.

McMullan, M., 'A Theory of Corruption', *The Sociological Review*, Vol. 19, 1961, pp. 181–201.

Merton, Robert K., 'Social knowledge and public policy', in R.K. Merton, *Sociological Ambivalence and Other Essays* (New York, Free Press, 1976).

Milne, Edward, *No Shining Armour: The Story of One Man's Fight Against Corruption in Public Life* (London, John Calder, 1976).

Miners, Norman, *The Government and Politics of Hong Kong* (Hong Kong, Oxford University Press, 1982, third edition).

Miyazaki, Ichisada, *China's Examination Hell: The Civil Service Examinations of Imperial China* (New York, Weatherhill, 1976).

Mockridge, Norton, and Prall, Robert H., *The Big Fix* (New York, Henry Holt, 1954).

Muir, J. Ramsay, *Peers and Bureaucrats* (London, Constable, 1910).

Naunton, Sir Robert, *Fragmenta Regalia* (London, Edward Arber, 1870).

Norton-Kyshe, J.W., *The History of the Laws and Courts of Hong Kong* (Hong Kong, Noronha, 1898), 2 vols.

Nye, J.S., 'Corruption and political development: a cost benefit analysis', *American Political Science Review*, Vol. 61, 1967, pp. 417–27.

Pareto, Vilfredo, *The Mind and Society* (New York, Harcourt Brace, 1935), 4 vols.

Peters, Charles, and Branch, Tayler, *Blowing the Whistle* (New York, Praeger, 1972).

Popper, Karl R., *The Poverty of Historicism* (London, Routledge & Kegan Paul, 1957).

Pott, F.L. Hawks, *A Short History of Shanghai* (Shanghai, Kelly & Walsh, 1928).

Potter, Stephen, *Lifemanship* (London, Rupert Hart-Davis, 1950).

Pringle, Patrick, *Hue and Cry: The Birth of the British Police* (London, Museum Press, 1955).

Purcell, Sir Victor, *The Memoirs of a Malayan Official* (London, Cassell, 1965).

Rabushka, Alvin, *Value for Money: The Hong Kong Budgetary Process* (Stanford, Calif., Hoover Institution Press, 1976).

Rear, John, 'Godber', *Hong Kong Law Journal*, Vol. 3, 1973, pp. 249–53.

Reynolds, G., and Judge, A., *The Night the Police Went on Strike* (London, Weidenfeld and Nicolson, 1969).

Richardson, James F., *The New York Police: Colonial Times to 1901* (New York, Oxford University Press, 1970).

Rose-Ackerman, Susan, *Corruption: A Study in Political Economy* (New York, Academic Press, 1978).

Rubinstein, Jonathan, *City Police* (New York, Farrar, Straus and Giroux, 1973).

Sayer, G.B., *Hong Kong: Birth, Adolescence and Coming of Age* (London, Oxford University Press, 1937).

Schur, Edwin M., *Crimes Without Victims: Deviant Behaviour and Public Policy* (Englewood Cliffs, NJ, Prentice-Hall, 1965).

Scott, James C., *Comparative Political Corruption* (Englewood Cliffs, NJ, Prentice-Hall, 1971).

Shector, Leonard, and Phillips, William, *On the Pad* (New York, G.P. Putnam, 1974).

Sherman, L. W. (ed.), *Police Corruption: A Sociological Perspective* (Garden City, New York, Anchor Books, 1974).

_____ *Scandal and Reform: Controlling Police Corruption* (Berkeley and Los Angeles, University of California Press, 1978).

Sampson, Antony, *The Literature of Police Corruption, Vol. 1. A Guide to Bibliography and Theory* (New York, The John Jay Press, 1977).

Simpson, Gwyn, 'The Godber affair: premature cheers', *Far Eastern Economic Review*, 6 May 1974.

Sinclair, Kevin, *Asia's Finest: An Illustrated Account of the Royal Hong Kong Police* (Hong Kong, Unicorn Books, 1981).

Skolnick, Jerome H., *Justice Without Trial: Law Enforcement in Democratic Society* (New York, John Wiley, 1975, second edition).

Smelser, Neil J., *Theory of Collective Behaviour* (London, Routledge and Kegan Paul, 1962).

Smith, Ralph L., *The Tarnished Badge* (New York, Thomas Y. Crowell, 1965).

Sprenkel, Sybille van der, *Legal Institutions in Manchu China* (London, Athlone Press, 1962).

Steffens, Lincoln, *The Shame of the Cities* (New York, McClure, Phillips, 1904).

_____ *Autobiography* (New York, Harcourt Brace, 1931).

Stone, Christopher D., *Where the Law Ends: Social Control of Corporate Behaviour* (New York, Harper and Row, 1975).

Sutherland, Edwin H., 'White collar criminality', *American Sociological Review*, Vol. 5, 1940, pp. 1–12.

Swart, Koenraad Walter, *Sale of Office in the Seventeenth Century* (The Hague, Martinus Nijhoff, 1949).

Symonds, Richard, *The British and Their Successors: A Study of the Government Services in the New States* (London, Faber and Faber, 1966).

Tappan, Paul, 'Who is the criminal?', *American Sociological Review*, Vol. 12, 1947, pp. 96–102.

Tasker, Rodney, 'Beneath the corruption iceberg', *Far Eastern Economic Review*, 16 January 1976.

_____ 'Year of the crunch for super police', *Far Eastern Economic Review*, 13 February 1976.

_____ 'Vice squad goes underground', *Far Eastern Economic Review*, 26 March 1976.

_____ 'The honeymoon is over for graft fighters', *Far Eastern Economic Review*, 26 March 1976.

_____ 'Police bitter about graft probe', *Far Eastern Economic Review*, 21 May 1976.

_____ 'The accused', *Far Eastern Economic Review*, 3 September 1976.

Templeton, J., 'Rebel guardians: The Melbourne police strike of 1923', in J. Iremonger, *et al.* (eds.), *Strikes* (Sydney, Angus & Robertson, 1973), pp. 104–5.

Thurber, James, *Further Fables for Our Time* (London, Hamish Hamilton, 1956).

Tilman, Robert, 'Emergence of black-market bureaucracy: administration, development and corruption in the New States', *Public Administration Review*, Vol. 28, 1968, pp. 437–44.

Tomkinson, Martin, *See The Red Light, The Pornbrokers, The Rise of the Soho Sex Barons* (London, Virgin Books, 1982).

Trebitsch-Lincoln, J.T., *The Autobiography of an Adventurer* (London, Leonard Stein, 1931).

Truman, David, *The Governmental Process* (New York, Random House, 1951).

Walker, Samuel, *A Critical History of Police Reform* (Lexington, Mass., D.C. Heath, 1978).

Ward, Robert S., *Asia for the Asiatics? The Techniques of Japanese Occupation* (Chicago, University of Chicago Press, 1945).

Watt, John R., *The District Magistrate in Late Imperial China* (New York, Columbia University Press, 1972).

Wesley-Smith, Peter, 'Graft Amnesty and the Law', *Far Eastern Economic Review*, 30 December 1977.

_____ 'Legislation', *Hong Kong Law Journal*, Vol. 8, 1978, p. 241.

Williams, Robert H., *Vice Squad* (New York, Thomas Y. Crowell, 1973).

Wilson, James Q., *Varieties of Police Behavior: The Management of Law and Order in Eight Communities* (Cambridge, Mass., Harvard University Press, 1968).

Wodehouse, P.G., *Blandings Castle and Elsewhere* (London, Herbert Jenkins, 1935).

Woollacott, Martin, 'Hard Graft on Treasure Island', *South China Morning Post*, 3 October 1973.

Wraith, Ronald, and Simpkins, Edgar, *Corruption in Developing Countries* (London, Allen and Unwin, 1963).

BIBLIOGRAPHY

Reports

Defalcations in the Treasury, Sessional Paper No. 32 of 1893.

Report of the Commission to Enquire into the Existence of Insanitary Properties in the Colony, Hong Kong Sessional Papers 1898, pp. 445–576.

Report of the Food Supply Commission, Hong Kong Sessional Papers 1901, p. 173.

Report of the Commission to Enquire into the Public Works Department, Sessional Paper No. 3 of 1902.

Report of the Commission to Enquire into and Report on the Sanitary and Building Regulations, Sessional Paper No. 10 of 1907.

Report of the Housing Commission, Sessional Paper No. 10 of 1923.

Butters, H.R., *Report on Labour and Labour Conditions in Hong Kong*, Sessional Paper No. 3 of 1939.

Commission of Inquiry into the Immigration Department, Sessional Paper No. 5 of 1941.

Report on the Riots in Kowloon and Tsuen Wan, October 10th to 12th, 1956 (Hong Kong, Government Printer, 1956).

Reports of the Standing Committee and the Advisory Committee on Corruption (Hong Kong, Government Printer, 1961).

Report of the Working Party Set Up to Advise on the Inadequacy of the Law in Relation to Crimes of Violence Committed by Young Persons (Hong Kong, Government Printer, 1965).

Kowloon Disturbances 1966, Report of the Commission of Inquiry (Hong Kong, Government Printer, 1967).

The City District Officer Scheme, A Report by the Secretary for Chinese Affairs (Hong Kong, Government Printer, 1969).

City of New York, Commission to Investigate Allegations of Police Corruption, and the City's Anti-Corruption Procedures (New York, 1972) (Knapp Commission Report).

Chong Hing Mansion Report 1971 (Hong Kong, Government Printer, 1972).

Blair-Kerr, Sir Alastair, *First Report of the Commission of Inquiry under Sir Alastair Blair-Kerr* (Hong Kong, Government Printer, July 1973).

———— *Second Report of the Commission of Inquiry under Sir Alastair Blair-Kerr* (Hong Kong, Government Printer, September 1973).

Report of the Prime Minister's Committee on Local Government Rules of Conduct, Cmnd. 5636 (London, HMSO, 1974) (Redcliffe-Maud Report).

The Interim Report of Inspectors into the Affairs of Paul Lee Engineering Company Limited (Hong Kong, Government Printer, September 1973).

Second Interim Report of Inspectors into the Affairs of Paul Lee Engineering Company Limited (Hong Kong, Government Printer, January 1975).

Report of the Royal Commission on Standards of Conduct in Public Life, 1974–1976, Cmnd. 6524 (London, HMSO, 1976) (Salmon Report).

Report of the Commission of Inquiry into Inspector MacLennan's Case (Hong Kong, Government Printer, 1981).

Government Publications

Annual Departmental Reports by the Commissioner of Police.

Annual Report of the Activities of the Independent Commission Against Corruption (1974 onwards).

Civil and Miscellaneous Lists, Hong Kong Government.

The Hong Kong Civil Service List.

Hong Kong Government Annual Reports.

Hong Kong Hansard.

INDEX

ABUEVA, JOSÉ, 8
Advisory Committee on Corruption, *see* Standing Committee on Corruption
Anti-Corruption Branch (ACB), 87, 92
Anti-Corruption Office, 98
ARP scandal, 40 ff.
Auden, W.H., 66
Audit, Director of, 178, 212

BAILLIE-STEWART, LIEUTENANT NORMAN, 45
Baker, Russell, 186
Barber, Noel, 49
Becker, Howard S., 198
Benson, Harry, 34 ff.
Bernacchi, Brook, 55, 59
Bidmead, Kenneth, 77
Blair-Kerr, Sir Alastair, 89, 92, 97, 160
Boxall, Walter, 93, 173 ff.
Buisson, Émile, 50
Butters, H.R., 48

CADETSHIPS, 25 ff.
Cameron, Nigel, 25
Cantlie, Sir James, 32
Capone, Al, 4
Carlyle, Thomas, 17, 26, 125
Cater, Sir Jack, 101, 106–7, 134, 191
'Caterer', 122–4
Chang Chung-li, 12

Chatham, William, 36
Chau Yu-kit, 169–70
Cheng Hon-kuen, 112
Cheung Tak-sing, 121
Chiap Hua Manufactory Company, 44
Chinese Board of Censors, 19
Chinese examination system, 13
Chinese Manufacturers' Association, 187 *passim*
Chinese officials, 10 ff.
Chong Hing Mansion affair, 160 ff.
Ch'ü T'ung-tsu, 19
Community Relations Department, ICAC, 3, 150, 186, 188
Compradors, 180 ff.
Corruption, definitions of, 16
Corruption Prevention Department, ICAC, 133–4, 176–8
Corruption syndicates, 117 ff.
Cowperthwaite, Sir John, 197
Crane, J.W.D., 149, 153
Cressall, P.E.F., 43, 47
Crosland, T.W.H., 29
Cultural Revolution, 69, 200–1
Cunningham, Cecil, 93

DOIG, ALAN, 220
Doolittle, Revd Justus, 180
Drury, Commander Kenneth, 173
Duncan, James, 167
Durkheim, Émile, 93

EATES, EDWARD, 98
Elliott, Mrs Elsie, 55 ff., 129
Endacott, G.B., 48
English, Jack, 124
European inspectorate, 28 ff.

FAIRBANK, J.K., 205
Forrest, R.A.D., 38 ff.
Francis, John Joseph, 30

GASS, SIR MICHAEL, 76
Gide, André, 15
Gift, the, 28 ff.
Gilman and Company, 184, 191
Godber, Peter, 69, 93–8,
    111–12, 114–15, 200, 205
Goodstadt, Leo, 28, 73, 220
Grantham, Sir Alexander, 87,
    162, 207
Greene, Graham, 203
Gregory, J. Maundy, 10

HADDON-CAVE, SIR PHILIP, 166
Haig, General Sir Douglas, 142
Hao Yen-p'ing, 180
Harding, President, 4
Harknett, Gerald, 109, 117, 168
Heath, Henry, 59 ff.
Henderson, L.J., 197
Henry, Roy, 144–5, 153
Hogan, Sir Michael, 58
Holmes, Sir Ronald, 67, 102
Homosexuality, 60, 62, 126 ff.,
    154 ff.
Hore, Thomas, 35
Ho Tung, Sir Robert, 181
'Hunger Striker', see So Sau-
    chung
Hunt, Ernest, 61 ff., 112, 130
Hutchison House incident,
    138–141, 156

IMMIGRATION DEPARTMENT
    SCANDAL, 38 ff.
Independent Commission
    Against Corruption Ordi-
    nance, 104
Informers, 120
Inglis, Allan, 162

JUNIOR POLICE OFFICERS'
    ASSOCIATION, 138, 154–5

KENNARD, EDWARD, 168 ff.
Key, V.O., 5
Knapp Commission, 167
Kot Siu-wong, General, 72

LAU CHONG-CHOR, 121
Lau, Miss Mimi, 44 ff.
Lee, Mary, 172
Lee, Paul, 165 ff.
Leff, Nathaniel, 7
Le Play, 3
Leys, Colin, 3
Litton, Henry, 155
Liu Po-shan, 162 passim
Lo, Sir Man Kam, 84
Locard, Dr Edmond, 115–16
Lockhart, Sir James Stewart, 28
Lo Kei, 58, 63
Luddington, Sir Donald, 151
Lui Lok, 142

MACGREGOR, SIR ATHOLL, 39,
    46
MacIntosh, Duncan, 84
MacLehose, Sir Murray, 75, 80,
    98, 101–3, 105–7, 142 passim,
    199 ff., 214 ff.
MacLennan, Inspector John,
    127, 147, 157

MacMullan, M., 21
McNeice, Louis, 94
Marconi scandal, 19
Mark, Sir Robert, 100–1
Marsman, Jan, 42
Marx, Karl, 130
May, F.H., 30 ff.
Merton, R.K., 184, 196
Misdemeanours Punishment
  Ordinance, 1898, 37
Mitchell-Innes, N.G., 39
Muir, Ramsay, 17

NAUNTON, SIR ROBERT, 10
Norman-Walker, Sir Hugh, 165
Northcote, Sir Geoffrey, 39, 47
Nye, J.S., 21

O'BRIEN, WILLIAM SMITH, 156
Olivetti (Hong Kong) Ltd., 185
Operations Target Committee,
  192

PARETO, 25
'Partial amnesty', the, 142–3
Paul, Jean, 119
Pennefather-Evans, John, 84
Pepys, Samuel, 10
Police Commercial Crimes
  Office (CCO), 188, 213
Police 'mutiny', 129 ff.
Police Public Relations Branch,
  66
Police strikes, 71
Pong-paân, 27, 35
Popper, Sir Karl, 218
Potter, Stephen, 28
Poulson affair, 19 ff.
Prendergast, Sir John, 117, 128,
  151

Prevention of Bribery Ordi-
  nance, 1971, 92, 182
Prevention of Corruption Ordi-
  nance, 1948, 74, 182
Proto-corruption, 10 ff.
Public Works Department
  (PWD), 36
Purcell, Sir Victor, 40

QUINCEY, INSPECTOR, 31
Quinn, Michael, 61

RABUSHKA, ALVIN, 197
Rachman, Peter, 123
Redcliffe-Maud Report, 19
Reform Club, 59
Riots, Star Ferry, 57 ff.; 1956
  riots, 57–8; 1967 distur-
  bances, 69–70
Robinson, Sir Hercules, 25, 37

SACKVILLE, LORD RICHARD, 10
Salmon Report, 19
Secretariat for Chinese Affairs,
  67–8
Sexual Offences Act, 1967, 126
Shanghai, 48 ff.
Sherman, Lawrence, 156
Simpkins, Edgar, 2, 5
Singapore, 74
Skolnick, Jerome, 108
Slevin, Brian, 132, 137–9, 152
Smalls, Derek (Bertie), 113–14
Smelser, Neil, 66
Smith, T. Dan, 20
So Sau-chung, 54
Standing Committee on Corrup-
  tion, 88–92
Stanton, William, 31
Starkey, R.D., 27

Station sergeants, 93, 118 ff.
Steele-Perkins, Wing Commander A.H.S., 41 ff.
Sutcliffe, Charles, 68, 70, 99–100, 132
Sutherland, E.H., 210–11

TAAI-PAÂN, 35
Tannenbaum, Frank, 115
Tappan, Paul, 211
Target Committee on Corruption, 91
Teapot Dome Scandal, 4
Television Broadcasts Ltd., 185
Thurber, James, 169
Tilman, Robert, 7
Trebitsch-Lincoln, 50
Trench, Sir David, 70, 75
Triads, 71 ff., 132
Trotsky, 125
Truman, David, 119
Tsang Kai-wing, 124
Tsang Shing, 126–7
Tsui, Paul, 26

'Turf Frauds', 34 ff.
Tweed, Boss, 4
Tyrer, Edward, 66

UMELCO, 186

VIDOCQ, FRANÇOIS, 90
Virgo, Commander Wallace, 172

WALLACE, EDGAR, 59
Ward, Robert S., 47
Wesley-Smith, Peter, 143, 175
White-collar crime, 210 ff.
Witchell, Job, 32
Wodehouse, P.G., 145
Wraith, Ronald, 2, 5

YAMEN, 13 ff.
Yang, Mr Justice T.L., 127
Yao, Raymond, 145, 153
Yau Ma Tei Fruit Market drug syndicate, 117
Young, Sir Mark, 46